Starting and Operating
A Woodworking Business:
How To Make Money With Your Skills

A. William Benitez

Starting and Operating
A Woodworking Business:
How To Make Money With Your Skills

Cover by A. William Benitez
All Rights Reserved. Published By

Positive Imaging, LLC
201 Stassney Lane
P.O. Box 405
Austin, Texas 78745
http://positive-imaging.com
bill@positive-imaging.com

Printed In The USA

First Paperback Printing January, 2008

ISBN 978-0-6151-8693-1

Covers

Front cover photographed and designed by A. William Benitez.

The China Cabinet was designed and built by A. William Benitez. It was designed around the stained glass pieces, which already existed. Making the doors was the first step in the project. Then the rest of unit was designed and built to fit the doors. Sometimes you may find customers who own pieces they wish to incorporate into a cabinet or furniture piece. It is important to have the flexibility to work with these customers.

Rear cover photographed and designed by A. William Benitez

Here are photographs of many projects constructed by A. William Benitez over the years. In the center is a photo of the sign he maintained on his truck for many years and it often brought in new business. At the top right and left are two pictures of a solid maple cabinet that was custom made to fit a customer's specifications. At the bottom right and left is a nine-module entertainment center designed to fit into a 6 foot wide by 9 foot tall wall opening.

At right and left center is a front and rear view of the podium/lecterns for the business discussed in this book. At top center is a foyer table and mirror frame for which there are complete plans and drawings and the same mirror, in a horizontal position, is shown used in a bathroom setting.

Contents

	Introduction	1
1	Is Self-Employment For You?	5
2	The Illusion of Security	6
3	Self Motivation and Discipline	7
4	Taking Full Advantage of Your Skills	9
5	Your First Steps	11
6	Advertising For Projects	12
7	Selling Your Woodwork	14
8	Customer Complaints	15
9	Staying In Business	17
10	Keeping Customers	20
11	Recordkeeping	22
12	Guarantees	23
13	Contracting For Projects	24
14	How Much To Charge	25
15	Expansion	29
16	Using Subcontractors	31
17	What Is Simplified Woodworking	32
18	Building Cabinets With Modules	34
19	Shop Space and Tools	36
20	Finishing Projects	40
21	Shop Notes	42
22	Drawings of Customer Projects	53
	Single Page Drawings	54
	Multiple Page Drawings	58
23	Sample Business Forms	62
	Letterhead	63
	Business Card	64
	Podium Sales Letter	65
	Woodwork Agreement (Contract)	66
	Specifications Addendum	67
24	Marketing and Selling Aids	68
	Accepting Credit Cards	68
	Creating a Photo Album	69
	Using A Web Site	69
25	Personal Assistance	71
	Safety Notes	71
	Ten Basic Rules For Success	72
	Fitness	75
	Final Notes	75

26	The Projects	77
	Bookcase Units	77
	Blanket Chest/Window Seat	84
	End Table/Desk Combo	88
	Entry Table	97
	Kitchen Range Shelf	103
	Laundry Cabinet	110
	Mirror Frame	117
	Study Desk	124
27	Bonus 1 - The Business Project	129
	Podium/Lectern Instructions	129
	Table Top Podium Drawings	144
	Standup Podium Drawings	145
28	Bonus 2 – Laminating Countertops	147
	Instructions - Laminating Tops	147
	Drawings Of Laminated Tops	159
	Glossary	164
	Other Books - Positive Imaging, LLC	171

INTRODUCTION TO THE WOODWORKING BUSINESS

Putting It All Together

Operating your own woodworking business can be an enjoyable and financially satisfying adventure. But, if you don't know what you are doing, it can be a financial and personal disaster. The goal of this book is to help you succeed financially and avoid a disaster. This is the kind of book that could have helped me avoid the many mistakes I made when I started my woodworking business. To help you avoid those mistakes, I created 28 chapters all based entirely on my first-hand experience.

The first chapter starts with a question that you need to ask yourself before starting any business. Your success in this business depends on being brutally honest with yourself and make certain your answer indicates that you are capable of self-employment.

What about security? So many people believe that security is only found in a good job, working for someone else. It is good to have an enjoyable job that challenges you each day, but it's not a guarantee of a secure future. If you are certain of your security because you work for a good company, remember that thousands of Enron employees and the employees of many other large corporations believed the same thing. Many of them lost their jobs and even their retirement savings. This is not to say that having a good solid job is not a positive thing, just that it does not guarantee security. There are no guarantees with employment or self-employment.

Self-motivation and discipline are critical for successful self-employment. This book explains the value of self-motivation and the important role that discipline plays in getting your business started and gaining long-term financial success.

One of the most important things you will have to do is accurately analyze your skills. In this book I help you to determine your strongest skills and how to develop those that are not as strong. There are many ways to make money with your skills and then spend time learning and expanding those skills. Success requires that you take full advantage of all your skills.

Those first steps, while getting started, are important and many people falter before they ever get going. You must know what to do and how to do it right from the start. Unlike some books, this important subject is not taken for granted here.

When people start a business they promptly realize that advertising is of critical importance. Without it, potential customers will not know that you exist. But it's easy to spend excessive amounts on worthless advertising and wind up in debt and with few if any customers. This book will help you to make advertising choices that you can afford while still bringing in customers.

Once you make contact with prospects, the next step is to convert them to paying customers. Many people hate selling, but if you plan to be self-employed you will have to get accustomed to selling everyday. If the sales person does not produce results, there will be no income and without it a business cannot survive. In a one-person business, you are the sales person. You must do the selling of every job and this book will help make selling easy and enjoyable.

If your woodworking business succeeds, you will have many customers. You will find valuable information in this book about how to deal with your customers on a daily basis. This information will help you to remain in business using the best, most sell them, it also provides complete instructions and drawings so you can build them in your shop. You are guided every step of the way so you can sell these podiums. And, you are not limited to your own community. I sold and shipped them to three cities. One of them was in another state. This section of the book alone could make you hundreds, even thousands in profit.

Some cabinets and furniture pieces require a plastic laminate top. This book includes a bonus book section detailing instructions for making quality laminate tops. Every step from tools needed to the cutting and application of the plastic laminate is covered with detailed drawings to help you understand each step.

The final section is a useful Glossary defining many of terms found in this book. As the book progresses it will put everything together for you so you can start your own business and succeed in just a few short months. I hope you find this book highly informative. All the information is based solely on my first-hand experience. It has all been tried and proven in practice and there is no reason it can't work for you. I hope you will jump right in and give it a try.

When you get started, please email me and let me know. Good Luck.

One

Is Self-Employment For You?

Since you purchased this book, it would probably be safe to say that you have a strong interest in starting and operating your own successful woodworking business. Before you take that big step, I want you to stop and ask yourself one important question.

"Do I really want to be self-employed?" Or, stated another way, "Am I suited to self-employment?" Considering that you invested in this book, this may sound like a dumb question. It's an important question and before you answer it I want to share some information with you.

The one-person business differs from other forms of self-employment in that you are the whole crew. You are the owner, boss, designer, accountant, receptionist, salesperson, cabinetmaker and cleanup person. You may have some relative or friend to help you with some of the work but you are responsible for all of it. It isn't an easy job and you must be up to it. If not, perhaps you should reconsider.

Also consider that your income comes in spurts, usually on completion and installation of a project. If the project is delayed so is the payment for that project. When you get sick, everything stops including the income. And, you have to pay for your own health insurance or do without. When you go on vacation or just take a day off to go fishing, everything stops including the money.

You are the sole contact for your customer, so expect calls at strange hours. There is no one else to listen to complaints. They all come to you. There are times that, despite your best efforts, things will go wrong and customers will turn to you. You will need much patience to deal with all the problems.

It is essential that you be organized to avoid wasting time because time will be at a premium. Even when you have projects you will be getting calls from people interested in contracting your services. You will have to leave for sales calls. Then you will have to design projects, before constructing them. In other words, it is a lot of work and you will be doing it all.

It may seem that I am trying to discourage you from starting this venture but that isn't the case. I did it for more than 20 years and found it enjoyable and challenging. What I am trying to do is paint an accurate picture for you. Unlike some who will hype the romance of self-employment without showing you the warts, I am going to let you see it all before you decide.

There is an important decision to be made, I hope you choose to start a woodworking business and I will help you as much as I can. If after reading all this you are still certain that this is what you want, then proceed without hesitation because now you know the worse.

Two

The Illusion of Security

If you have always been employed by some company, corporation or government agency, self-employment can be a frightening experience. Taking that giant step away from a regular salary is difficult. I experienced that once and it was one of the most difficult things I have ever done. The fear was overwhelming. What's most interesting is that I spent most of my youth self-employed. Then I got a good job with the government managing federally funded programs.

After more than twelve years I got tired of it and decided to start my own publishing and consulting business. My fear was that I would not be able to continue paying my bills and maintaining my insurance and a hundred other things that entered my mind. It was the fear of being insecure. It was bad because I had become accustomed to the illusion of security that came from having a good job.

If you believe that you are secure because of your job and your savings, you are not keeping up with the news. Read about the experiences of thousands of Enron employees, many that not only lost their jobs, but also their life savings. And they are not alone. Many other large companies laid off thousands of employees and made poor and often illegal decisions that adversely affected the jobs and retirement funds of all their employees. The greedy leaders of these corporations left with millions and wiped out everything for employees who had been producing for them for years.

To make matters worse, thousands of jobs are being eliminated by new technologies and by companies who close down plants in the U.S. to open new ones in foreign countries. With this strategy they save billions in labor cost. Some companies have even moved twice. They started by moving to Mexico and then dropped their Mexican employees to move to China and save even more. Do you think that your company is as concerned with your security as they are with their bottom line? I'm certain that you know better than that.

Since your circumstances can change at a moments notice, the only security you can count on is within yourself. Any other security is an illusion that will come back to haunt you. I'm not saying that self-employment is the best thing for you. I just want you to make the decision with the understanding that long-term security is a foolish illusion and decisions should be made accordingly.

Three

Self-Motivation and Discipline

These two topics are closely related. To me, self-motivation is what propels you forward to do things even when they are frightening. Self-discipline defines the ability to stick to it and perform in a consistent and organized way to attain your goals. They are both important if you intend to succeed in your woodworking business.

If you have been at a job for many years and perform well, come in on time and avoid wasting time during the day, you probably believe that you are self-motivated and self-disciplined. Perhaps you are but it is just as likely that you aren't. Here is a prime example of what I mean.

A friend of mine worked for a large cabinet company for many years. He was an excellent employee, always coming in on time and almost never missing work. His performance garnered him several merit raises. Despite his success with this company, he dreamed of owning his own woodworking business. He talked about it constantly with his coworkers and saved his money diligently. Gradually he started converting his garage to a shop and buying all the tools he needed for a woodworking business of his own.

Finally, he took the big step, quit his job and started his own cabinet business. Almost from the first day of self-employment he seemed to have lost his good working habits. He slept late every morning, seldom starting to work before 11 A.M. He would then work a few hours and take off to go fishing or to do other things with some friends. I could not believe my eyes. After all those years of starting at 7 A.M., suddenly he could not awaken early. What could have changed?

Actually, he did not change. Many people need an outside source of discipline to function well. His company required him to be there by 7 A.M. each morning and he met that requirement easily. Once the requirement was gone, so was the discipline. Even though he was motivated to become self-employed, he obviously was not disciplined for self-employment. It wasn't long before he closed his shop and returned to the company. They were glad to have him back and he was there on time as usual.

I know from many people who talked to me while my shop was open that they believed I had the freedom to do as I pleased. It seemed to them that I could come and go at any time. Although that was true, it was balanced by the fact that I had to make sure that all the work was finished and delivered on schedule. I could not do that and come in at mid morning and leave at mid afternoon. A schedule was essential as was the discipline to adhere to it. Anything short of that would have ensured my failure.

It should be clear now that self-motivation and self-discipline are essential elements for your success in the woodworking business. So how can you develop these skills if you don't already have them? It does take work but you can start by creating a schedule. Determine how many days a week you will be working and how many hours during each day. From that you can determine when you will start and end the day. Once you have developed that schedule stick to it as closely as possible. You don't want to obsess over it since there will be times when you will have to interrupt your work to handle some other business or personal activity. Take care of it and get right back on track.

During the first year you will probably work much more and much harder than you will later. As time goes by, you will learn how to make better use of your time and you will become more productive. When this happens you can cut back on your hours if you choose. Or, you can keep the same hours and make more money.

Another help for self-discipline is a simple "to do" list. At the end of every day take a few minutes to list everything you have to do the next day. Then number them according to their importance or priority. The next day start with task number one and go through the list. Even if you are interrupted and don't finish everything on the list, you will have completed the most important items because you took the time to set a priority for them.

While a schedule is important, you should not be compulsive about it. In my woodworking business I often had one or two large jobs going at once. Sometimes a small job that was a high profit opportunity would arise. Being a slave to my schedule I would have lost these profitable opportunities. Instead, I took them on and worked a little extra to get them out while slightly delaying the larger project. This allowed me to make the profit on the large project and add to it the profit from the small project. To give me flexibility I would always contract as much time as possible for the big jobs. This would allow me to quickly finish small and profitable jobs without adversely affecting the schedule of the larger job. If you set a longer schedule and then deliver early, no one will fault you. The problems arise when you do not deliver on time.

Organization is an essential element of self-discipline. Layout your workspace so that you are working efficiently and moving the project so that when it is finished it will be ready to load for delivery. Don't set your tools so that you have to move projects back and forth in your shop while you are working on them. Create a place for the storage of materials with the cutting area nearby. From the cutting area things can move to the assembly area and then to the finishing area. In some shops the assembly area and the finishing area will be one in the same. Regardless of the size of your shop, plan it as efficiently as possible. This will save you time, make your work easier and increase your profit.

Do your best to avoid unprofitable interruptions. If your shop is in your garage at home, you can expect many interruptions. There are always personal situations arising and since you are nearby, it is likely that you will be involved. Take the time to explain to everyone the importance of following your schedule. Make certain that personal interruptions during the normal workday are emergencies or at least highly important.

Most people who become self-employed were excellent employees for some organization. To ensure your success with self-employment, try to work for yourself at least as well as you did for your last employer. If you do this, success is almost inevitable.

Four

Taking Full Advantage of Your Skills

Woodworking involves a myriad of skills and most woodworkers have some skills that are stronger than others. It does not mean that they can't do the others, only that some are what they do best. These are the skills you want to concentrate on when getting started. You should learn and practice as many woodworking skills as possible but focus on your best.

As an example, I was born into construction since my father was a general contractor. I could build a house from the ground up but door work was my strongest area. I could hang doors from scratch faster than most of my contemporaries and I could diagnose and correct door problems easily. When I started my woodworking business I advertised for door work even before I had my shop ready to go. I got many small jobs that kept the money flowing while I finished my shop. What is your strongest skill and how can you take advantage of it? Answer that question and you will be making a profit from your business almost immediately.

Here are some other examples. Let's assume that you have built some fine furniture for friends and family. They like the furniture and it is obvious that you have skills in this area. You can start by advertising for furniture projects. If you built furniture then you can also repair furniture. Yet another possibility is building and repairing kitchen cabinets. Your furniture skills will extend to many areas and you should take full advantage of them. Did you do some carving on your furniture projects? If you did then you can do carving work. Advertise that skill to the local or nearby antique shops. They sometimes need small parts carved for pieces.

Just because you specialize does not mean that you cannot accept other kinds of work. Leave yourself open to other work but try to stick with your strong skills during the first year. This will be the most profitable way to proceed. It will also make you more comfortable during the initial time you are in business.

A simple rule to help you succeed during the first year is; Never accept a job if you are not confident that you can finish it properly. On more than one occasion I have been called to help a woodworker finish a project that was beyond his skills. Sometimes I was able to help finish it but other times it was necessary to start from scratch. You don't want that to happen anytime, much less during your first year. Not only will it cost you one or more customers, but it will also be a blow to your confidence.

To improve your skills, study the woodworking craft. Read everything you can find about building the kinds of projects you are most interested in. Don't just use the project plans, instead study them and then go to furniture stores and study the various methods they use to assemble cabinets. They use simpler methods and you want to learn to work as simply as possible. Once you have learned enough from both sources use the information to design your own methods that are simpler yet allow you to use the tools you have available. The simple methods described in this book will help you to save time and make more money. But, they are not carved in granite and you can improve on them. Since these methods are tried and proven, I suggest you start with them and then improve them as you see fit.

No matter what methods you use, work at being creative. Make changes to the ideas and make them your own. Be original and your work will have its own identity and higher value. There are many woodworkers who build projects using the instructions and drawings directly from magazines or some other source. I have never enjoyed working in that fashion. There are many good designs that I have worked with but I always change them to my own design. Most clients appreciate this originality and are usually willing to pay more for it.

While we are talking about skill levels, it is important to determine the size of jobs you will accept. I would always determine what I could do alone and that would be all that I would accept. I did consider larger jobs but only if I felt confident that I could finish them. During the first year stick to what you know you can do and then grow slowly as your skills increase.

Five

Your First Steps

Depending on the regulations in your community, the first step in getting started may be getting an occupational license. When I lived in Tampa, Florida a license was required to legally operate my woodworking business. When I moved to Austin, Texas, years later, it was not required. It is important to check the requirements in your community and adhere to them to avoid problems after you have started your business.

What about the name of your business? I suggest you simply use your own name and add the words woodwork, woodworking, cabinets or something similar that identifies what you do. But, you can also create a name for your business. For years I operated as the Cabinet Doctor. The important thing is to register the name as a fictitious name with your County Clerk so that no one else can use the name. This is easy to do and the fee is usually reasonable.

Sales tax is another requirement to consider. This can be confusing. For example, you may need to charge sales tax to customers who purchase furniture and other products. But, kitchen cabinets that will be permanently attached to the walls of a home may not be taxable since they are taxed as part of the real estate. You should register to collect sales tax as needed and then pay the collected taxes to the state on a monthly or quarterly basis.

Purchase or make your own business cards and stationery. There are many inexpensive software programs that do this easily. You probably have one on your computer right now.

Get a liability insurance policy to cover you for any potential problems that may arise. This policy should include coverage for completed and installed products. It should also cover anything that may happen during the installation process in a home. Shop around for this insurance coverage because the rates vary enormously. Unless you plan to do some high dollar jobs I would start out with a $100,000.00 policy.

Have a phone installed with a number especially for your business as soon as possible. Considering present low cost contracts. I suggest a cell phone so that you can keep it with you when you leave the shop. This way you will not miss any potential customers.

These few steps should get you started and then you can follow through with the other things covered in subsequent chapters.

Six

Advertising For Projects

Success in woodworking, as in almost any other field, is dependent on customers. Getting customers is especially important when starting out. Advertising is the key to bringing in customers during the early stages. Even though word of mouth will be meager at the start, it can still help. My first big job came to me because of a next-door neighbor who was familiar with my work. He told a friend of his who was opening a dry cleaning store about my skills and I got the job to build all the cabinets for the new store. Since most new businesses work with an almost non-existent advertising budget, this kind of help is invaluable.

There are many ways to get your message out without spending much money. You need business cards. If you have a computer and printer, I suggest that you make your own and print only the quantity you need. Use these cards to introduce your business to everyone you know. You can give the cards to everyone you run into and mail the cards with a brief letter about your business to every address you have. Send emails to everyone on your email list and tell them about your new business and encourage everyone to call you or email you about any woodworking job they have in mind. Also, ask them to forward the email to friends on their mailing list.

Print up flyers and take them to any location that will allow you to put them up. This may include home improvement stores, grocery stores, restaurants, churches and Laundromats. In some communities there are small businesses that specialize in delivering flyers to bulletin boards in various locations. One of these services may be able to spread your flyers to 100 or more locations.

Create some nice postcards with your computer and printer and then mail them to nearby subdivisions. You can get the addresses from directories at the local library. Some of these directories even describe the income levels of the subdivision. You can also visit subdivisions and other areas that seem to need a little work. Walk the area taking down addresses and meet and talk with as many people as possible about your business. You may not get immediate response from these cards and visits but people tend to keep the information in a drawer and you will get a call from them a year or two later. It may not help much now but in the long term it will. If you live in a subdivision, walk the neighborhood taking down addresses. Mail every address a postcard that shows you live right in the neighborhood.

There are companies that help you create postcards and mail them to specific zip codes in your area. The best one I found to handle this procedure is Quantum Mail. You can check them out at: http://www.quantummail.com/ . They have online software you can use to create the postcards and then they mail them for a reasonable price. It is much easier than putting a mailing together yourself.

Create an attractive wooden sign for the tailgate of your truck. Make a sign that shows off your creative and woodworking skills. It is surprising how many people over the years would follow me until I stopped somewhere and come talk to me about work. The back cover shows a picture of the sign on my pickup truck.

The newspaper is a good place to advertise but it can be costly. Use the service section of the classifieds. This is where people usually look for home-related services.

Place the largest ad you can afford but remember that consistency is better than large size. You would be better off running a small ad regularly than a large ad one time. Check out the weekly newspapers in your area. The advertising is usually cheaper and the ad remains available for a full week. This increases the odds that it will be seen.

Create and maintain a photo album of all your work. In this age of Internet access, it is also a good idea to have a web site to keep pictures of your work and information about your business. A simple web site can be made using a free program such as those available with Internet Explorer and Netscape. Or, you can download an excellent web creation software called NVU from http://www.nvu.com .

You can get a domain name for under $10 and the web hosting for a small monthly fee. Then you can use the website in conjunction with all your other advertising. If you have photos of your work and information about your woodworking skills on your website, you can use it with your other advertising. I recommend http://www.positive-imaging.com for domain name registration and web site hosting services.

Establish a regular budget for advertising, no matter how small. Each month determine how best to spend that amount to help build your business. Don't make it a haphazardous thing. Advertising is important to your success. Keep tabs on the success of your ads and stick with those that pull customers and drop those that don't.

If the quality of your work is high, the time will come when advertising is almost unnecessary. There is just so much volume a one-person woodworking business can handle. If you do quality work, after a couple of years you will be almost totally dependent on word of mouth recommendations from your customers. When you reach the point that you have all the work you can possibility do, save your advertising dollars. If things slow down during some periods, you can advertise for more work at that time.

Seven

Selling Your Woodwork

It is amazing how many small business operators hate selling. Many of these people seem to feel that most sales techniques are less than honest. There are sales techniques that are based almost entirely on fooling the perspective buyer but this is not representative of all selling. Dishonesty can be found in all areas of life not just sales.

You can have a successful sales technique that is based entirely on honesty. The first step is handling a product or service that is of real value and not some useless scam. Your woodworking will fit into this category. Second, you must believe in that product or service. If you don't believe what you are telling the potential customer, then you are being deceptive. Don't tell the potential customer anything that isn't true.

Avoid hard sell techniques. Do not badger your potential customer to get them to buy when they resist. Explain your work methods and techniques, tell the customer why they would be making the right decision to hire you for the job and share your ideas about what they want to do. Talk to them in a clear, concise and honest way and remain fully involved in the process even if they decide not to close the deal. Some people need time to absorb everything. They may not close that day and then call you a week later because you were the only one that listened to them and helped them with ideas.

During my years of woodworking I got many jobs when I was not the lowest price. On one occasion I got a job where the customer had obtained three bids and I was the highest. He still gave me the job. He told me this after I had finished the job. And, he said that I was the only one that he was confident would do a first class job. That is the kind of impression you want to make when you go to sell a job.

There are many books and tapes on good sales techniques. Take the time to check some of them out but be careful because some of them deal with superficial and phony methods. These are not conducive to the one-person woodworking business. Establishing an honest and trusting relationship with a customer early on is important.

The final part is one that many sales people miss. They are so busy trying to convince the potential customer to buy that they forget to listen. It is difficult to listen when your lips are moving. Failure to listen is the reason that many sales are lost. Often an individual is ready to buy, has given a clear signal that he or she is sold and the sales person continues to sell. You may want to let the customer know how great your work is but if you were recommended to them and they are ready to buy, it is time to stop talking and close the sale. Otherwise, a wrong word could lose the sale for you. Watch for the signal of acceptance and then proceed to close the deal. We all must sell to keep business going but let's give the customer time to express his or her feelings also. This will help you to understand the customer's needs and to give them what they want.

Eight

Customer Complaints

What should you do when someone complains about your work? This is a simple question and how you answer it will reflect on your level of success. If it is a product that can be returned easily, refund their money immediately. If they paid the cost of mailing it back to you, reimburse them. Make the situation as painless as possible for the customer. Let them understand that your main concern is always their complete satisfaction. By doing this you convert an unpleasant situation into a positive experience for the buyer. They lose nothing in the process and will certainly consider other products that you may be selling in the future.

If you are dealing with large woodworking projects the situation is more difficult financially, but the principal remains the same. It is essential to make the experience pleasant for your customer. This will bring you more business later even if you lose a little money now. Over my more than twenty years of running a woodworking business, I have had some opportunities to deal with situations that were less than pleasant. In all those years, which involved hundreds of pieces of furniture and cabinets, I can remember only one customer that was impossible to satisfy. And that was not completely my fault although I was certainly a participant.

The situation was complicated by the actions of a general contractor. He tried to serve as a middleman and made a real mess of things. Even in this case, the only real disagreement had to do with the price and not the quality of the work.

All the other cases where problems arose ended with the customer completely happy and giving me additional work. In one case I built a conference table for a law firm and they were not happy with the way the top turned out. I asked them to use the top for the next two weeks while I made a new top that would meet their requirements. After I delivered the new top they commented on my professionalism and gave me another large job. It was obvious that they had been through several unpleasant experiences with other firms.

So what happens when someone tries to take advantage of you? Certainly there are people out there who would abuse your honesty. Well, each case must be reviewed on its own merits to determine what is best in the particular situation. Let's take a simple contractor or homeowner situation. Many homes have storm or screen doors and the screen portion is sometimes left open when the weather is ideal. What if a homeowner calls you during the one-year guarantee period because their screen has been ripped. Obviously you will be responsible for a manufacturers defect. If it seems that the screen is defective, replace it promptly and without question. What if it is obvious that either a dog or a child has simply jumped through the screen? That is abuse and you are not responsible for the damage. The individual should pay for the repair.

These situations are not always clear-cut. If there is any doubt as to how the screen was torn, I would replace it without question. If this person has been in the house for almost a year and has never called you about anything else, you might replace it anyway, just as a courtesy. On the other hand, if this person is always calling with problems that are obviously caused by abuse, it may be time to say no. No one can say what is best for a specific situation except the person facing it at the moment.

So what can you do during these uncomfortable situations? Start by listening. When a customer is upset, they want someone to take the time to listen and appreciate their problem. So even if you can't help, the person will realize that you are interested. This will often diffuse a situation. Next, find out what the person wants. You may think they want something replaced and they may simply want you to patch it for them. It could be that five minutes of work would resolve a serious problem. If that's the case, it would certainly be better than a conflict. View complaints as an opportunity to prove that you are a reliable and honest professional. Many merchants dread complaints and make things difficult and unpleasant for the complainers. Any business handling complaints in this manner will suffer for it.

Nine

Staying In Business

Starting a new business can be difficult. You will probably face many problems and most of them will be financial. It is important to be prepared for discouraging situations. During the beginning, cash flow may not keep up with expenses and you will have to get as much work as possible to keep things going.

It is important to have some reserve funds before getting started and to keep adding to those funds as time progresses. You should be depositing at least 10% of your gross income into a reserve fund to handle those unforeseen situations and to keep you from getting behind on paying your expenses. If you do have to use some of these funds during one month, you should make every effort to repay the fund as promptly as possible. This fund may well keep your business afloat if you have some slow times.

I suggest you do your own accounting using an accounting application on your computer and do it regularly. Keep up with all income and expenditures so you will have a good idea how things are going at all times. Watch the expenses and cut out any unnecessary costs. Avoid waste even if you can afford it. Save the money instead, to help overcome those tough situations.

Open a separate business bank account and keep close track of funds by using online banking. It is easy to do now and very inexpensive. Perhaps you can have a family member do the accounting. However you do it, make certain it gets done regularly so you know where you stand when an expense or an opportunity arises.

Many small businesses fail because of tax problems. You would probably be surprised by how many small businesses are having problems with income taxes. Some of them are making payments to the Internal Revenue Service for taxes from the previous year. Some are even paying for several previous years. Don't let this happen to you. Make certain that you begin depositing a percentage of your income to pay your taxes. Create a saving account just for this purpose. Better yet, get the forms from the IRS and pay estimated taxes every quarter. At the end of the year your taxes will be paid and all you have to do is complete and submit your tax forms. It certainly makes things much easier and you will be able to use your money for profit instead of past due taxes plus interest and penalties.

Don't mess around with the IRS. Pay your taxes every year when they are due. If you do have a problem and can't afford to pay the IRS, complete and submit your income tax form on time and with a check for whatever amount you can afford. The IRS will bill you for the balance and will probably work out a payment arrangement for you. Pay as much as you can as quick as you can. It can be a real drain paying past and present taxes.

Income taxes are high for self-employed persons. Right off you have to pay the full 15% for Social Security, unlike employees who only pay half that amount. Then you have to pay a percentage on your income depending on the amount you make. These two figures can add up significantly. Plus, if you live in a State that collects income taxes, you have yet another percentage over and above those two.

I've noticed that most people believe that IRS employees derive pleasure out of ruining people financially. That has not been my experience. I was audited once and on two occasions I had to arrange monthly payments to finish paying my taxes. During all of that time the IRS employees I dealt with were helpful and non-threatening. It seems to me that we get back what we put out. I suggest that you be honest, courteous and concise in your dealings with the IRS. Chances are you will be treated in the same way.

I've stressed the importance of good and consistent accounting practices. There is one area of accounting that requires special attention. That area is accounts receivables. This is the money you have coming for your work. I strongly suggest that you avoid billing except for long term regular customers that you have come to know for many years. In all other cases the contracts should be handled with a 50% deposit when the job is contracted and the balance upon completion of the work.

I know you are probably thinking that this 50% deposit policy will lose you many potential customers. Well, the truth is it will cut out some customers. You will probably not be doing any work for government agencies since they are not willing to pay deposits. And, you may not be doing any work for general contractors who most often like to pay you after you have signed a lien waiver and they have received their draw from the bank. This is not as bad as it sounds. In the first place, government agencies are known for being slow payers. I once did a job for the Internal Revenue Service and it took them more than three months to pay me after I completed the work. And, contractors are notorious for agreeing to one amount and then trying to reduce the amount once they see that their profits are too low on a house or building that they are constructing. A contract and a deposit will help protect you from these situations. The important thing is that you will cut out all the customers that could fail to pay you.

I've had many friends in the woodworking business that got beat out of some or all of the funds on jobs because they simply did the work and then submitted a bill. That is not the best way to handle woodworking jobs under contract. It is definitely not the best way to make certain that you collect the full amount owed to you. During the beginning it is critical that you get paid in full for every job. You can't afford to come up short. You are much better off without these customers instead of risking a loss. Wait until you are on firm solid financial footing before you consider any billing.

In my more than 20 years as a one-person woodworking business I never failed to get paid for a job. I did lose a few jobs that I would have enjoyed getting because of my deposit policy but I did not lose money. On two different occasions I bid jobs for large firms and was awarded the bid. Then I insisted on the 50% deposit and they refused. I walked away from the jobs. Both of the jobs came through because I had been highly recommended and they decided to relent and pay me the deposit. With this deposit, even if something happens and you fail to collect the rest, at least your costs will have been covered so all you lose is your labor. Don't be foolish and compromise on this. If you do it could place your business at risk.

Even with a 50% deposit, you must pay close attention to accounts payable. When the job is completed, make certain you collect. One of the problems I faced with one customer is that he gave me a bad check for almost $300.00. For a long time I was unable to collect for that check because he kept giving me excuses. I started dropping by his bank every time I was in the neighborhood and I would try to cash the check.

One day, almost two months after he gave me the check, I went into the bank and he had just made a deposit. They cashed my check. The next day I got a call from this customer. He was angry because a very important check of his had bounced because I collected mine. Now that guy had some nerve but I would never have collected without persisting. As it turned out he called me for another job six months later and I refused the work. He persisted until finally I told him that I would do the job if he would pay me in full and in cash up front. He was offended and I did not do the work. It is up to you to take care of yourself. Doing a lot of work does you no good unless you collect for it.

Profit is very important to a business. You must keep an accounting of all your expenses in order to determine if you made a profit. Remember, to pay yourself a good salary for all the work you do. There are many self-employed persons who calculate all of their costs except for their own time and then say that they made a good profit on the job. If you did not figure in the hours that you worked at a fair hourly rate, your profit figures are overstated. Profit is the amount that is left when the job is finished and the labor, materials and expenses have been paid in full.

I suggest that you pay yourself a good living wage and stash all the profits in the reserve account during the first year or two. This will help you build much needed capital for tools or even a better workspace.

Remember that time is money. When you are self-employed you will probably have to run your own errands. This will consume many valuable hours. If you have someone who can run those errands, it is better to spend your time building projects. If you do run your own errands, set aside a certain time of the day when the traffic is most ideal to run the errands. Do them quickly and get back to work on the projects.

It should be clear that you have to keep track of many things when you are self-employed. It is difficult but worth the effort because it will ensure your success.

Ten

Keeping Customers

Success in a woodworking business depends on keeping your customers. It's time consuming and costly to get new customers so it's critical to do everything possible to keep a customer once acquired. In addition to having the customer continue doing business with you, it is important that he or she value your products and service enough to recommend you to others.

To be recommended to others you must establish a reputation for quality work and customer service. This is done by always delivering high quality work and prompt professional service. This does not mean that you will never make mistakes. It isn't critical that you not make any mistakes. What is important is how you handle mistakes when they happen. If you admit your mistakes and immediately take steps to correct them without being forced to do it, your customers will be impressed. In these cases being right is not important. The really important thing is how your customer feels when the incident is over. That will determine whether they will return and recommend you to others.

Good customer service is the key. It is more important now then ever because it is becoming very difficult to get good service. Think about the last time you got really good customer service at any business. If you are like me, it was memorable because of the poor service you normally get. That is what you need to do for your customers. Make it impossible to forget the experience of doing business with you.

Here are a couple of examples from my personal experience. One is about how to lose a good customer and the other is how to keep a customer even when a problem arises. The first happened to a competitor of mind. He had contracted to build a custom desk for a customer. He completed the desk and the customer told him that the desk should have had a lock on one of the drawers. My competitor insisted that it was not part of the price. He finally installed the lock and billed the customer for an additional $16.00. The customer paid it but was disturbed by being billed. My competitor refused to give the customer any satisfaction on the issue.

About a month later I received a call from this company to quote them for some office furniture. They were opening a second office and wanted several pieces of custom furniture including custom desks and a file cabinet. I submitted a quote and got the job. I later found out that my price was higher than my competitor's price for the same pieces but I got the job because the manager was still upset about the $16.00. So, for this small amount he gave up a contract of several thousand dollars. Of course, I was glad that he had to be right since it got me a very good contract. More importantly, it got me a good customer who ordered products from me many more times after that first experience.

On another job, I built a conference table for a law office and they did not like the appearance of the top. I was going through a bad financial time but I told the customer to use the existing top for a couple of weeks and I would build a new one for them just the way they wanted it. Two weeks later I arrived with a new top and switched it out. They were well satisfied with the new top and gave me a contract to install crown molding throughout the entire office. The original top was acceptable but it just wasn't the way they pictured it and it was obvious that I didn't understand what they had wanted. In addition to the new work, I got recommended to other law offices. As to the top that I took back, it served me for many years as an assembly table. I just placed it on a couple of sawhorses in my shop.

Good customer service pays off and it's the right thing to do. I suggest that you put yourself in your customer's shoes before making a decision on any customer service issue. Determine how you would like to be treated if you were facing the same situation and treat your customer at least as well.

Eleven

Recordkeeping

To handle the income and expenses of your business, open a business checking account and a savings account. These accounts should be separate from your personal accounts and used exclusively for your business. Use the checking account to deposit income and pay bills. Use the savings account to save the funds you will need to pay your taxes and to keep a reserve fund for unforeseen situations. I also suggest that you maintain a small petty cash fund to pay for small items that may become necessary.

Also purchase some accounting software to keep track of all your income and expenses. I highly recommend Quickbooks Pro but there are many others. Before purchasing your accounting software, check with your bank. Many banks now allow synchronization of your accounting software with your bank records. I did this for many years using Quickbooks Pro. There was a small additional fee for this service but it allowed me to easily balance my accounts. It is also wise to use this software to write the checks for your expenses. This allows for one time posting and avoids having to enter information later.

Microsoft has come up with an excellent accounting program called Office Accounting 2007. I mention it as an alternative to Quickbooks Pro because at this writing Microsoft is offering a free version for small businesses. This is not a trial version that stops working after a few months, it is completely free and works very well. I suggest that you google Microsoft Office Accounting 2007 to check it out before investing in your accounting software.

Whichever software you choose, use it to handle your invoicing and to maintain a customer list with complete details. This way you won't need to purchase printed invoices and your sales will be automatically posted to you accounting software when the invoices for each job are created. All of this valuable technology will save you time and help you make more money but it can become a waste of time without proper backup. Make certain that you backup your accounting software every time you use it. It is not uncommon for people to use good accounting software for years and never make a single backup. Losing all this information after several years can be a disaster. Don't let that happen to you.

Initially, you can avoid the expense of accounting software by taking advantage of online banking. With online banking you will get a record of every payment and deposit. This record can be printed weekly or monthly and become your accounting record. To use this method, devise a numbering system for your expenses. For example, use 1 for auto expenses, 2 for utilities, 3 for rent and so forth. Once you print out your online transaction record, identify all the expenses with the appropriate number and place the form in a folder. At the end of the year you will have a record of all income (deposits) and all your expenses (payments). You can then separate the expenses into the correct categories by using the code numbers and this will provide you with the information you need for your income taxes and will serve as evidence if necessary. Using this method you will have to handle your invoices manually but it will save you money. Once you are established, you can purchase and use accounting software.

Twelve

Guarantees

Most of your potential customers will not know you. Unless recommended to the customer by a friend or family member, you are a stranger and your customer is risking a loss. If they are paying a deposit or paying for something in advance, there is always the possibility that they won't receive it. Even if they do receive it, they could be disappointed in the quality.

The main purpose of guarantees is to allay the fears of new customers. They are attracted to what you have to sell but are afraid to spend the money with an unknown. A guarantee will usually relax them and ensure that they are willing to purchase your product. Make your guarantee clear so that it is easy to understand. If it seems that your guarantee is too complex people will tend to avoid doing business with you.

Check out the market and you will notice that even the largest items have guarantees. When a contractor builds a home he provides a one-year guarantee for building defects. Most appliances and automobiles have extensive guarantees. A good solid guarantee is part of the marketing process. It would be foolish to run a woodworking business without providing all your customers with a comprehensive guarantee.

No matter how good your work is, something can go wrong. The buyer should not have to suffer because of some problem that you can correct. Certainly your customer will have to maintain the woodwork and you cannot provide an endless guarantee, but you can make certain that the product provides real value.

I suggest you follow the example of homebuilders and give a one-year guarantee for everything except abuse. If a cabinet becomes loose because of a glue failure or some fittings came loose, by all means fix it promptly. On the other hand, if a table surface was obvious damaged by someone beating on it with a hammer, there is little that you can do to resolve such problems. They definitely do not fall under the guarantee.

Thirteen

Contracting For Projects

Prepare a simple contract document for your customers to sign before beginning a job. It is essential to get a signed contract together with a 50% deposit with every job before you start. You will probably hear or even believe that it is difficult to get a 50% deposit from your customers. I did this for over 20 years and seldom met with any resistance. Even when I was first starting, it was no problem to get a deposit as long as I carefully explained the work, presented clear and concise drawings and a fair contract form. Once you develop a reputation it will be even easier to obtain a 50% deposit from your customers.

A contract with a customer is based on trust. If a customer is unwilling to sign a contract and give you a deposit, then trust does not exist. The customer does not believe that you will follow through and perform as you promised. On the other hand, if you proceed without the deposit, you can't be certain that you will get paid. The 50% deposit is a compromise of sorts. The owner will be certain that you will do your job in order to get the rest of the money. You will be certain that you will get paid because the owner has contracted with you and given you a good faith deposit. If this much trust doesn't exist, you are better off not doing the work. Later in this book there is a section with sample forms that includes a copy of the contract that I used for many years. You may consider getting an attorney to prepare a simple contract for you but do not allow it to become a 10 to 20 page nightmare of legal jargon. This will just make it much more difficult to sell your work.

No matter the form of your contract, you will run into potential customers who absolutely refuse to pay the 50% deposit. They will sometimes come up with various alternatives. One of my prospects tried three different alternatives with me including a 10% deposit and depositing the total amount in escrow with a bank. Even after a recommendation from a neighbor, they would not give me a deposit. They continued to call me for a couple of months trying to get me to relent on my policy. I finally had to tell them not to call me anymore. I strongly recommend that you set a policy regarding the 50% deposit and apply it to everyone. Unless you can afford to lose money on projects, it is the only sensible thing to do.

Remember that this policy will eliminate almost all general contractors as customers. Contractors want to have the work done and then pay you after they get their draw from the bank financing the work. Again, this is a slippery slope that can cost you a lot of money. Some contractors will actually try to cut your price after the fact because they realize that the home or building is costing more than they estimated. If you stick with your policy, only contractors who have the financial ability to pay the deposit up front will do business with you and your odds of collecting the balance when the job is done are greatly increased.

Fourteen

How Much To Charge

Setting a price for your work is always difficult because there are so many variables. There is a concise method for calculating the price of any project or product but all the variables must be taken into account. Probably the most important question, and one that is often overlooked, is: How much do I want to make from this product or service. How can you possibly decide how much to charge without answering this critical question?

Start with an hourly figure so it can be applied to any project or product. Remember, this should be the figure you want to make for yourself before taxes. Do not consider material or overhead cost. Try to balance reality with desire with this figure. That is, what you want balanced with the reality of what is possible. Let's say you want a minimum of $20 per hour for your time. Please remember that you must decide this figure. It can be more or less depending on what you feel is right. There is no wrong answer.

The next step is the cost of your shop. You may be fortunate and use your own garage or utility building. Even if you do, consider the cost of shop space. When you go into business, your garage and driveway will become busy. Neighbors may complain and local regulations may force you to move the business into a commercial location. To determine this cost, check out commercial spaces of similar size. Use this figure to calculate the monthly rent and add for utilities such as electricity, water and telephone. If you don't have a separate line for your business, use a portion of the home phone cost. For example, take twenty percent of a total rent (or mortgage payment), electric and telephone bill of $1,000.00. The total would be $200.00 per month. For the sake of simplicity, assume you will be working 160 hours per month. Divide the $200.00 rent figure by 160 for a total of $1.25 per hour.

Woodworking requires an extensive collection of tools. Some are large stationary power tools including table saws, radial arm saws, band saws, lathes, thickness planers, jointers, etc. Others are portable power tools such as circular saws, miter saws, saber saws, sanders, biscuit jointers, etc. Still others are hand tools such as hammers, mallets, chisels, rasps, saws, knives, planes, etc. These tools not only involve an initial investment but they must be maintained in good working order. Over the years they may require replacement with newer or better models.

All these costs must be considered. The simplest way to deal with the cost of replacement is a depreciation schedule. Tools should be depreciated over several years for replacement and income tax purposes. Long after a tool has been depreciated for income tax purposes, the depreciation schedule should continue to ensure that funds are available when a tool must be replaced. For example, a good table saw may serve you for twenty years with proper maintenance and sharp blades. The easiest way to do this is to establish an annual depreciation figure based on the total cost of your tools and the years you expect them to last. Let's assume that this figure is $2,800.00 per year. This means that you should be putting aside $233.00 a month for the replacement and maintenance of tools. Using the 160-hour figure we established earlier, this would require $1.45 per hour.

The same thing goes for a work vehicle, plus you must consider maintenance and fuel. First you must take into account the cost of the vehicle. This cost is handled as depreciation. Let's assume that your vehicle cost $15,000.00 and you expect it to last for five years. Divide the $15,000.00 by 60 months and then divide that sum by 160 hours. This gives us a total of $1.56 per hour. The best way to determine your maintenance and fuel cost is by keeping good records. Let's assume that it will cost $300.00 per month to keep your vehicle properly maintained and fueled. This would require $1.88 per hour.

Insurance is a high cost item that must be considered. This includes keeping your vehicle properly insured, plus fire, theft and liability insurance for your business, your shop, job sites and completed products. Health insurance is also costly causing many self-employed persons to remain uninsured. This is a decision you must make but I recommend that you maintain at least major medical insurance coverage. It is unlikely that you will be able to obtain all this insurance for less than $450 per month requiring $2.80 per hour.

We all face federal income taxes and it is not uncommon for small businesses to have problems with the IRS. These problems often occur because no provisions were made to set aside funds for the payment of income taxes. If possible, pay your taxes quarterly as required by the IRS. If not, at least open a savings account to save a portion of your income to pay your taxes. This amount should be at least ten percent of your gross income. Ten percent may seem low but remember that we are working from gross income not from income after deductible expenses. It is difficult to estimate the exact amount of your income taxes but you will probably pay from twenty to thirty percent of your net income. Social Security alone will require a payment of fifteen percent. A net income of $30,000.00 per year could cost you $8,000.00 and this would require at least $4.20 per hour. This figure can vary considerably depending on your allowable deductions but it is better to save too much than not enough. And, don't forget your State income taxes.

Consider overhead costs for time spent figuring jobs, preparing drawings and bid presentations. This should also include picking up materials, running errands, accounting costs and related items. The will require some guesswork but the figure can be adjusted in the future. Get paid for this time spent by including them as part of your hourly charge. Start with $400.00 per month for an hourly amount of $2.50.

Profit is critical to any business. It is the motivator for all businesses. There are two ways to calculate profit. You can make the profit part of the hourly figure or calculate it separately. A higher percentage must be used if it is part of the hourly figure since the calculation does not include materials. If you add it to the hourly figure, use at least twenty five percent. Otherwise, twenty percent is acceptable.

Now, let's put all these sample figures together to get an idea of how to determine pricing. Start by using your drawings and related information about the project to prepare a materials list. Then, assign an accurate price to each item. If in doubt, price the item higher rather then lower. Any mistake here will come out of your pocket. You may need to contact some of your suppliers to get updated prices. Also, remember to add a waste factor. Most hardwoods come in random sizes and you will have waste. For this project we will assume the materials will cost $500.00 and the work will take 28 hours.

Check out the chart below for a breakdown of hourly charges. Let's calculate our hourly charge by listing all the items discussed previously.

Hourly Wage (Your must decide this)	$20.00
Shop Cost ($200 divided by 160 hours)	$01.25
Tools ($233 divided by 160 hours)	$01.45
Vehicle ($15,000 cost/60 months divided by 160 hours)	$01.56
Maintenance and Fuel	$01.88
Insurance ($450 divided by 160 hours)	$02.80
Taxes ($8,000/12 months divided by 160 hours)	$04.20
Misc. Overhead ($400 divided by 160 hours)	$02.50
TOTAL PER HOUR	**$35.64**
Profit (25% of Total Hourly Figure)	$08.91
TOTAL CHARGE PER HOUR	**$44.55= $45.00**

Since there is some guesswork involved in setting the various hourly amounts, round off the final figure to $45.00. Take 28 hours times $45.00 and it equals $1,260.00. Add this amount to the $500 for materials for a total of $1,760.00, which would be the total price of the job. If you prefer to add the profit separately, use the $35.64 figure times 28 that equals $998.00. Then add the $500 for materials for a total of $1,497.00. Calculate twenty percent of $1,497.00 and it equals $300.00. Add $300.00 to $1,497.00 to total $1,797.00. Notice that the figures are close.

You can do one final check to determine if your estimate is accurate. For jobs of average difficulty, you can multiply the cost of material times 3.5 to get a fairly close estimate. This figure is $1,750 and indicates that your calculations may be slightly high but definitely a safe bid certain to leave a fair profit upon completion. More complex jobs take more time and the checking multiplier should be larger.

There are several things to remember about these figures. They are not necessarily accurate for your area. Determine the going rates for your area and use them. This is especially important if they are higher as you may wind up charging too little for your work. Remember the rule of supply and demand. Your prices can and should reflect the demand for your work. This is common practice in many businesses. Check hotel rates during peak and slow seasons to see how they vary. If you are getting more work than you can possibly do increase your prices until the work levels off. This formula shows how much you must charge to make a living.

Your customer's willingness to pay determines how much you can charge above this amount. The right price for any project is the amount that a willing buyer will pay a willing seller. Beyond that, there are no limits.

For some reason, there is a preconceived notion that a self-employed woodworker can only make wages. Further, that we must be prepared to sacrifice a decent income, medical benefits and vacations to do the work we love. If you believe this is inevitable, it probably will be true for you. There is no question that it is true for many wood-workers. First hand experience has proven this to me. It doesn't have to be that way.

If you have the skills to produce a good product and charge enough for it, you can make a good living as a self-employed woodworker.

FINAL NOTES ON PERCEIVED VALUE AND SUPPLY AND DEMAND

Don't limit yourself by what the competition charges. You may be worth much more to the customer. Some people are making $5.00 per hour while others make over $500.00 per hour. There may be a significant difference in skills but what often makes the difference is the value the customer perceives. A clear example of this is the art world. One canvas may look beautiful and not be worth the value of the canvas materials. Another canvas of the same size may look worthless to you or me and bring thousands from art lovers. This is all value perceived by the customer who is willing to pay the price.

This is applicable to woodworkers. There are woodworkers who struggle to get a few hundred dollars for a really nice rocking chair and others who are getting thousands for a similar chair. Plus, the one that is getting thousands has a long waiting list. Perhaps one of those woodworkers is much more skilled than the other but more likely they are at similar levels. Perceived value is the key ingredient. Use perceived value to your advantage. If people really love your work, then charge as much as the market will bear.

If you want to be in business in a free enterprise system such as ours, you must remember that the price of everything is based on supply and demand. The maximum price of any product or service is the maximum amount that a customer is willing to pay for it. If you have a problem with the idea of perceived value and supply and demand, I suggest that you avoid running your own business because you will probably not make much money.

Fifteen

Expansion

How often have you heard the term "grow or die"? For most small businesses the goal seems to be to grow the business from a one-person operation into some kind of large corporation. If this is what you want, proceed carefully because businesses are very vulnerable during periods of extreme growth. You should probably look elsewhere for information because this book is geared to the one-person business. However, check out the list below for some of the things that are involved with expansion to a large business.

Accounts receivables become a large part of your business. You will have to develop good collection methods to make certain that your company gets paid for all of its work in a timely manner. You can't let things pass because that affects cash flow adversely. Without sufficient cash flow you won't be able to pay the bills that will continue to come in regardless of how collections go. This kind of situation can lead to bankruptcy because you are unable to pay your debts.

Expansion always involves hiring employees and this brings many new problems into play. First, of course, you must make certain that you hire good, productive employees who will care about their work. You also have the problem of payroll deductions and payroll payments to the IRS. This means your entire accounting system must be upgraded to deal with this in a way that meets government standards. And, we still have not covered the additional cost of insurance and the large cost of worker's compensation. The result of all of this means that an employee that works for $10.00 per hour will probably wind up costing you more than $20.00 per hour.

My experience with expansion in my woodworking business was not good. I decided that if I hired a competent woodworker I would have more time to concentrate on projects and the other woodworker could also increase my overall productivity. I really believed that it would free me up to do other jobs. Unfortunately, it did not work out that way.

I hired a professional woodworker and started sharing the work with him. I would do the designs and even create the cut lists and drawings. As it turned out I never had enough time to just concentrate on my projects. Instead I wound up overseeing his work to make certain that it met my standards. This drained time away from my work and reduced the benefits significantly.

Because of my consistent and stressful pushing, I got a lot more work done during the first six months. My gross income was somewhat higher for that 6 months period but the amount of profit was the same as when I worked alone. And, percentage wise, my profit margin was actually lower. I decided at that point to just work alone and simply hire someone to help me deliver and install projects.

Working alone I completed fewer projects but I made just as much money and avoided all the stress of dealing with an employee. Plus I avoided all the payroll hassles. I continued in the business for many years without employees.

One of the reasons that I explored the employee route was that my volume of work had increased significantly. At one time I had a project backlog of more than eight weeks. After my experience with hiring an employee I decided to deal with my large

Seventeen

What is Simplified Woodworking

Simplified woodworking is a name that I coined many years ago when I wrote my first book on the woodworking business. It is nothing more than the use of methods that are simpler, easier and faster than what most consider traditional methods. This does not mean that there is anything wrong with traditional methods and I am not putting them down with this book. These are alternative methods that I have worked with for many years and other woodworkers may find them useful. The main objective of the simpler methods that I describe in this book is to facilitate the quick completion of woodworking projects to increase profits without reducing quality.

It is very difficult to convey an exact definition of simplified woodworking beyond what I have given above. However, it may help to discuss how these methods evolved and some of the basic techniques. Many years ago, when I started my woodworking business, it became evident that it would be difficult for me to make a good living using traditional woodworking methods. The time involved in building projects using these methods tended to price me out of the market. It was either that or a low wage that was not acceptable to me.

There are a few woodworkers who do well financially building projects using traditional methods. Most of these become well known and supplement their income by writing books and creating videos about their work. Unless you become this famous, it is unlikely that you will be able to make a good living using traditional methods. The only exception to this is if you can develop a high dollar clientele making reproductions and restoring valuable antiques. These are both tough fields to break into.

I decided to develop methods to complete my work faster and at a lower cost while still maintaining a high degree of quality. I began compiling ideas that would make things simpler and therefore faster. One of the major questions during this effort was "What kind of joinery can I use on my furniture jobs?" This was an important question because mortise and tenon, dovetails, finger joints, dados, etc. comprise excellent joinery methods but are all time consuming.

I did not consider using dowels even though many woodworkers believe that dowels are a good alternative for these other joinery methods. My own experience and that of several other woodworkers indicates that dowel joints are inherently weak because they lack adequate long grain glue surface. Dowels are round and most of their glue surfaces wind up against the end grain of boards. Glue does not adhere well to end grain. Therefore, the only part of the dowel that is actually holding is that portion that is glued to the long grain of the wood and this causes weak joints.

Many woodworkers mistakenly use dowels when gluing up boards to create a wide surface. This almost always causes joints to crack when the boards move and the dowels remain in place. In addition to these problems, they also make alignment of pieces difficult and time consuming. Actually, when a set of boards are glued up properly to make a wide surface, the glue joint becomes stronger than the board itself. To test this yourself, glue up four or five pieces of boards six inches long and clamp it up. When the glue dries, hit the boards over a sawhorse or some other hard surface until it breaks. It will always break in a board not the joint. Since the glue joint is stronger than the board, it is pointless to use dowels or anything else for any purpose except ease of alignment.

Nails and screws provided an alternative for some cabinets such as those in kitchens. Screw holes can be plugged and nail holes filled. The combination of nails for assembly and screws for strength worked quite well for many kitchens. However, this was definitely not the best answer for fine furniture. Although with shop made plugs it did give an acceptable appearance.

I concluded that building furniture projects economically required a simple joinery method. Butt joints are very simple and fast but have little strength and are frowned upon by many traditional woodworkers. My answer was to use the biscuit joiner or plate joiner to reinforce the butt joints. That is the reason this book covers the use of biscuit joiners in depth. This one tool will help you build many beautiful projects quickly and easily without nail or screw holes to plug or fill.

To help you better understand how best to use the biscuit joiner, all of the projects in this book were constructed using a biscuit joiner and the methods for each project are explained in detail in the instructions. It takes a little effort to learn how to use a biscuit joiner effectively and efficiently but once learned, it will speed up your work and create strong joinery.

Eighteen

Building Cabinets With Modules

Over the years, I have worked with many woodworkers. One of the most common mistakes they make is building large projects as one piece. I have seen entertainment centers that would barely fit through a doorway even when turned on the side and kitchen cabinet units that were over eight feet long. Some units were so heavy that it took six people to move it.

It is much simpler to build cabinets and furniture in modules that one person can carry. At worst, two people should be able to carry the biggest module. Building in this manner makes the job much easier and facilitates the final installation.

One of my contracts involved building all the cabinets for the data center of a large corporation's branch office. The units had to accommodate six people with their computers, storage and regular desk space. Plus, it included divider walls to afford limited privacy to each of the employee. The entire job was built at my shop. One person could carry each piece. The installation took two people because some of the cabinets had to be installed a few feet above the floor. Once assembled, it appeared to be one very large unit.

I think the resistance to modules stems from the aversion to cabinets that seem to be assembled from a bunch of pieces. This problem is easy to overcome with good design features and a little care. First, the design should be such that the final appearance gives the impression of one large piece. Secondly, it is essential to assemble the modules in the shop to see that everything fits properly. Problems should be corrected at the shop. Don't wait till you get on site to find out that there is a problem with the modules fitting together.

One of my projects several years ago was a very large entertainment center. It was constructed of MDF (Medium Density Fiberboard) covered with black, high gloss plastic laminate. The unit included space for television and video recording equipment, plus a complete audio setup and some storage. The complete unit was 6' wide, 6' 6" tall and 26" deep. The extra two inches of depth beyond 24 were to accommodate a wire chase so that the myriad of wires necessary for the various components would be completely hidden. They could not be seen from inside or outside of the unit. The unit had casters so it could be moved from the wall for uncovering the wire chase and making changes.

Since the unit would be in three stacked modules covered by high gloss laminate, it was essential that the modules line up perfectly. I accomplished this by assembling the units at the shop without the laminate and then using a belt sander to make certain that all the modules lined up at all points. Once the MDF had been sanded into perfect alignment, I covered the outside surfaces with the high gloss black laminate and checked the final fit by reassembling the modules. The final unit looked like one very large entertainment center with the joints almost invisible.

It was difficult for two people to carry the three modules because of the weight of the MDF with the laminate. It would have taken a large crew to move this cabinet as one unit. The final unit took twelve carpet casters in order to roll easily and smoothly.

Take the time to design cabinets as modules. I suggest making a sketch of the entire unit and then determining the best way to divide it into workable modules. Once this is decided, you can proceed to make the final working drawings for the unit. Remember to divide the modules at the point that will be the least conspicuous so the final appearance will give the impression of one unit.

One final trick for building cabinets in modules involves the use of reveals. Sometimes it just isn't possible to assemble the modules so the unit appears as one large unit. In this case you do something to make the joints part of the design. One method I have used is to adjust the size of the cabinets to accommodate reveals. I make 1/4" thick strips that I place between the modules and recess them about 1/4". You can make these a different color as an accent but I have found that they work fine the same color as the project. The recess creates a shadow making the recess darker and it gives a very good appearance. It simply takes attention from the module joints by converting them to design features.

Nineteen

Shop Space and Tools

It's not necessary to have a large shop space to start a woodworking business. Obviously, the larger the space the better it will be for your work. An ideal situation would be to start in your own double garage. This can be done in some communities but in others it is prohibited either by City ordinances or deed restrictions in specific subdivisions.

The important thing is to keep costs down initially. If you can use your garage or a large storage building on your property, the costs will remain low. If you must rent a space, search for a bargain. Your rent will be a monthly and never-ending expense so it's important to keep it reasonable.

Don't worry about the location initially. What you want is as large a place as you can afford even if the area is less than desirable. Remember that most of your customers will not come to your shop. They will see you in their home when you sell them, take all your measurements and then deliver and install the project.

I have run into woodworkers who do not have a shop. They work by building cabinets for customers on site. I don't believe this is the best way to do business. It is very inconvenient for the customer. Instead of a cabinet job, it is basically the same as major remodeling. You will do much better if you have a place to build the cabinets and then come for one or two days and just replace or install the cabinets. Customers will appreciate the limited inconvenience.

I believe that an ideal size for a shop is 20' X 24' or larger. It is important to layout your shop space efficiently. I won't provide shop space drawings in this book because many different designs will work well and you need to decide what will work best for the kind of work you will be doing. The important thing is to develop a layout that accommodates the flow of the work. For example, you want one side, close to a door, to bring in and store materials. From there you want to have the cutting area and move to the assembly area. The final step is to a finishing area that should also be near a door so you can load the finished projects onto your vehicle for delivery and installation. You don't want to have to haul projects back and forth across your shop as you complete each aspect of it. You should probably include a space to park projects midway in their construction in case you have to stop one to complete another for some special case.

If possible, find a shop space that has a separate room that can be used for an office. Of course, you can use a room in your home for an office but it is helpful to have it at the same location. A small office area would also be easy to heat and air condition and it would provide a nice brief haven for you to take breaks away from the heat, cold and dust of the shop floor. Naturally, it would be great to have an air-conditioned shop space but that is not always possible. The office would also serve as a place for design work and to figure the price of various jobs.

Tools are critical to the woodworker. It is important to have the best tools that you can afford to purchase. On the other hand, it is possible to do fine work with consumer brand tools. Don't give up just because your tools are not all trade models. I encourage woodworkers to start with the tools they have and then buy more and better tools as the money begins to come in.

There are many tools of critical importance but the heart of a shop that builds cabinets or furniture using sheet materials is the table saw. A good table saw will be of enormous help in getting all the parts for your projects accurately cut. It is also important for the table saw to have a good size work area. It is very difficult to cut down 4' X 8' plywood sheets alone if all you have is the table saw. You need support benches surrounding the two sides and the back of the table saw. For best results, I suggest that the overall work table of your table saw be about 8' X 8'. This will allow you to easily run plywood sheets through the saw without strain. When not in use for your table saw, this work area serves for the assembly of projects.

The tables that surround the table saw can also be cabinets that accommodate storage space for the tools and supplies you need in your shop. You can build some very nice cabinet tables for your table saw area. I suggest you cover the tops with laminate to make them smoother so the sheet goods will slide easily.

An excellent accessory for your table saw is the custom fence. Most table saws come setup to cut about a 24" wide strip. There are times when you will need wider pieces. You can cut these pieces by deducting the width and then cutting the other piece off but it is better to have that extra control that a custom fence affords. Most good custom fences will allow you to cut about 48" wide pieces. This will accommodate any sheet goods you may need to rip or crosscut.

Purchase a set of carbide-tipped blades for your table saw. High-speed steel blades cannot maintain their sharpness and you will be wasting your time sharpening blades every few cuts. Carbide-tipped blades remain sharp for months under normal use. I suggest a 24-tooth blade for ripping lumber, a 60 to 80-tooth blade for cross cutting lumber and a triple chip model for cutting fine hardwood plywood faces or laminates.

For many years my favorite power tool for crossing cutting lumber was the radial arm saw. Now I prefer the sliding compound miter saw. I like these saws better for a couple of reasons. The first is that they seem to be more stable across the entire cut. The second is that the location of the beginning of the cut line does not change when you move from a 90-degree cut to any other angle. With a radial arm saw the entire arm moves and the beginning of the cut line changes location entirely. This can make things more complex. With the sliding compound miter saw changing the angle does not affect the cut line start.

The band saw is one of my favorite tools. You should have as large a band saw as you can afford. There are several models in the 12" to 14" size that work well for most work. I would keep a ½" wide blade for cutting thick woods, a ¼" wide blade for most general work and a 1/8" wide blade for scrollwork. Most of these band saws will cut a board up to 6" thick. I suggest the two wheel design band saws because my luck with three wheelers was not good. However, some of the more expensive three wheelers may work fine.

Sometimes a circular saw will come in handy and I would definitely have one in my shop for those occasions. A circular saw is more a carpenter's tool for cutting wood for construction and remodeling but it can be helpful in a woodworking shop. It often serves an important role during installations.

The router is a critical tool for a woodworker. You should definitely have a powerful model that will allow you to do all kinds of decorative work. This is a tool that fa-

Twenty

Finishing Projects

Most of the project plans have information on finishing. This chapter covers just a few of the products and methods that I have used. You can use these and try other things that may work better for you. My favorite finish for natural wood is simply a clear coat. Before the clear coat, you can apply a stain. Wood stains come in many types and colors. I like the MinWax brand but there are many others. Most stains require overnight drying before you can apply the clear coat but you can get water based stains that dry in one hour.

When selecting a stain color remember that it will look different depending on the color and grain of the wood. So, your project may turn out a little darker or lighter than the sample that you saw in the store. I suggest using a scrap piece to test the color. Before beginning, stir the stain thoroughly. The pigment has a tendency to settle to the bottom of the container. Using it without stirring will give a washed out and splotched look. Splotching appears on many wood surfaces. To avoid splotching, apply a pre-stain coat. This can be mixed from your clear coat but I would advise you to purchase a pre-stain product to keep things simple. Remember that this product will seal the wood slightly to keep the stain on the surface from splotching. This will also cause the stain color to be lighter and more than one coat may be required.

To prepare for staining, uniform sanding is critical. Sand the entire project evenly. Do not apply excessive pressure to the sander during this job. This causes shiny spots that will not take the stain well causing lighter areas on the surface. To avoid this, change sandpaper often. Friction builds up when using a power sander and if the sandpaper gets worn it will simply shine the surface instead of sanding it. It is a false economy to use sandpaper beyond its effective life.

Once the stain is applied, wipe off the excess with good t-shirt rags. Wipe the surface completely making certain no streaks are left. If the stain dries before being wiped, the streaks can only be removed with paint or lacquer thinner and this will require additional staining. After wiping, allow the stain to dry overnight, unless the instructions indicate otherwise. Once the stain is dry, apply the clear coat according to the instructions on the container. Do not sand the stained surface before applying the first coat of clear. Sanding at this time can cause unsightly lightened areas.

If you prefer water-based clear coats, MinWax makes an excellent product called Polycrylic that dries fast. To get a good finish with this product, make certain you use a polyester brush, preferably one of the specialized brushes sold by MinWax, and do not apply it when the temperature is below 60 degrees. Most clear coats should be brushed carefully. Brush only with the grain of the wood and do not over brush. Just spread it as evenly as possible, thick enough so it will flow out but not so thick that it runs. When using fast drying clear coats, do not go back to completed areas with the brush. These will already be semi dry and brushing will leave deep and unsightly brush marks.

Another finishing option is painting. Small projects can painted with spray cans. Whether you spray or brush, always use a primer for the first coat and then sand all the surfaces smooth before applying quality enamel.

It has been my experience that spraying finishes with HVLP (high volume low pressure) equipment works well for woodworking projects. However, spraying has its complexities and safety issues. There is a learning curve involved in learning how to use a spray gun competently. It is important to practice until you become proficient before using spray equipment to finish projects.

With all finishes you must also consider harmful vapors and flammability. This is especially true of lacquer finishes. I suggest that you avoid spraying lacquer unless you have a safe, adequate, properly ventilated area in which to finish your projects. In addition to having good ventilation and a high quality respirator, you need to make certain that your equipment is designed so that it does not cause sparks that could set off the combustible sprayed lacquer. I strongly suggest that you learn how to use lacquer products properly and safely before spraying any project with them.

Twenty-One

Shop Notes

This section is devoted to notes that I have compiled over many years of building woodworking projects. You should be able to glean some helpful suggestions for handling various aspects of building woodwork projects.

Purchasing Hardwoods - Purchasing hardwoods can be confusing if you purchase from a regular lumber company or a home improvement center. I suggest you purchase from a store that specializes in hardwoods. Many communities have one or more such stores. You can find them listed in the yellow pages of your phone directory. Hardwoods are most often sold by the board foot. In many cases, it comes rough on all four sides, and must be planed and straight lined before use. If you have the equipment and the time to plane and straight line your hardwood, this is the best and lowest cost way to purchase it. However, if you don't have this equipment, many hardwood stores will plane and straight-line hardwood boards for a reasonable fee.

Some stores purchase hardwood that is already planed and straight lined from distributors. This practice can create problems for you because the straight lining may have been done weeks earlier, and the boards may have dried crooked. If this is the case, the straight lining is of no value even though you are paying for it in the price of the material. If you are allowed to handpick your boards, you may be able to save money by buying such merchandise. I have been to hardwood stores that have two prices on planed and straight lined hardwoods. One is based on random boards picked and loaded by their employees, the other higher price based on you picking out the boards. You must decide which way is best for you. If you need only one or two boards for a project, I suggest you pay the higher price and pick out the boards yourself.

If you have a thickness planer, the least expensive way to buy hardwood is in its rough state. Each step taken by the hardwood stores or the wholesale distributor will increase the board foot price of the wood and the ultimate cost of your project. Usually I prefer to purchase surfaced hardwood and straight line it myself when I am ready to use it. I do this because I often purchase the 100 board foot minimum in order to keep the price down, even if my current project requires less wood. Since I will be using the excess for some other project in the future, it saves me money. I prefer to straight line it myself because even if I have it straight lined just before I pick it up, the hardwood that is set aside for other projects will probably get a little crooked by the time I use it. Sometimes, however, when my time is limited, I let the dealer straight line it for me. One hundred board feet costs me about $6, and it is well worth it.

Quarters - Hardwood thickness is measured in quarters. Each quarter is ¼ ". For example, 4/4 lumber is 1" thick, 6/4 lumber is 1 ½" thick, 8/4 lumber is 2" thick, and so on. The hardwood you will use for most projects is 4/4 thick with 8/4 being used for legs and other thicker parts. The hardwood is most often planed to 13/16" thickness. However, many hardwood stores will plane it to 7/8" thickness. Others will plane it to the thickness you request. Some stores will stock planed lumber for those who want their standard thickness, and rough lumber for those who want a specified thickness or who have their own thickness planers.

Straight Lining - Whether you purchase the hard wood surfaced or rough from these stores, it will seldom be straight lined. Many stores have straight lining machines in their mill and will gladly straight line your boards for a fee. Usually this fee is five to ten cents per lineal foot. If your time is limited, this is the best way to handle this job. Remember, many stores have a minimum fee for this service, based on 100 board feet. But it may still be worth it to save work and time.

Straight lining can be done in various ways with various tools. I prefer to use my table saw. I made an 8' long jig that easily accommodates almost any board that I will use. This jig consists of a ¾" thick plywood board that is 10" wide and 96" long. A second ¾" thick strip that is 2" wide and 96" long is screwed to the top of the first board. The exact placement of this strip is determined by the width of the boards to be straight lined. Four hold-downs made from thin solid wood or plywood are then screwed on top of this strip. These are evenly spaced and positioned so that they lap over the edge of the top strip.

This straight lining jig is used by placing the board to be straight lined on the bottom plywood and against the edge of the top strip. The four hold-downs are then swung over the hardwood board and tightened down. This will hold the board in place while you work on it. Now measure from the outside edge of the jig to the outside edge of the hardwood board. Do this in three places: on each end and in the middle. Take the smallest dimension and deduct ¼" to ½"" from it; use this dimension to set the rip fence on your table saw. The last step is to place the outside edge of the jig against the rip fence and run the jig through the saw as you would to rip any board. Make certain that the blade is set high enough to cut through the hardwood board in its elevated position.

During the rip it is essential to keep the edge of the jig tight against the rip fence. As the blade cuts through the hardwood board, it will leave a straight line to use for all future ripping. Before starting to rip the pieces for your project, straight line all the pieces you will need. Do not straight line any more than you need. Instead, wait until you are ready for the next project to straight line the pieces for it. Once you have straight lined pieces, ripping is relatively easy. I suggest that you use a sharp 24-tooth carbide blade for ripping.

Ripping - Ripping hardwoods can be difficult. The first step is to straight-line your board. Some lumber companies have a limited selection of hardwoods, including oak, ash, and maple in nominal sizes just like other lumber. If you purchase these, straight lining may not be necessary. Nevertheless, it is important to remember that straight lining is the method used to create a straight line on one edge of boards to facilitate straight and even ripping. Since many boards that come in nominal sizes are crooked, straight lining may still be necessary to ensure straightness and accurate ripping.

Remember that inexpensive blades are no bargain. They are not as well balanced, their arbor holes are not as precisely drilled, and the carbide on the teeth is not as large as on a quality blade. The initial cost of a quality blade is much higher, but it will last indefinitely and it will seldom need sharpening. If you will be ripping only hardwood or just a few short pieces of 4/4 lumber, you can use a good crosscut carbide blade. I keep a 60 tooth, triple chip carbide blade on my saw for ripping plywood and laminates. It easily and cleanly rips a few pieces of hardwood, but I still use my 24-tooth rip blade when I do a lot of ripping.

To rip the pieces you need, set the rip fence to the desired dimension. If you have an accessory fence with an accurate measuring system, by all means use it. If not, set the correct distance between the blade and the fence by measuring from the fence surface to a tooth on the blade that is beveled toward the fence. Remember to allow for planing or sanding after the ripping. You should add at least to 1/16" to the finished size that you want. Set the height of the blade approximately 1/4" higher than the thickness of the wood, and you are ready to rip. Before starting, prepare a short, sharp pointed wedge and keep it within reach. Place the edge of your piece squarely against the fence and approach the blade slowly but consistently. If your table has a splitter installed, you will not need the wedge. Otherwise, watch the cut as it leaves the blade to determine if it will begin to close up. If it does, carefully place the little wedge in the cut and proceed. This will stop the cut from closing up and tightening up on the blade. Failure to do this can cause friction that is bad for the wood and the blade. It can stop the saw and, more seriously, it can cause a kickback and injure you.

Safety Notes - The splitter is part of the blade guard on many table saws. I recommend that you use it for all cuts whenever possible. However, I must acknowledge that many people do not use the splitter or a blade guard because the blade guard is highly inconvenient for many cuts. But blade guards do provide valuable protection. Extra care is definitely called for if you decide not to use a blade guard. Table saws are inherently dangerous and can cause serious injuries that can maim you for life.

Every cut you make has the potential to hurt you. There is no place for overconfidence or carelessness when you are using a table saw. Your mind must be fully on the work you are doing. Stay aware of where you are standing in relation to the work piece. When ripping a narrow piece, avoid standing directly behind the work piece.

Read the instruction booklet that came with your table saw. It contains valuable safety information. Read other books on how to make the best use of your table saw. Become familiar with every part of your table saw and its potential uses. Avoid obviously dangerous cuts. Many cuts that would be somewhat dangerous on the table saw can be done safely on a band saw. Watch your hands always. It may sound silly, but I always consciously check the location of both my hands before starting any machine.

Become totally aware of the machine and yourself before starting any cut. Then analyze or visualize the cut from start to finish before making it. This may well show you some trouble spots. Once you are completely clear about the cut, go ahead, but don't divert your attention for any reason. Do not allow anyone to speak to you during a cut. If they persist, run them out of your shop. Your attention must be 100% on the cut. Use push sticks as necessary to keep your hands from coming too close to the blade. Don't let anyone convince you that you are going overboard on safety; you cannot be too safe. Set your rules and follow them to the letter every time you make a cut. Discipline is essential because there are no second chances. Being maimed by a machine can seriously affect both your livelihood and your life.

Crosscutting - Crosscutting plywood sheets is more difficult than crosscutting normal size lumber. Sometimes you will be crosscutting a piece that is as much as 24" wide and often over 12" wide. My favorite tool for crosscutting now is the sliding compound miter saw. I used to crosscut with a radial arm saw but found that a good sliding compound miter saw is more stable and easier to use.

You can crosscut plywood pieces that are 24" or wider by using the table saw with a standard or after market fence but it is tricky and can be dangerous. It is essential to take great care when making these cuts. You must maintain good alignment with the blade and feed the material slowly so the blade does not bind. You also need to have a fine carbide-tipped blade and a fresh throat plate on your saw to avoid tear out on the plywood surface. Always make these cuts with the best side up.

Pieces that are narrower than 24" should not be crosscut on the table saw unless you have a large sliding table. These tables work well but they are expensive. Some inexpensive table saws have a sliding table but it is quite small and not suited for large plywood panels. If you don't have a sliding table there are a couple of options. The simplest is to use a circular saw and clamp guides to the pieces to make certain all the cuts are correct. Some woodworker supply stores offer aluminum guides with built in clamps that work quite well.

Another option is to build a sliding crosscut jig for your table saw. You can find complete details about a large crosscut jig at http://woodworkdoctor.com together with a lot of other valuable how-to information.

Assembly with nails - Kitchen cabinets can be assembled quickly and easily using nails and glue with butt joints. Many other joints are possible and will certainly provide an excellent job but they are unnecessary. Some craftsmen will frown on using nails. Some call them metal dowels. What's really important is how you want to build your project. Woodworking involves diverse methods, and you will always find people to agree or disagree with many of the methods. So the best thing to do is to make your own choice. I choose nails for many projects. Sometimes even when I use joinery I may use a nail or two in lieu of clamps.

I have found that using nails increases the speed of building any project. Even with certain pieces of furniture, nails can be used in out-of-the-way places where they won't be seen after the project is complete. I like to use #6 galvanized casing nails which have a larger head than finish nails but are still small enough to set and fill without difficulty. The easiest way to nail the parts together is to make certain that the piece you are nailing into is against something such as a wall or floor to keep it from sliding around under the impact of the hammer. Depending on the depth of your cabinet, use four or five nails across each piece. Drive the nails until they are almost flat with the surface, then use a nail set to finish driving them and set them so they are ready for wood filler.

Pneumatic nailers – Nailers are great tools that can save an infinite amount of time. You can easily nail a cabinet together without placing any part of it against the floor or wall for support. Pneumatic nailers are costly and unless you are building cabinets with nails regularly this expense is not justified. A good small compressor and a quality finish nailer will cost between $300.00 and $500.00. Some home improvement stores carry nailers and compressors at a lower price and sometimes they are on sale. You can also get a better price by purchasing used equipment. Just make certain to check it out carefully before you buy it.

If you do purchase a compressor and nailer, remember that safety is very important with this tool. Do not remove the safety apparatus from a pneumatic nailer, it may save time, but it could lead to a painful injury to you or someone else. I find it comforting to know that my nailers cannot fire unless they are pressed against the wood. They cannot go off by accident when I pick them up or put them down. These tools also require maintenance if they are to last. The compressor will need an oil change once in a while unless you purchase an oil-less unit. The compressor tank must be drained regularly so that moisture build-up in the tank will not cause rust. Most nailers requires a little oil prior to every use and should always be kept clean and free of dust so that the parts will function properly and not get jammed. There are some nailers that are oil-less so you should check the instructions.

Scribes - These are helpful in fitting cabinets to walls. They are especially useful when fitting cabinets between two walls. A scribe is a facing strip that creates a space between the cabinet sidewall and the wall that it will be installed against. This space makes it possible to compensate for crooked walls. It is called a scribe because the strip is often scribed to follow the shape of the wall. The size of the scribe is optional and normally based on the quality of the walls. If the walls where the cabinet will be installed are quite straight and level, a ¼" scribe will probably be adequate. If the walls are crooked and out of level, a ½" or even 1" scribe may be appropriate. To use the scribe strip, place the cabinet against the wall and level it properly. Then check how the scribe strip fits the wall. If it isn't a tight fit, you mark or scribe the strip at one or more points, then cut it along the line to make it fit the wall. Now the cabinet can be installed to fit tightly against the wall, giving you a very professional job. It would be impossible to shape the side of the cabinet itself in this manner.

Anytime you are building a cabinet to fit between two walls or in a tight place, remember to measure the diagonals. This is important because it can be costly and embarrassing to try to install a cabinet when it won't fit through a doorway or between moldings.

Building a cabinet that won't fit into a doorway can be embarrassing. One of my jobs involved building all the cabinets for the home of an attorney. All the cabinets fit perfectly until I reached the last cabinet. It was a bathroom cabinet with a built-in clothes hamper that was to be installed in a small water closet room within the bathroom. When I was ready to install it, I got it into the bathroom but it would not fit through the door to the water closet space where it belonged. I finally had to take the cabinet back to my shop and cut it in half to make it fit. Fortunately, everyone just got a good laugh at my expense. So be sure to check these things before you complete your design.

Another useful purpose for scribes is to fit cabinets around baseboards and other moldings. By having a large enough scribe you can simply scribe around the molding and still get a very built-in look for your cabinet This can be done with the scribe on the cabinet during Installation or attached after installation depending on what works best for the situation at hand.

Hang rails - When building cabinets to be hung up or built-in on your walls, hang rails are very important. They give strength to the fasteners that will hold the cabinet to the wall. Most cabinets have thin backs that are too flimsy to hold the weight of a cabinet and everything that it will contain. But by placing a hang rail at the top and bottom of a cabinet the installation screws can go through the hang rail and the back and have more than enough strength to hold the weight. The simplest and quickest way to install hang rails is nailed from each side inside the cabinet before the back is attached. Some cabinetmakers attach the back to the cabinet first, and then attach the hang rails behind the back. In this case the cabinet sides, top and bottom must be ¾" narrower to accommodate the hang rail spacing. And any side of the cabinet that will show must have a molding or other facing to cover the edge of the hang rail because it will show. Cabinetmakers who use this method prefer it because once the cabinet it installed the hang rails are not visible. Another advantage to this kind of hang rail treatment is that there is a large hollow space behind the back between the hang rails. This space can be used to advantage when you install cabinets on very crooked walls. With both methods the hang rails serve the same function of insuring a strong and safe installation.

Iron-on Veneer - Iron-on veneer is an excellent and easy-to-use product. It can be applied without special tools, but special edge banding machines are available to make the job faster and easier. These machines range in price from about $280.00 to thousands of dollars, depending on their level of automation. They help you attain great speed, but you can do an excellent job with just an old household iron. I suggest buying an old iron from a flea market or Goodwill. New household irons have all kinds of safety features that will automatically turn them off if they sit for any length of time unused. This can be very inconvenient when you start to veneer and the iron is no longer hot. Older irons are free of all these features. You also need a utility knife, a mill bastard file and some 100 or 120 grit sandpaper for the final touch. I also highly recommend one other inexpensive tool: the Virutex edge trimmer that costs about $15. This wonderful little tool trims both edges of the veneer flush with the flat surfaces in one quick pass. It has two blades on each side that are completely adjustable so you can cut the veneer as close as you want. The first blade cuts the veneer flush with the surface. The second blade follows about an inch behind and bevels the veneer to a 45 degree angle leaving it ready for final filing or sanding. If you set this machine properly, the filing and sanding are very easy and quick to complete.

To apply the veneer, set the heat on the household iron on medium to high. Since every iron is different, test this setting and adjust it as needed. If the veneer does not stick well, make the iron hotter. If the veneer surface burns, even though you have kept the iron moving, make the iron cooler. Cut your veneer strip slightly longer than the edge to be covered. Hold the veneer in place with your hand about six inches from the end of the piece. Make sure that the first six inches of veneer are properly aligned with the edge and then place the iron flat on this section and press. Watch your fingers to avoid a severe burn. If you allow this section to cool for a moment, it will remain glued while you work the rest of the strip.

Keep the iron moving. Align the veneer with the edge with one hand as you move forward and press down with the iron in the other hand. When applying the veneer you can tell right away if it has not been heated sufficiently. When you lift the iron, the veneer will curl up. Once you have heated it adequately, it will stay put. Remember to apply pressure to ensure a good bond.

When you reach the end, check the entire strip to make certain that the veneer covers all the edges. The veneer is slightly wider than the edge, and it should be either flush with the edge or overlapping. If there is any edge showing, go back over that section with your iron and quickly force the strip into alignment while it is still hot. You may need a glove for doing this, because the glue and the surface are very hot. Allow the piece to cool completely before trimming. If you are doing several pieces, veneer them all, then go back to the first one to start trimming.

To trim the veneer, place the edge with the veneer face down on a table. Use the utility knife to cut the excess veneer flush with the ends of the piece. Next, trim both edges of the veneer along the surfaces of the piece. This can be done with a utility knife, using great care. If possible, buy the Virutex Edge Trimmer, and adjust it carefully. It will do a first class job.

You can also do the trimming with a regular utility knife. Before starting, install a new blade because a sharp edge is essential. Lay the piece to be trimmed flat on a surface and place the utility knife on the surface so the blade is flat or parallel with the surface. Cut into the veneer until the blade touches the plywood surface and then proceed to cut off the excess veneer while keeping the blade squarely against the plywood surface. Do not cut at an angle because the blade will cut into the plywood and damage the surface. The goal is to cut only the excess veneer.

After the trimming, remove any excess left by the blade with a mill bastard file and then smooth it out with sandpaper. You can just use sandpaper, but the glue will quickly build up on it. It builds up on the file, but it can be easily cleaned off with a file card or a wire brush. You can see when the edge sanding is finished by the way it looks. There should be no visible line at the corner.

This veneer is easy to use and does an excellent job when properly installed. It is available in 13/16" width that is perfect to cover the edge of 3/4" plywood. It may be purchased in small shrink-pack rolls or in 82' and 250' rolls. Some stores even sell it by the lineal foot so that you can buy exactly what you need. If you cannot find it locally, you can find it in many woodworking catalogs.

Butt Joints - Simplified Woodworking methods involve using reinforced butt joints. Other methods of reinforcement can be used. The simplest is to use nails and screws. Although frowned on by some woodworkers, this method is quick, easy, and looks smooth and professional when properly done. For precision in using this method it is important to clamp the project pieces tightly together and then drill and drive your screws. You can use drywall screws, countersunk and covered with flat or round plugs. Or you may prefer to use trim screws and fill the holes with matching filler. Trim screws are exactly like drywall screws except that they have very narrow heads, only slightly larger than those of finish nails. Drive them in until they are slightly countersunk and fill the holes after the first coat of clear finish has been applied. Use color putty that closely matches the wood. Clean the excess putty from surrounding surfaces. When the putty has dried, fine sand all surfaces and apply the last two coats of finish. Your screws should be almost invisible.

Drywall Screws - Drywall screws are self-tapping and easy to drive, even by hand. But if you use screws frequently I recommend that you purchase a rechargeable drill/screw gun. This tool along with the magnetic bit holder and appropriate bits (Phillips and square head) will speed up your work.

Euro Hardware - Blum hinges and drawer slides are available in most communities and through several websites and woodwork catalogs. In order to learn to use them properly, obtain a copy of the Blum catalog that describes all of Blum's products and provides helpful information on installation and adjustments. I use Blum products because over the years I have had no callbacks on them. Other companies, such as Mepla and Grass, offer similar products that are also reliable and should be used if they are readily available to you. These European style hinges are adjustable in all directions. If your doors do not fit perfectly, you simply make minor adjustments with a Phillips screwdriver to align them.

The drawer slides are based upon a system called captive roller. The ball bearing roller on one side is held captive while the roller on the other side is allowed to run free. Even if your drawer is a little narrow for the space, it will still run smoothly without cocking or locking up. With this hardware your drawers and doors are easier to install and work more smoothly than they would with ordinary hardware.

The 35mm (1 3/8") hole for the concealed hinges should be drilled with a drill press using a Forstner type bit to avoid damaging the face surfaces. Test the drilling and the depth of the hole on a scrap of the same thickness before you drill the hole. The depth and location of the holes is critical to the proper fit and function of the hinges.

Staining - Staining is a critical step in finishing your project. My preference, whenever possible, is to avoid using a stain. I like the natural color of wood and many of my projects are finished without stain. However, stains can add much to a project if the wood used has little character. If used properly, stain will not detract from an attractive wood grain. The single most common mistake made when staining is inadequate wiping off of excess stain. Various stains have different instructions, but for the most part staining involves applying the stain, allowing a little drying time, and then wiping off excess stain. The important thing to remember is that all you want from the stain is the color. It should not contribute lines to the grain pattern of the wood. If it does, you have not wiped enough or you allowed it to dry too long so that it will not wipe off.

Apply stain with a brush or a rag and then wait and watch. Do not walk away and come back in a few minutes. Watch the drying process. If you are staining a large project, plan your staining in delineated sections. Wipe each section as soon as it is ready. I prefer to start wiping as soon as drying begins even in just a small section. It is preferable to wipe too soon than to wait too long. Keep fresh rags handy and replace them when they get so loaded with excess stain that they will not wipe without streaks. Wipe vigorously with the grain until all evidence of the stain, except the color, is gone. The grain of the wood should be prominent through the stain without streaks. If stain dries and streaks, you can usually remove the streaks and much of the stain with lacquer thinner. This also works well if the color is too dark. Just wet a rag with lacquer thinner and wipe the surface evenly.

Some stains come with varnish in them and are applied like varnish. I like one of these called Bartley's Gel Varnish. It comes as a gel in clear or a variety of stain colors. It is applied with a rag. Once again, removing the excess is critical. Once it has been wiped off, buff your piece lightly with a clean cloth. Using Bartley's is a minimum two-coat process. If you like the color after the first coat, use clear Bartley's for the second coat. If the color is too light, recoat with Bartley's Stain/Varnish. Or you can even use a different color to alter the final color of the project. You can also color clear Bartley's or alter the color of the stain using oil base colors.

Remember, the key to successful staining is the wiping.

Finishing – I like Deft finishing products and they work well if the instructions are followed correctly. Start by sanding all parts of the project using 220-grit sandpaper. Make certain that all the edges and corners are smooth and then clean off the surfaces completely. To do this, brush all the dust off the surfaces and then wipe them with a rag. Now apply the first coat of Deft Clear Wood Finish or Wood Armor. If you use Deft Clear Wood Finish be certain to work in a well-ventilated area or use a good respirator. You can tell your respirator is working well if the smell doesn't get through. If you don't use a respirator, use a fan to blow the vapors towards an open door or window.

You won't have this difficulty with Wood Armor because it is water based, but you should still work in a well-ventilated area. Once you have applied the first coat, allow it to dry for at least two hours. After it is dry, feel the finish. If you are applying it to solid hardwood, it will probably feel fairly smooth, so sanding will not be required at this stage. But if you are finishing plywood, the surface will probably feel quite rough because the grain has been raised considerably. If this is the case sand all the surfaces by hand using 400-grit sandpaper. Feel the surface for smoothness as you proceed. Make certain the entire project feels smooth. Brush off all the dust and then wipe with a rag or paper towel. Finally wipe the entire surface carefully with a tack cloth to remove all the dust from the surfaces. Now apply the second coat. You want to lightly comb this coat out carefully because it is more likely to run this time since the wood has been sealed. However, do not go back to areas that are beginning to dry. This action will cause large ugly brush marks and won't resolve the problem.

Allow this coat to dry for at least two hours and then repeat the process. This time sand both the solid wood and the plywood using 400 grit or finer sandpaper until the surfaces feel as smooth as glass. Feeling the surfaces is the only way to make certain they are smooth. Now clean all the surfaces just as you did after the first sanding. Make absolutely certain that no dust is left on any of the surfaces.

Now apply the third coat and allow it to dry completely. Your project is finished. For additional luster or strength you can apply one or two more coats, but this is not essential. Using this system you will get consistently good results. Remember that as the temperature gets colder the drying times get longer, so you may need to wait more than two hours before recoating. Also remember that Wood Armor is a water-base product and will not perform well at temperatures below 65 degrees. I have used Deft Clear Wood Finish successfully in 40-degree weather, so if the weather is cold you may have to use it instead of Wood Armor. Deft Clear Wood Finish is flammable and should not be used around heaters that have a flame of any kind.

Sanding all surfaces before assembly makes your job much easier. When using Deft finishing products it is unnecessary to sand finer than 150 grit before staining or applying the first coat of clear finish. Because the liquid raises the grain, finer sanding is a waste of time at this point. Fine sanding should take place after the clear finish is applied. For a really smooth finish, sand with 400 grit after the first coat of clear and then with 600 grit after the second and subsequent coats.

Belt Sanders - The handheld versions are excellent tools that can speed up your sanding of solid hardwoods. However, belt sanders can also damage your project if used carelessly and should not be used to sand a plywood face. They come in various sizes and power ratings. The most common sizes are 3x21, 3x24, and 4x24, but there are others. It is best to buy one of the common sizes because sanding belts in these sizes are readily available from most dealers.

If you are in the market for a belt sander, purchase a good one. Rockwell (Delta), Ryobi, Makita, Freud, Bosch, Milwaukee, AEG and others make good belt sanders. The prices vary, but you will probably have to spend well over $100 for a quality unit. An industrial grade sander will cost well over $200, some even $300, but you should be able to buy an excellent sander in the $140 to $200 range. Shop around locally for what you might like. Once you find a model you want to buy, check the ads in woodworking magazines. In many cases you will find exactly the same model for less, and in many states you will not have to pay sales tax. You can save up to 25% in this way.

There are several important things to look for in a belt sander. The first is balance. This is a very personal thing and differs from one woodworker to another. Find a tool that feels well balanced to you, one that is easy for you to keep flat on the surface being sanded. If one end tends to tilt, you will gouge your wood surface with it. The next thing to check is weight. With a belt sander, lightweight is not an advantage. The sander should do the sanding with its own weight. It should not be necessary to press down with it on the surface. Pressing down will create excessive friction for the belt and overwork the motor and the bearings. It also causes gouging and can easily ruin a surface or edge. With a light sander people have a tendency to press down to speed up the cutting. A hefty sander with a good belt will cut smoothly, evenly and consistently without gouging.

Next, check the tracking. The belt should track accurately and maintain its position. Inexpensive belt sanders often have cheap tracking devices. You can see this by the way they are designed. Some have a cheap little wire between the adjustment knob and the actual adjusting mechanism. This connection has too much play and the belt often over reacts when it is adjusted. Or, it does not initially react at all which causes over adjustment and a moment later the belt is out of adjustment in the opposite direction. This can be very frustrating. With a lot of practice you can get accustomed to these peculiarities, but it is neither easy nor necessary. These inexpensive sanders are obviously poorly designed and bulky. They do not feel good in the hands and are not a bargain. It is best to wait until you can afford a quality belt sander.

Sanding belts can be purchased from many manufacturers. Price is not always a good guide to quality. You can get good belts at bargain prices, especially if you are willing to buy them in boxes of ten or more. Check around for prices. Check the ads in woodworking magazines and catalogs. Call other woodworkers in your area about sources for sanding belts. You can save a great deal of money in this way.

When sanding, use gum belt cleaners. They work well to clean saw dust from belts, and they help you get much more use from each belt. Use fresh belts always. There is no advantage to using worn belts. It is not economical, and it can cause you to ruin your project and your sander. I seldom use a belt rougher than 100 grit. Anything rougher scratches the surface and creates more work. If the surface requires that much sanding, I prefer either to cut it or plane it before I sand. For most projects, I sand using a 100-grit belt on my belt sander, then switch to my orbital sander to start the final sanding.

When you are sanding with a belt sander, it is important to keep the sander flat and square with the surface of your wood. If you do this and sand with the grain, a 100-grit belt will leave you with a smooth even surface ready for final sanding or other milling. Some belt sanders come with an attachment frame that helps keep the sander flat on the surface. This is probably a valuable accessory, but learning to keep the sander flat and square is important even if you use the frame. It's also important to keep the sander moving while it is running. Do not stop in one place because the sander will immediately begin to dig into the surface. When working large surfaces, keep moving forward, backward and slowly to the sides at the same time. Do not press down; let the weight of the sander do the work.

The only time that it may be appropriate to use sandpaper rougher than 100-grit is when working with glued up boards. If there is a lot of excess glue and the boards are not very even, it will take a great deal of sanding. In this case your best bet is to sand with a heavy grit paper across the grain until the boards are reasonably flat. Then you can start your smooth sanding. However, if you take enough time when gluing up boards, making sure they are even, flat and free of excess glue, this may not be necessary.

Compound Miter Saw - My choice for mitering and crosscutting is the compound miter saw. This saw is easy to set to various angles and makes short quick work of mitering. If you don't have a miter saw and plan to purchase one, I strongly recommend the compound miter saw. If you already have a miter saw, by all means, use it. If you have never checked the accuracy of your miter saw, do it first thing. It should also be the first thing done with a new miter saw. Start with the blade; the blade that comes with most miter saws, even if it is sharp, is inadequate for mitering. A quality sixty-tooth carbide blade is best for the job, but a forty-toothed blade is adequate. You will notice the immense difference in how your miter saw works immediately after installing a good carbide blade. Don't skimp here; there is a difference in blades. I have used many $15 to $20 blades on my 8 ¼" compound miter saw. Usually I have to compromise and purchase an 8-8 ¼" blade. That means the blade is actually 8"—a little smaller than what the saw should have. Recently I purchased a high quality forty-tooth blade for $45. The difference was pronounced. The saw cut much easier, more importantly, my cuts were cleaner and smoother.

Keep all the moving parts of your miter saw clean and lubricated so that everything functions smoothly without requiring excessive pressure. I have used miter saws so corroded that immense pressure was required to move from one setting to another. Now check the settings. The lines on most miter saws are inaccurate, and the stops at the 22½ degree, 45 degree and 90 degree angles are also usually inaccurate. On some saws it may be possible to better adjust these stops. Read the instructions for your saw. For example, my miter saw has a good adjustment for the compound miter setting at 45 degrees, but any other part of the scale requires checking. I also marked the exact place on my miter saw where the blade cuts at exactly 45 degrees either side and at 90 degrees. This is done quite easily.

Let's do the 90-degree check first. Take a scrap piece of wood about two feet long and 2" to 4" wide. Place it on your miter saw and cut it at 90 degrees. Now take one of the pieces and flip it over, keeping the cut together. Make certain both pieces are against the fence and tight against each other. If the cut is tight all the way across, your saw is set at 90 degrees. If the cut is open on one side or the other, the 90-degree stop on your miter saw is inaccurate. Make minor adjustments, tightening the blade in place each time. Keep making test cuts until the pieces meet squarely when one is flipped over. Now take your scratch awl and permanently mark the scale of your saw directly under the arrow. Or, if the arrow is adjustable, move it until it points to the 90-degree mark when properly set.

These random shop notes were collected while working on projects. They should be helpful when building the projects included in this book or any of your other projects.

Twenty-Two

Drawings of Customer Projects

Notice that the drawings that follow are not complex. The important thing is to make them as clear and easy to understand as possible. Many customers have a difficult time visualizing how the finished cabinet will look from a drawing. Making the drawing too complex contributes to the problem.

These drawings are copies of the actual drawings that I used. I did not make new drawings because I wanted the reader to see them exactly as they were and not cleaned up or formalized. Obviously, you can make your drawings as neat and formal as you choose but drawings like these worked for me for many years.

The drawings on the next page are for a floral cabinet in a large, local health food market.

FLORAL DESIGN CABINET

DRAWN BY
A. WILLIAM BENITEZ

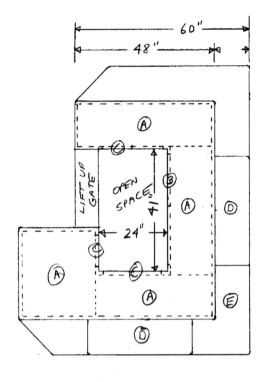

Ⓐ - CABINET STORAGE SPACES
Ⓑ - LOCKING DOORS
Ⓒ - DOORS
Ⓓ - DISPLAY SHELVES
Ⓔ - CONTINUOS DISPLAY SHELF

SPECS
- CONSTRUCTED OF 3/4" MAPLE PLYWOOD
- EDGES OF SOLID MAPLE
- TOPS & SHELVES COVERED
  WITH PLASTIC LAMINATE
- CONCEALED, SELF-CLOSING HINGES
- FINISH - 3 COATS CLEAR
- ADJUSTABLE SHELVES INSIDE
  OF CABINET
- UNIT CONSIST OF 4 CABINETS
  AND SHELF UNITS
- TOP ONE PIECE EXCEPT
  GATE SECTION

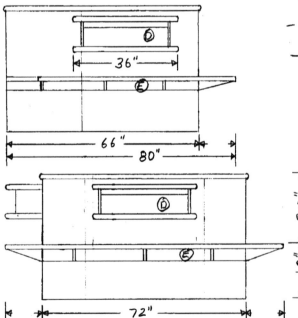

These are desk units that I designed and built for the purchasing and receiving office in a large hotel.

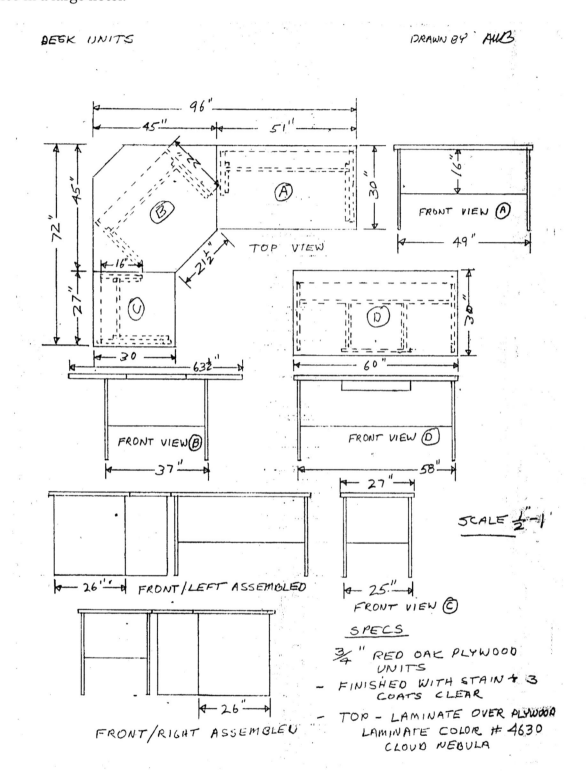

These are plans for a set of simple end tables and a coffee table.

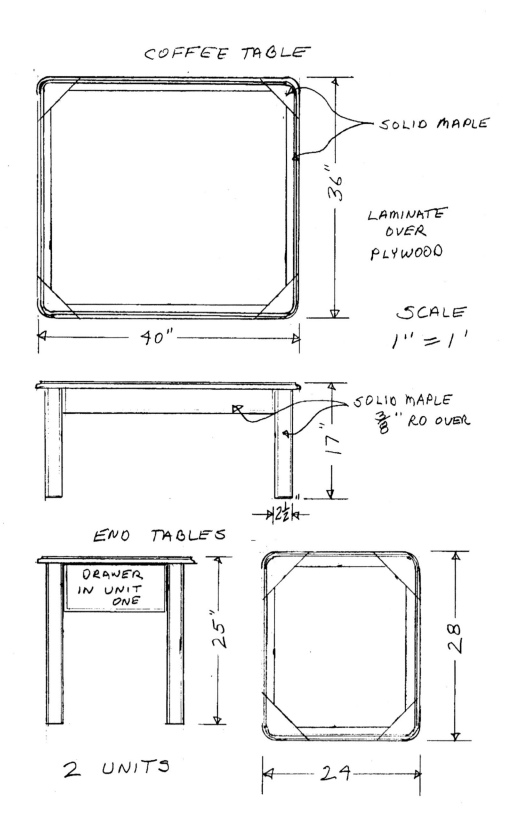

COFFEE TABLE

SOLID MAPLE

36"

40"

LAMINATE
OVER
PLYWOOD

SCALE
1" = 1'

SOLID MAPLE
$\frac{3}{8}$" RO OVER

17"

$2\frac{1}{2}$"

END TABLES

DRAWER
IN UNIT
ONE

25"

28

2 UNITS

24

This is a conference table built of solid maple and maple plywood.

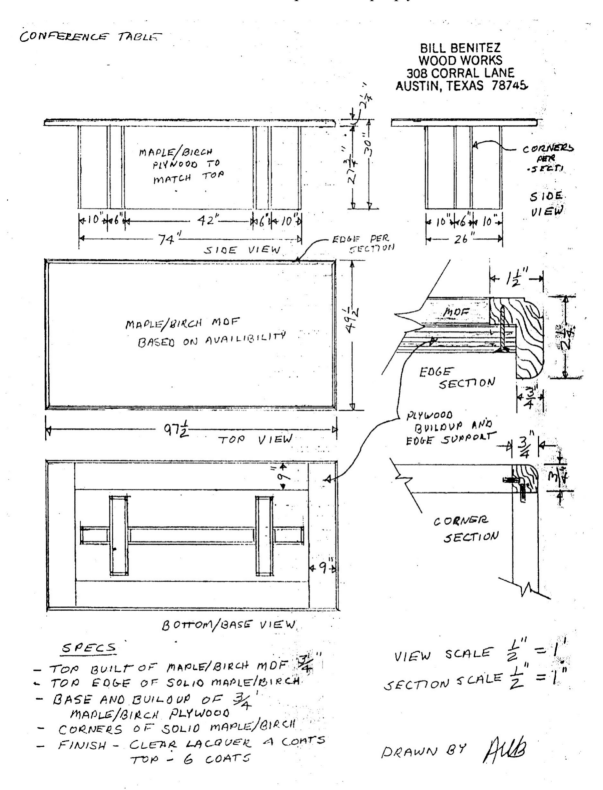

A. William Benitez Woodwork Services   **JOB DRAWINGS**
Entertainment Center/Bookcase   Unit # 1

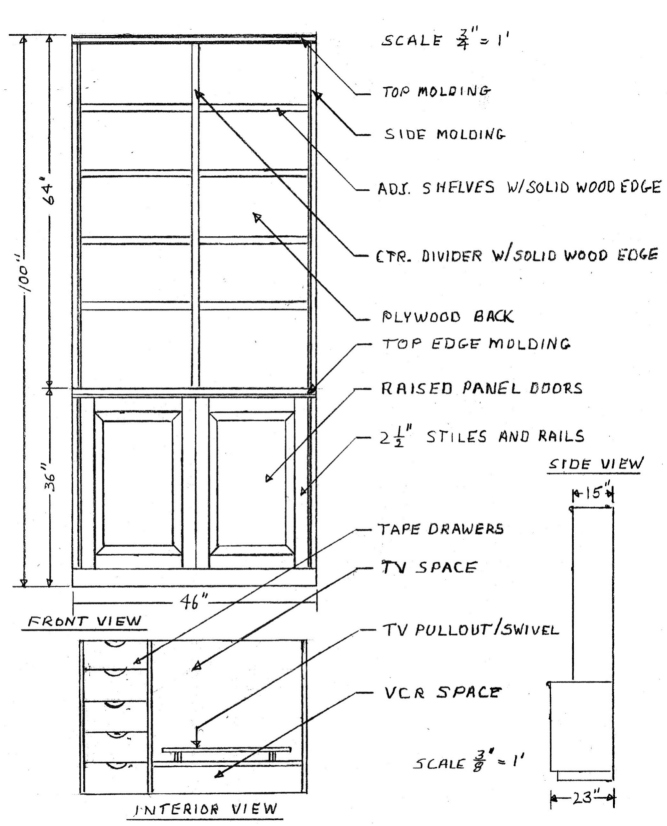

SCALE ¾" = 1'

TOP MOLDING

SIDE MOLDING

ADJ. SHELVES W/SOLID WOOD EDGE

CTR. DIVIDER W/SOLID WOOD EDGE

PLYWOOD BACK

TOP EDGE MOLDING

RAISED PANEL DOORS

2½" STILES AND RAILS

SIDE VIEW

15"

TAPE DRAWERS

TV SPACE

TV PULLOUT/SWIVEL

VCR SPACE

SCALE ⅜" = 1'

23"

100"

64"

36"

46"

FRONT VIEW

INTERIOR VIEW

A. William Benitez Woodwork Services
Entertainment Center/Bookcase   Unit # 2

JOB DRAWINGS

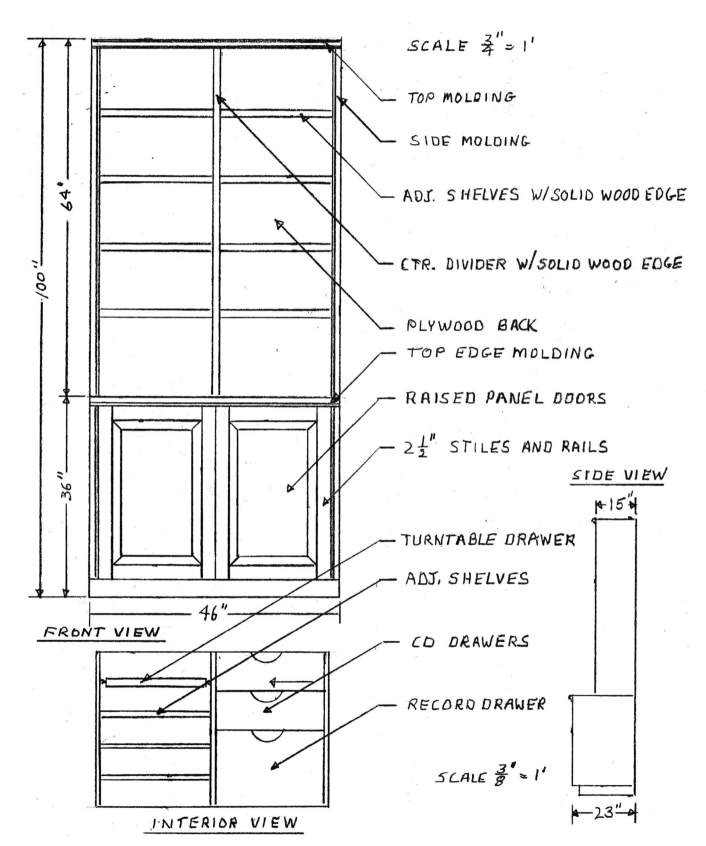

SCALE $\frac{3}{4}" = 1'$

TOP MOLDING

SIDE MOLDING

ADJ. SHELVES W/SOLID WOOD EDGE

CTR. DIVIDER W/SOLID WOOD EDGE

PLYWOOD BACK

TOP EDGE MOLDING

RAISED PANEL DOORS

$2\frac{1}{2}"$ STILES AND RAILS

SIDE VIEW

15"

TURNTABLE DRAWER

ADJ. SHELVES

CD DRAWERS

RECORD DRAWER

SCALE $\frac{3}{8}" = 1'$

23"

64"

100"

36"

46"

FRONT VIEW

INTERIOR VIEW

59

A. William Benitez Woodwork Services
Bookcase   Unit # 3

JOB DRAWINGS

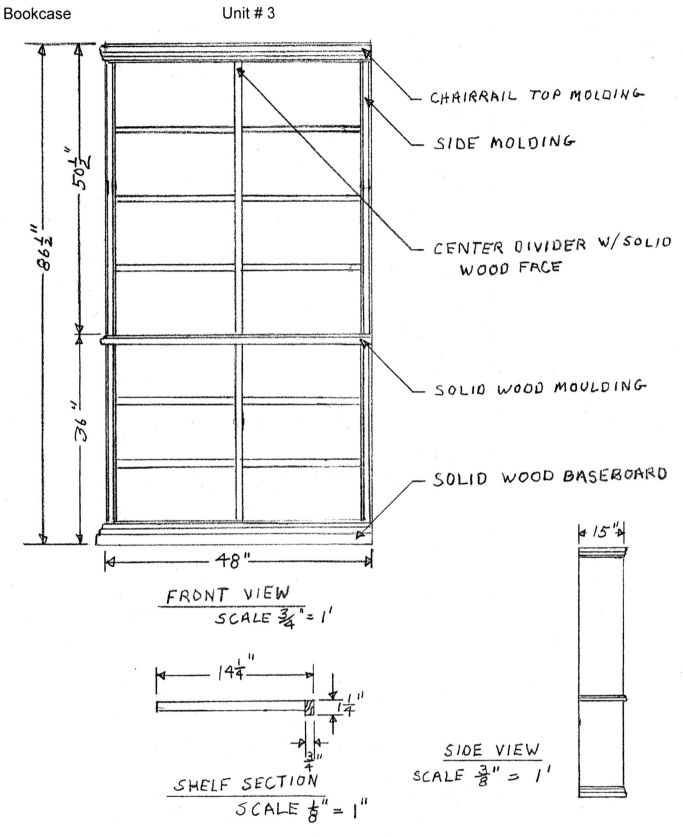

CHAIRRAIL TOP MOLDING

SIDE MOLDING

CENTER DIVIDER w/ SOLID WOOD FACE

SOLID WOOD MOULDING

SOLID WOOD BASEBOARD

$50\frac{1}{2}$"

$86\frac{1}{2}$"

36"

48"

15"

FRONT VIEW
SCALE $\frac{3}{4}$" = 1'

$14\frac{1}{4}$"

$1\frac{1}{4}$"

$\frac{3}{4}$"

SHELF SECTION
SCALE $\frac{1}{8}$" = 1"

SIDE VIEW
SCALE $\frac{3}{8}$" = 1'

A. William Benitez Woodwork Services

JOB DRAWINGS

Kitchen Cabinet Doors   Unit # 4

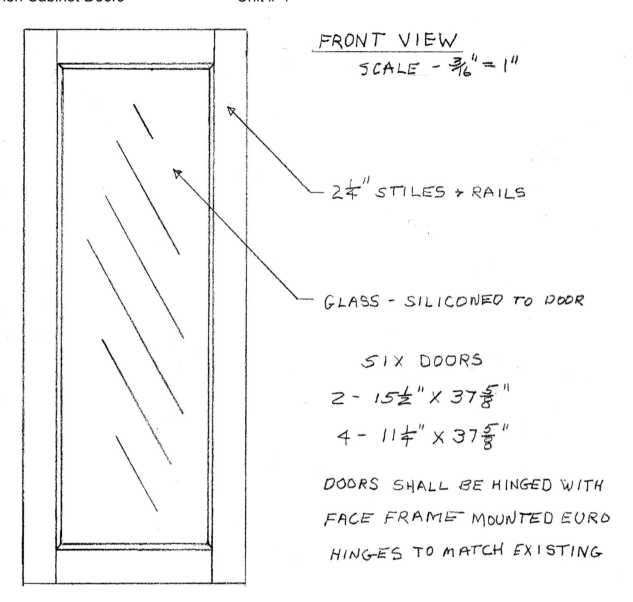

FRONT VIEW

SCALE - $\frac{3}{16}$" = 1"

$2\frac{1}{4}$" STILES + RAILS

GLASS - SILICONED TO DOOR

SIX DOORS

2 - $15\frac{1}{2}$" X $37\frac{5}{8}$"

4 - $11\frac{1}{4}$" X $37\frac{5}{8}$"

DOORS SHALL BE HINGED WITH FACE FRAME MOUNTED EURO HINGES TO MATCH EXISTING

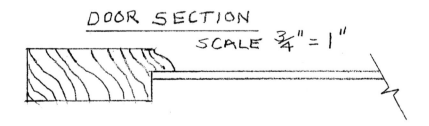

DOOR SECTION

SCALE $\frac{3}{4}$" = 1"

Twenty-Three

Sample Business Forms

In this chapter I have included a random selection of business forms that I used in my business over the years.

The forms include a standard contract form that I used for many years and a specification addendum form for more complex jobs. I have also included a copy of my letterhead, the letter I used to sell podiums and my business card.

Most forms are 8.5 X 11 inches in size, the exact size of the pages in this book.

Letterhead

Business Card

Podium Sales Letter

Woodwork Agreement

Specification Addendum

A.William Benitez Woodwork Services

402 Corral Lane   **447-4744**   **Austin, Texas 78745**

This is a very generic letterhead. You can use something like this or use stationery creation software, Word templates or some other program to create an attractive and original letterhead.

This is a sample of the business card I used many years ago. I don't purchase business cards any longer because I prefer to make them myself. There are many inexpensive software packages that you can use to make your own card. This way you can make only the number that you need instead of investing in a large quantity.

On the next page is the sales letter that I used to sell my podium/lecterns to many local hotels.

A.William Benitez Woodwork Services

402 Corral Lane   **447-4744**   **Austin, Texas 78745**

TO: Director of Engineering
Anytown Hotel

Are your podium/lecterns looking a little rough? Do you have enough available for your scheduled events. Our podium/lecterns are easy to move from one location to another and are designed to prevent damage. If you have avoided purchasing solid wood podium/lecterns because of the potential for costly damage, take a look at our damage resistant design.

We now have podium/lecterns handcrafted of solid wood products and reasonably priced. Our design not only reduces the potential for damage, it also facilitates quick and easy repair of any limited damage.

Each unit is individually assembled by hand and finished to match the stain color of your choice. This design has handsome, solid wood bumpers all around to protect the various panels from damage. These same bumpers can be repaired easily with a touch of finish or with sanding and refinishing if damaged seriously. The panels remain untouched.

Enclosed are photographs illustrating this podium/lectern design. I would appreciate the opportunity to speak with you regarding these podiums. In addition to our regular single unit prices, we are glad to quote on larger quantities. Every handcrafted unit comes with a one-year warranty against defects.

Within 20 miles of our shop, delivery directly to your location is included in our prices. For longer distances we will quote shipping prices or you may make arrangements to pick the units up at our shop.

Thanks for you attention. Please don't hesitate to call with any questions or send email to: billbenitez@ureach.com

Sincerely,

A. William Benitez

A.William Benitez Woodwork Services

402 Corral Lane   **447-4744**   **Austin, Texas 78745**

AGREEMENT FOR WOODWORK SERVICES   Date:___June 14, 1993

This agreement is made as of the date above between A. William Benitez, a sole proprietor, and_____
of Austin, Texas 787___ , hereinafter called the Owner. For and in consideration of the mutual promises and covenants hereinafter set forth, the Owner and A. William Benitez agree as follows:

ARTICLE I: A. William Benitez will perform the work described herein: Build, finish and install all the units described in the attached drawings as Unit #1, Unit #2, Unit #3 and Unit #4 and the attached specifications. All work shall be done in accordance with the attached drawings, specifications and additional notes. All units shall be completed when sanded and ready to paint. This contract does not include the painting of any of the units described.

ARTICLE II: The work shall be completed and installed as indicated above within 30 days of the execution of this agreement.

ARTICLE III: The Owner shall pay to A. William Benitez, in the manner described below, the total of $5,370.00 plus $429.60 sales tax for the work listed in Article I.

Total Price of the Work...$5,370.00
Sales Tax..$ 429.60
Total Price including Sales Tax...$5,799.60
Deposit: Due upon execution of agreement.............................$2,800.00
Balance: Payable in full upon completion of the work..............$2,999.60

ARTICLE IV: Additional items of agreement: Drawings and specifications attached.

ARTICLE V: Miscellaneous: A. William Benitez shall furnish all materials and labor for this work unless described to the contrary in Article I. All work shall be performed in a workmanlike manner to meet or exceed industry standards. This document and its attachments as listed in Article IV, constitute the entire agreement between the Owner and A. William Benitez, and it may be altered, amended, or repealed only by mutual agreement and a duly executed written instrument.

IN WITNESS WHEREOF, the Owner and A. William Benitez execute this Agreement as of the date stated above.

OWNER   **A. WILLIAM BENITEZ**

_____   _____

A. William Benitez Woodwork Services   SPECIFICATIONS

ENTERTAINMENT CABINETS, BOOKCASES, AND KITCHEN CABINET DOORS:

For_____Address_____

The following specifications shall apply to all the woodwork being done for this job. Additional notes listed below specifications shall also apply. These notes shall be added by mutual agreement prior to the execution of the contract.

All units shall be constructed of ¾ inch maple plywood.

All exposed plywood edges shall be covered with solid wood edging or molding as shown in the drawings.

All shelves except for VCR shelf shall be adjustable with brass standards and brass clips Brass standards shall be recessed to be flush with cabinet surfaces on all exposed areas.

All unit doors shall be raised panel of solid maple with 2 ½ inch stiles and rails. During installation all units shall be trimmed to the walls.

Doors shall be hinged with self closing, concealed euro hinges.
TV space shall have a swivel pullout unit.

Component section shall have a pullout drawer for turntable.

All drawers shall be constructed of ½ inch plywood with ¼ inch plywood bottoms except for the record drawer that will have a ½ inch plywood bottom.

CD, record and tape drawers shall have appropriate plastic dividers.

Doors in kitchen shall be standard stile and rail design except stiles and rails shall be 2 ½ inches wide and panel shall be standard glass adhered with clear silicone. These doors shall be hung with face frame mounted, self-closing euro hinges.

ADDITIONAL NOTES:

Twenty-Four

Marketing and Selling Aids

Accepting Credit Cards

Setting up for the acceptance of credit cards can make it more convenient for customers to pay you. It's important not to get caught up in the hype about credit cards. There are many companies out there selling credit card services that will tell you that you cannot get along without accepting credit cards. In the woodwork business this is far from true. You can get along quite well without accepting credit cards.

I conducted my business for years without credit card acceptance and it was never a problem. Then I set up to accept credit cards and used the service very rarely. Most people expect to pay a small business owner with cash or check. This is especially true of large items such as cabinets and furniture.

There are some advantages to using credit cards. It appeals especially to those customers who are accruing airline miles. They like to make large purchases with credit cards even when they can afford to pay with a check. By using the card they gain miles that can be used for free flights. Having the ability to accept credit cards will please these customers and reduce resistance to your pricing in some cases. However, it is unlikely that you will ever lose a project simply because you do not accept credit cards.

If you spend anytime on the Internet, you have already heard about getting set up with merchant account status for accepting credit cards. There is a tremendous amount of hype on this subject. Plus, there are many companies offering merchant account status at absolutely outrageous prices. Avoid these companies at all cost. Instead, check out the article written by my friend Walt Boyd. He has been doing business on the Internet for years and knows about all the scams you must avoid. He wrote this article to help his customers avoid being ripped off when setting up a merchant account. Just connect to your Internet connection and then click the link below and it will take you to this article. Before setting up merchant account status, read it carefully. It could save you thousands.

http://sohostore.com/freeinfo/creditcards.html

Now it is easy for any business owner with a computer to set up for credit card use with PayPal, an Ebay company. Most people familiar with PayPal think that using them for a credit card payment requires the customer to be a member of PayPal. That is no longer a requirement. With PayPal you can now send an invoice to your customer for payment with a credit card even if they are not members of PayPal. To do this you must become a verified business member of PayPal at a one-time cost of $49.95.

I suggest that you start your woodwork business without credit card acceptance until you are established. Then, if you feel that you need it, contact your local banker and set up merchant account status at your local bank. You will save a lot of money and do business with someone that may be able to help your business in other ways.

Creating A Photo Album

Unless a satisfied customer has recommended you, a potential customer will not be familiar with the quality of your work. A showroom is a costly but effective way to show off your work but a photo album will serve just as well at a much lower cost.

Before starting in business you should have already built a number of projects for yourself, family members and friends. Take good pictures of all of these projects and include them in an album to show your customers. This is a valuable tool that most prospects appreciate.

When a customer is going to spend a substantial amount to purchase custom cabinets or furniture, they want to make certain that they get value for their money. Pictures of previous projects go far in proving that you produce quality work. So, as your business grows, take more pictures and add them to the album. Keep the album current with pictures of your latest projects. It might also be helpful to include a text page with information about the project.

Your album can also include samples of your contract, some drawings and details about your specialty. The important thing is to give your potential customers an illustration of the kind of work you do so they will feel more comfortable doing business with you.

Using A Web Site

As a writer/publisher I use web sites extensively in my business. I presently own and operate over twenty web sites and manage others. Web sites can be a valuable marketing tool for some businesses but I only see limited uses for a website in the woodwork business.

A web site will probably not bring you a lot of local business unless you spend the time and money to market the site. This would be time and money better spent to market your woodwork services directly.

On the other hand, I believe that a small and simple web site would serve you well as a selling tool when visiting or talking to prospects for your work. Today most people have computers at home and most of these computers are connected to the Internet. Why not take full advantage of a ready-made marketing tool by having your own simple web site.

In this section there is information about creating a photo album of your work to show potential customers. Your web site can be a 24/7 photo album of your work. This can be a place where potential customers can learn about your business at their convenience.

Your web site should include brief information about you and your skills. It can explain how you handle each job and the details of your guarantee. It should include several pictures of your best projects including some close-ups of the details that show off your woodworking skills.

You could develop a section for frequently asked questions about your work and even a few testimonials from satisfied customers. These can be included with a picture of the customer and the project with the customer's permission. You should also include a link so potential customers can send you email to request information.

Your web site can be your silent sales person day or night just waiting to answer questions when you are not available. You get people to this web site simply by adding it to any advertising effort. It can be on your business cards and other stationery. It should be included in classified ads or flyers and, of course, you can give it to potential customers by word of mouth.

You don't need a web site to succeed in the woodworking business but it can be a great tool to make marketing easier and available at all times, even when you are not.

Like the merchant account, web sites can be problematic and expensive if you are not careful. Here are a few details that will help you get started on a small budget.

The first step for a web site is to register a domain name. There are many registrars out there offering many different price levels. I use Positive Imaging at http://www.positive-imaging.com because it is reliable, inexpensive and easy to use. You can register your web site name with them in minutes. Choose a simple name for your site and consider using your own name because that gives you name recognition.

The next step is to create a web site. There are many tools for web site creation. If all you want is a simple one page site with a few pictures and a little information, you can set this up with Positive Imaging for only $14.95 a year. You would assemble your site using your own pictures and Positive Imaging's online site creation software. This price includes the hosting of the site.

This is a good place to start but you will probably want to have a more comprehensive site as your business becomes established. Positive Imaging has inexpensive design and hosting services for web sites of up to 5 pages. Positive Imaging Web Design services can also help you with larger web sites.

Web sites can be designed using different software applications including those that come free with Internet Explorer and Netscape. I use the free NVU web site creation software to create my websites. This software is free at http://www.nvu.com.

For web site hosting I highly recommend Positive Imaging. They have an excellent hosting package for only $3.99 a month. You can get complete details at: http://positive-imaging.com .

Twenty-Five

Personal Assistance

Safety Notes

POWER TOOLS ARE INHERENTLY DANGEROUS! Any tool that can cut wood can also cut skin and bone. Keep this in mind every time you use a power tool. Plan every cut carefully before starting the tool. Clamp work pieces securely before cutting, routing or sanding. Read and adhere to the safety guidelines that came with the power tool. These guidelines are written to help you avoid serious injuries.

Here are a few more simple hints that will also help you avoid injuries

If you are using a power tool with one hand, always check the location of the other hand before starting the tool. This may sound silly but it is a good way to keep all your fingers.

Visualize the complete procedure before you start. This will help you avoid potential kickback or other injury causing incidents.

Never use power tools if you are tired, taking medications or using alcohol or drugs. This is a sure way to get hurt.

Always use ear and eye protection and dust masks when needed.

Woodworking is an enjoyable hobby and it can be profitable as a business. Don't let a moment of carelessness ruin it for you. Think before turning on any power tool and take good care of yourself and others around you.

NOTE ON TABLE SAWS: The table saw is probably the most commonly used stationary power tool for woodworking. It is a tool that has many diverse uses. With the right kind of jigs it can perform amazingly well. It can also be dangerous. More than 90% of shop injuries involve the use of a table saw. These machines can injure you seriously.

Using a table saw, and any other power tool, requires your total attention. In addition to the potential for cutting you, when improperly used, a table saw is capable of kicking pieces back at astounding speed. These pieces can cause serious injuries. It is not my intent to frighten you; I just want everyone to understand the power of these machines. Always give your work on any power tool your full attention. Take the time to learn the safety rules for your machine and adhere to them. It only takes one mistake to cause a serious injury. Please be careful.

Ten Basic Rules For The Woodworking Business

ONE - Some People Are Not Cut Out For Self-employment. Unflinching self-analysis is important before taking the step into self-employment. It definitely is not for everyone. Take a good long look at yourself and be honest. Are you self-disciplined and motivated. Remember, as a self employed person you are the boss and the employee. You must set your own hours, plan and stick to your work schedule, and meet your deadlines.

There is no boss or manager to check on you and make certain that things get done. In the beginning especially, you will have to put in long hours to take care of all the numerous details required. Many people need someone to tell them how, when, and where to work. Are you one of them?

Self-employment requires the courage to face uncertainty and the unknown. You will have to give up regular paychecks and bonuses. You will have to handle your own health care coverage and retirement benefits. To be successful you must have perseverance because it will take time to develop your business. The rewards can be great but there is always the risk of failure. The question is, do you have what it takes? It is essential to be honest with yourself when answering this question.

TWO - Is woodworking the right business for you? Just because you enjoy building things for yourself doesn't mean you will enjoy doing it as a business. Many years ago photography was my hobby. I loved taking pictures of everything. I took courses and read everything I could find on the subject. I became a very proficient photographer. Then I took pictures of a friend's wedding and it was very lucrative. I decided to start a part-time wedding photography business. For two years I did over sixty weddings a year and then I just quit. I couldn't stand to do it anymore. Now I seldom handle a camera. It lost its joy for me. This may not be the case for you but realize that a hobby is not the same as a business.

THREE - Learn all you can about woodworking. I run into people everyday who have stopped learning. They already know all there is to know about their field. This is a serious mistake. Keep your eyes and your mind open. Read about woodworking methods. Study the work of others and see how things are put together. It is amazing how much you will learn if you simply look and listen. Learning is a never-ending process and your work will be made easier and more lucrative by the many lessons you gain. I have always made it a habit to observe the work of others and then finding ways to do it better or more efficiently. This makes it possible to complete projects rapidly. Reducing the time required on a project increases the profit.

If you can find a mentor who you respect, take the time to learn all that he or she has to offer. There are people willing to take the time to share their knowledge with you, so don't pass up the opportunity no matter how much you already know. The more you know about your business, the more successful you will be.

FOUR - Be prepared by calculating how much capital you will need to get started. If you are going into woodworking full-time, this figure should include enough to cover your living expenses for at least six months and preferably a year. This is not always possible, but do the best you can. In the beginning, most of what the business generates will be put back into the business for marketing and unforeseen expenses.

Once you get the capital together, find a good location for your business. Work from your own garage or utility building if possible. If you do have to rent, avoid getting a lease for more than one year. If you do work from home set aside the space especially for your business. This will be important to get the deduction on your income taxes.

Secure the necessary permits or licenses. You can get this information by calling City Hall and your County Courthouse. You may be required to collect sales tax. For information about this call your State Comptroller. These things vary from city to city and state to state.

Purchase all the supplies and equipment that you will need to operate. Remember to watch your budget. Check everything you already own to determine if it can be used in your business. Look at used equipment and buy only what is absolutely necessary to get started.

FIVE - Keep it SIMPLE! Set up as modestly as possible. Keep a tight hold on your spending. Be on the lookout for bargains, but make certain that the product is in good condition. Be careful with your reserve funds. You can begin simply and then move up to luxury much easier than the other way around. Most people start off their business with far more space, supplies, and "splash" than they need. Avoid opening accounts until your business is established.

SIX - Advertise consistently. Advertising can take a big chunk out of your reserves but you can take a simple route. Advertise in the small weekend or weekly papers, rather than a large daily paper. The rates are lower and the message is in the potential customer's hands for a week instead of just a day. Pass out and post flyers in all available locations. Tell everyone you know and meet about your business and pass out business cards.

Prepare and send out press releases about your business to local newspapers, radio stations, and TV stations. If you do something interesting that they find newsworthy, the publicity you get from this will be much more valuable then all your advertising.

Open your doors for business and give outstanding service. Your best advertising will come from the mouths of satisfied customers.

SEVEN - Honor your customers. Remember that customers are the most important part of your business and always treat them with respect. They need your service or product, but you need them more. One of the greatest joys in having your own business is the joy of serving or doing for others. Give your customers the benefit of the doubt and handle their complaints quickly, efficiently, and compassionately. Be there to help them and let them feel that you genuinely care about them. Remember; if you keep customers coming back you can reduce or even eliminate a lot of your advertising cost.

EIGHT - Avoid hiring employees, especially during the beginning. The best form of self-employment is a one-person business. If you need help, get family members to assist you. Otherwise, hire subcontractors and make certain you adhere to the IRS rules for subcontractors. Having employees is stressful and costly. With employees you have the extra costs of withholding tax, social security, worker's compensation, and even health care. Finding good employees is difficult and you often have to deal with people who are incompetent, or simply don't take pride in their work.

Many very successful self-employed people use subcontractors. It's simple; all you have to do is make certain they are competent. Keep focused on your goal to be self-employed. You made this decision in order to have freedom, to be your own boss, to do what you really want to do. If you choose to expand and hire employees, then also hire an accountant to handle all your payroll requirements and advise you about laws and rules concerning employees. Then prepare yourself for a lot more stress.

NINE - Charge enough for your work. Many self-employed individuals undercharge for their work. This happens through a lack of knowledge of actual costs or a desire to be very competitive. Undercharging can create serious problems for your business. It is foolish to be competitive if you are losing money. Calculate all your costs carefully. There are many costs to consider including rent for your business space and the equipment in that space. You must also consider the costs of operating your business vehicle. Insurance is always a costly item and must be included in your calculations. There are many overhead items that are overlooked. Check these carefully in your figures.

Don't forget to consider your income taxes. You should be setting aside funds for this purpose. Make certain you are charging enough for your time and the time of any subcontractors. Then add a profit to keep your business going. Your profit should be at least 20% and preferably more.

TEN - Be a good householder. Keep good, up-to-date records from the very beginning (this may be a part of the business that a family member can handle). Many self-employed people put off record keeping for months at a time. When tax time comes, you will have to spend days putting everything together. Develop some kind of regular bookkeeping system using your computer. There are many accounting software programs. I use and highly recommend Quickbooks but many others will do the job for you. Bring your accounting up to date at least once a week. To make the process easier, you can use your computer to write and print your checks. You can also establish online banking with your local bank and this will keep your checking account reconciled at all times.

Take care of your equipment with regular maintenance. Woodworking equipment requires regular care if it is to serve you for many years. Perform regular maintenance and keep all blades and bits sharp.

Draw a conservative amount from the business for your salary. Keep as much money going back into the business as possible. As time passes and your business grows your salary can increase and even include bonuses.

Pay your income taxes when they are due. Preferably, pay your estimated tax quarterly so you will not face a large tax bill at the end of the year. You would be surprised how many self-employed people are behind on their income taxes. This always leads to costly interest and penalties.

Start by doing business on a C.O.D. basis, but once you do open accounts, pay all your bills on time. Maintain a savings account for your reserve funds. Try to make deposits regularly even if they are small. This money will help during tight periods.

Always get a 50% deposit on contracted work. Upon completion, collect the rest. If they can't pay you, do not deliver the product until they can. Collecting your income is as important as delivering a good job. It is pointless to be in business if you are not paid for your work.

BONUS RULE- Be good to yourself. Take care of your health, both physically and emotionally. Being self-employed requires lots of stamina, emotional stability, and persistence. Eat well, exercise daily, get plenty of rest, and take time off for relaxation and play. It's very important to leave your business, both mentally and physically, at regular intervals. Now go for it and have fun in your woodworking business.

Fitness

Fitness is important for your business survival. I am not speaking solely of physical fitness but also mental and emotional. There will be times when things are tough and hard decisions will have to be made. There may well be times that you'll think about quitting and going back to work for someone else. The decisions made during these times will have much to do with your fitness. This kind of fitness goes beyond exercise. It involves healthy living and a positive attitude.

Healthy living requires good eating habits. When you are self-employed you will tend to eat out a lot. It's important to be very selective and stay away from the fast food places with all their high fat content. Avoiding junk food all together is a good start. First thing in the morning have a good breakfast instead of two donuts and some coffee. Not only will this help to keep your weight down, it will help to keep you healthy.

Avoid cigarettes, alcohol and drugs, they are the nemesis of good health. Addiction to alcohol and/or drugs reduces stamina, clarity of mind and your chances of success in your woodworking business.

Stress is detrimental to your health. Meditation can help you to reduce your stress level even when things are not going well. Try meditating once a day for just 20 minutes. This will definitely reduce your stress level and help you to see things more clearly. It doesn't matter what method of meditation you use. The objective is simply to quiet the mind which is usually chattering consistently with all kinds of useless information. At first it will seem that the meditation is doing no good because your mind is still running at full speed. That will change in time. Don't worry about it, just keep up the meditations every day and soon you will notice the difference.

Putting in the many hours required to get a woodworking business going can be very tiring. It requires a lot of stamina and you need to be in reasonably good shape. While going to a gym is good, it isn't necessary to maintain physical fitness. A good walk every day before going to work or after work will help a great deal. Exercise not only contributes to physical fitness but also helps you mentally. You will be refreshing your body and your mind and this will help you remain alert and open to new ideas.

Then feed this alertness and openness with books, magazines, journals and other publications on woodworking and related fields. Keep yourself in a learning mode at all times and your work will continually improve and become easier and more profitable.

Final Notes

To be really profitable it is important to be a recognized expert in your field. In this case the field is woodworking. Strive to be the best woodworker in your area. It's not as difficult as you might think. Look around and see how many people really excel. Most people simply do nothing more than what is absolutely required. All around you, mediocrity reigns supreme.

Those in the top 5% of their field are in demand and are paid the most. To be in that top 5% there are two basic things you need to do. First you must have or develop excellent communications skills. You must be able to get your message across clearly. If you already have those skills you are head and shoulders above most other woodworkers. If you don't have those skills, work to improve your vocabulary and your communications skills. There are colleges, adult education programs and even home study courses to help you with this.

The second thing is to learn everything you can about your field. It isn't enough to know how to build a few things. You need to be prepared to help your potential customer to design what they want or need. You have to be able to visualize and explain how you will create the product or furniture they want. Magazines, books and trade journals help. Go to trade shows and talk with other woodworkers. Learn what others are doing and how and why they are doing those things. Find out if these methods will work for you. Or, perhaps they will serve as the basis for some new methods of your own. Don't just accept existing methods as the end all. Create your own ways to do things.

When you are visiting a furniture store of any kind, study the furniture in detail. You will be surprised how many great ideas will come to you from studying even cheap furniture that you would not consider buying. Not that you will use their methods but something will make you think and could lead to some really useful information.

You will probably be driving to various locations to bid jobs. Instead of spending that time listening to news or music or letting your mind chatter away, listen to motivational tapes. There are many good ones on the market. Wayne Dyer has some excellent tapes. Earl Nightingale, who died many years ago, had many excellent tapes. His tape set entitled Lead The Field is my favorite. You can probably get a copy from the Conant Company or at some used bookstore. These tapes help to instill the values that are important to any one but especially to self-employed persons.

Go the extra mile for your customers. Don't nickel and dime them for small items. Price your work so you don't need to sweat the small stuff. Never make promises that you can't keep. Always deliver what and when you say that you will. Treat customers as if they are the most important people in your business because they are. Be confident and positive with your customers because it builds trust.

Don't criticize your competition to your customers. Sell yourself and your work in a positive manner. If your competitor is doing poor work, his reputation will follow him. Mentioning or dwelling on the quality of a competitor's work will just diminish your rapport with a customer.

Be open to new and unique methods. Explore new possibilities and be creative. There are many ways to do things. Some people are so hung up on their "right" way to do things that they are not receptive to new ideas.

Simplify everything. There is almost always a simpler way to do things if we just take the time to find it. Simpler methods save time and that translates into more profit.

Twenty-Six

The Projects

Find photos and additional information about all of the following projects at:
http://www.woodworkingbusinessbook.com/projects/projectsmain.html

Basic Bookcase Unit

This project is an easily built single bookcase unit with adjustable shelves. The construction method is quite simple. More importantly, however, the same methods can be used for an infinite variety of bookcase designs. For example, you might multiply this unit in order to cover an entire wall with book storage. Whether you build a single unit or multiple units, you can alter the design by adding moldings of various kinds. You can even add doors to the lower section. You can build stationary or adjustable shelves or a combination of these. You can make a low bookcase with a top for display. The variations are limited only by your creativity and your needs.

Single Bookcase Materials List

A	2	Sides	¾" X9 ¼"X84"	Hdwd Plywood
B	7	Shelves	¾" X9 ¼"X30 ½"	Hdwd Plywood
C	4	Frt and Bk Supports	¾" X3 ¼"X30 ½"	Hdwd Plywood
D	2	Sides/Top/Support	¾" X3 ¼"X7 ¼"	Hdwd Plywood
E	2	Sides/Bottom	¾" X3 ¼"X6 ¼"	Hdwd Plywood
F	1	Top Molding	½"X3/4"X30 ½"	Solid Hardwood
G	35	Iron-On Veneer	13/16" wide	To match plywood

Below are complete details on a number of variations that you might want to use to build bookcases.

Five Variations On The Basic Bookcase Unit

Bookcase Variation Number 1: Wall of Bookcases

Instead of a single bookcase unit, you can cover an entire wall with bookcases. Or perhaps you have a window in your wall and prefer bookcases on either side of the window. You can even place smaller bookcase units over and under the window to cover the entire wall around the window. To make multiple bookcases you merely have to make additional top and bottom support structures. You also need additional part A's. The first step is to determine the size of your units. Measure the space, then figure the number of units it will take to cover the space. Keep in mind that you want each unit to be at least 18" wide but no more than 32" wide. For example, if your wall space is 96", you will need three 32" units. If your wall space is 120", you will need four 30" units.

To determine the size of the top and bottom support structures, you must calculate the shelf space after deducting all the Part A (uprights). For example, if the size of your wall is exactly 122" you would make the following calculations: First, subtract the space on each side of the bookcase. Let's say you will leave 1" on each side. Deduct 2", leaving 120". It will take four units to cover this space. A four unit bookcase requires five Parts A. Each Part A is ¾"thick. Multiply ¾" times five and then subtract the result of this calculation from 120". This leaves 116¼" that is then divided by four, resulting in 29 1/16". This is the size of the top and bottom support units. You must change the size of the Parts B and Parts C to 29 1/16". Everything else remains exactly the same as described in the materials list, except that you will need a greater number of each part: You will need five Parts A, 28 Parts B, 16 Parts C, 8 Parts D and E, 4 Parts F, and almost four times as much iron-on veneer. You drill the holes for your supports, sand and assemble the bookcase in the same way you would for the one unit project. Just clamp the units together, and then attach with screws. Once the multiple units are assembled, you can fasten them to the wall as you would a single unit.

For the space below the window, build a low bookcase in the same fashion as the full sized single units. Depending upon the width of the window, you can use either a single, double or triple unit. You will need to make a top for this part of your bookcase because the top supports on the taller units are open. Your top can be finished like the rest of your bookcase, or it can be laminated with a plastic laminate of an appropriate color. These units should be built the size of the window opening plus approximately 1" to accommodate the space between the tall bookcases and the window. The space might be larger if you want to accommodate curtains or drapes.

The area above the window can be left open, or it can be decorated with a bridge from the bookcase on one side of the window to the bookcase on the other side. This bridge can be built simply as a top support structure spanning the full width of the space between the bookcase units. If you add a face board, it can serve as a valance for a curtain rod. Or you can make it a light bridge by using 3" canister spots to light the top of the lower bookcases. If you want indirect lighting in the room, you can install fluorescent light units in the support opening. If the bookcases are floor to ceiling, the top section can serve as a bookcase only, or as a combination of bookcase, valance, or light bridge.

Remember, when building a floor-to-ceiling bookcase, you must allow for the bookcase to fit the space on the diagonal. It is quite embarrassing to build a bookcase that will not fit into your room because the diagonal measurement is too large to allow for standing it upright. The simplest way to deal with this problem is to convert the bottom support into a toe space arrangement. That is, it is built separately, and the size of the toe space unit plus ¾" is deducted from the floor to ceiling measurement. This will then be the overall actual measurement of the bookcase. Instead of fastening a bottom support inside the two Part A's, you merely attach a Part B to form the bottom shelf.

The toe space is built in the same way as the bottom support unit, but the Part B is not attached since it is now a part of the bookcase. The toe space may be constructed the same size as the bottom support would have been, and this will provide for a recess around the base of the bookcase. Or you can enlarge these dimensions to make the toe space unit the same size as the bookcase and then install a decorative baseboard. If you do not plan to use a baseboard to cover the toe space, I suggest that you cut and assemble the toe space unit using miters at all the corners so the end grain of the plywood will not show.

Using the toe space arrangement makes installation of a floor-to-ceiling bookcase quite simple. You merely stand the bookcase up and place it in the proper location. Then push the unit up to the ceiling and slide in the toe space. Now fasten the bottom Part B to the toe space unit with screws.

For safety, tall bookcases should always be fastened to the wall. If the bookcase is the height described in our plans (84"), this is easy to do. Using a stepladder to reach the top of your bookcase unit, drive a screw through the back Part C of the top support directly into a stud. If possible use two screws, but if the distance between studs makes this impossible, just make certain that the screw is solidly into the stud. If you are building a floor-to-ceiling bookcase, it will not be possible to put a screw into the back of Part C because the top of the bookcase is too close to the ceiling. There are two ways to deal with this situation. You can install a ¾" strip of solid wood on the bottom of the Part B that was fastened to the top support unit. This strip is called a hang rail in cabinets because its sole function is to provide a place through which the cabinet can be screwed solidly to the wall. This is the preferred method, but you can also use a small metal "L" bracket in the same location and fasten it to a stud. This will work, but it will not look as neat.

Bookcase Variation Number 2: Moldings

Moldings can be used in many ways to change the design. One basic way is to use moldings at the top and the base of the bookcase. For example, a wall of bookcases can be changed completely by Simply altering the top and bottom supports. By increasing the size of Parts D and E by ¾", Part C will be flush with the front of Parts A at the top and the bottom. Then you can attach a solid molding to the top and bottom supports. You can use a one piece molding such as a bed mold or a crown mold along the top. Along the bottom, you can use a piece of Colonial base mold or some other molding style that you like. This alone will make a significant change in the look of the bookcase.

Bookcase Variation Number 3: Edge Moldings

Solid wood edge moldings provide another way to change the appearance of your bookcase. There are a few ready-made ¾" solid wood moldings that you can use on the front edge of your shelves. If you choose a decorative edge molding, make your shelves (Parts B) about ¾" narrower so that the ends of the molding on the front edge of Parts B will butt against the sides of Parts A. Otherwise, the molding on Parts B will butt unevenly against the sides of the molding on Parts A This will look unprofessional. You can also use solid wood to make square edging. The wood you use for this purpose should be at least ¾" thick, but can be any width that you like. If this strip is left square, there is no need to cut the shelves (Parts B) narrower. However, if you decide to round over the edge strips, you should narrow the shelves as described above.

Bookcase Variation Number 4: Face Frames

Face frames can significantly alter the appearance of your bookcase. I prefer bookcases without face frames, but many people like them. If you decide to use face frames, I suggest that you make them 2" or less in width. Also I suggest that you put face frames only on Parts A and on the top and bottom supports, leaving the shelves recessed. This gives a pleasant appearance, yet still allows the shelves to be adjusted easily. If you must have face frames on all the edges including the shelves, I suggest making the shelves non-adjustable.

Solid wood moldings and face frames can be fastened in various ways. The quickest and simplest is with finish nails; drive them, set them, and then fill the holes with wood putty. You might also use screws and plugs. In my shop I use nails when working on kitchen and bath cabinets. When building furniture, I use my biscuit joiner to attach moldings. With either technique I recommend that you also use glue. Unfortunately, with glue there is almost always a degree of squeeze-out that must be thoroughly cleaned up, but this problem is minimized with the biscuit joiner. By using glue sparingly and only in the biscuit slots, you have the advantage of glued joints without the problem of squeeze-out. On face frames you can use the biscuit joiner with the small #0 wafers to assemble all the face frame joints. The strength of these little wafers is amazing.

Bookcase Variation Number 5: Doors

Doors can be a worthwhile addition to your bookcase. Installing them on the bottom section of your bookcase can provide valuable, dust-free storage for many things. With a few minor changes to the basic unit design, you can easily install doors. First, determine how tall you want your doors to be. At the chosen height, fasten one of the Parts B permanently. This provides a non-adjustable shelf that forms the top of the cabinet that will be covered by your doors. Next determine how many of the Parts B will be in the bottom section of the bookcase. In order to fit behind the doors, these shelves (Parts B) must be ripped to a size at least 1" narrower than the rest of the Parts B.

As to the design of the doors, there are several options. The simplest is a flat, plywood door with iron-on veneer edges for an attractive, yet functional appearance. Or you might install a decorative, surface-mounted molding on each door. You can also use a fancy brass or antique brass pull to add a little character to the door.

To make the doors for each bookcase section, use the following steps. First, measure and list the width and then the height. Get an exact measurement. To determine the size of the doors, deduct ½" from the width and then divide this result by two. This will give you the width of each of the two doors in a unit. The ½" is deducted to provide 1/8" on either side and 1/8" between the doors. This totals 3/8". The other 1/8" is to allow for the thickness of the iron-on veneer of approximately 1/32" thick. One piece on each side of each door adds up to four thicknesses of veneer or 1/8" The 1/8" gap may seem a little large, but remember that your cabinet will have three coats of varnish on it. This makes a total of twelve coats of finish and can be rather thick. The height of the door is determined by measuring the exact size of the opening and then subtracting ¼". This will give you the exact size of the door. Once you have the sizes, cut the doors to these dimensions.

Next apply the iron-on veneer to all edges. Trim and sand the door, and apply finish before hanging it. Use Blum or other brand European concealed hinges on your doors. To install them, drill two 35mm (1 3/8") diameter holes exactly ½" deep in the back of each door. The holes should be centered exactly 3" from each corner and 7/8" from the edge of the door. You must use a Forstner-type bit to drill these holes because regular bits have large tips that may protrude through the front of the door and ruin the face of the door. The 7/8" measurement is not critical, but your latitude there is minimal. If the center of the hole is less than 13/16" or more than 15/16" from the edge, the hinges may not function correctly.

To hang the door on the cabinet, fasten the mounting plates to the hinges, then place the door in its proper position. Use a small shim (wedge) to raise the door from the bottom to insure proper spacing. Make certain that the distance between the top and bottom of the doors and the cabinet is the same. Determine if your doors will be flush or recessed. Make certain the door is held in place with the hinge edge against the side (Parts A) of the bookcase. While the door is in its proper place, reach into the cabinet and install screws into the mounting plates. Now open that door and follow the same steps with the other door. Once both doors are installed, take a Phillips screwdriver and adjust the doors, so they fit exactly in the opening.

NOTE: Remember you can choose to make the bottom part of the bookcase deeper than the top part. It would involve building a base cabinet unit separately, then making a shorter bookcase unit to place above it. These are just a few of the possible bookcase designs variations. Certainly there are many other designs possible. Let your imagination roam, and you may come up with original designs.

There are two easy ways to cut the recesses in Parts A for the metal standards. If you have an edge guide for your router, set it so that the edge of the recess will be 1" from the edge of Parts A. After the edge guide is set, adjust the depth of the router bit. It should be set to cut slightly deeper than the thickness of the metal standard. Now carefully align the router and guide on the edge and feed the router through the cut from left to right. Try this on a scrap piece or two first. If the router pushes away from the edge, you are cutting in the wrong direction. You should maintain pressure against the edge, but not an excessive amount. Another way to make this recess is to clamp a long plywood guide to Part A. The guide should be measured to ensure that the bit will cut the recess 1" from the edge. With the guide on the side of the router away from you, make your cut from left to right.

Attach the metal standards after the bookcase is assembled and finished. The standards should be attached with the nails provided for that purpose. Some metal standards are attached with screws and others may require specialized staples.

Iron on the veneer edging and then trim all the edges. File the edges with a mill bastard file. You could sand these edges, but the file is faster. Glue build-up can be removed from the file with a file card. The surfaces to be covered with the edge veneer are as follows:

The front edge of both Parts A

The front edge of all Parts B

Assemble the top and bottom support structures. These are basically butt-jointed boxes as shown on the drawings. Assembled them by fastening Parts C to Parts D for the top support structure and to Parts E for the bottom support structure. Once again, you must decide how to fasten these together. You can glue them and nail them with finish nails, then set the nails and fill the nail holes. Or you can use dowels or biscuit wafers. If you do a careful job filling the nail holes, nailing will be quite adequate for this project.

Sand all components completely before you assemble the bookcase. This makes sanding easier, faster and more thorough because you need not sand into corners where it is difficult to sand with the grain.

Complete the top and bottom support structures by fastening a Part B to each support. A Part B should be fastened to the top support structure with the best face showing. It should be aligned flush with the back of the support and overlapped over the front of the support. It should be flush with the ends of the support structure. A Part B should be aligned with a 1" overlap on the back of the bottom support structure and a 1" overlap on the front of the support. The Parts B can be fastened with finish nails and glued on. Use the glue very sparingly to avoid having it squeeze out. These Joints do not require heavy gluing. If you do have some glue squeeze-out, remove it all promptly, or it could ruin the appearance of the stain. Squeeze-out can be avoided on these joints if care is taken.

Finishing the bookcase is the next step. Use a quality stain and Deft Clear Wood Finish or Bartley's Stain/Varnish. By doing the finish work before assembly, you will get a more professional looking job. Finish the two Parts A, the five Parts B and the top and bottom support structure. Remember, you need finish only the front and the shelf surface on the top and bottom supports. You can finish both sides and the front edge of all Parts A and Parts B by standing them on edge to dry. By driving two finish nails into the ends of all the parts, you can stand them on end and they won't touch the floor. It isn't necessary to finish any of the ends.

Final assembly of the bookcase is easy. Drill four holes close to each corner of Parts D and E. Assemble the bookcase by clamping it together in the appropriate manner. The top support structure should be clamped to the top with the open end of the support to the top and flush with the top edge of Parts A. Make certain the Part B affixed to the support structure is flush with the front edge of Part A. Do the same thing with the bottom support structure except that the opening goes down and the support structure goes flush with the bottom of Parts A. Once everything is clamped together, use 1¼" drywall screws from the inside of the support sections. Countersink these screws about 1/8" (not to exceed ¼") to afford a stronger grip. These screws will fasten the support sections to the Parts A. After these sections are fastened together, the clamps may be removed, and the unit is complete except for the shelves.

When you install your bookcase, secure it by placing a screw or two into the back of the top support section and into a stud. This will keep tall bookcases from tipping forward even when heavily loaded.

Drawings on next page.

Contact me at bill@woodworkbusiness.com with any questions.

Bookcase Drawings

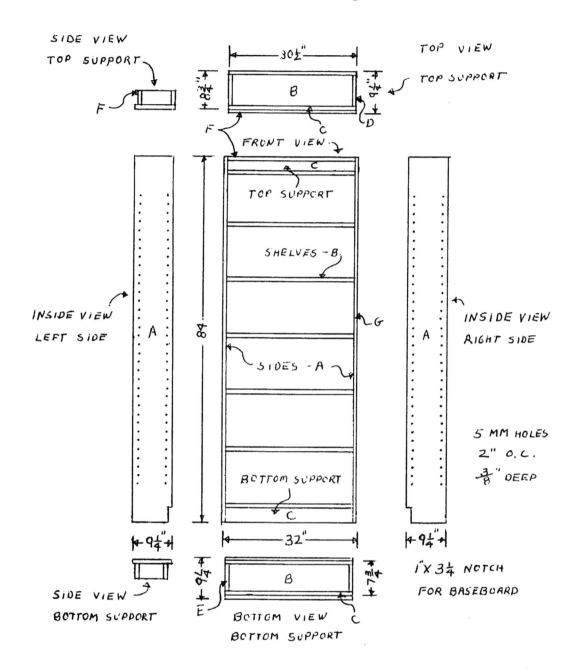

SIDE VIEW
TOP SUPPORT

TOP VIEW
TOP SUPPORT

$30\frac{1}{2}$"

$8\frac{3}{4}$"

$\frac{3}{4}$"

F

B

C

D

FRONT VIEW

C

TOP SUPPORT

SHELVES - B

INSIDE VIEW
LEFT SIDE

A

84

G

A

INSIDE VIEW
RIGHT SIDE

SIDES - A

5 MM HOLES
2" O.C.
$\frac{3}{8}$" DEEP

BOTTOM SUPPORT

C

$9\frac{1}{4}$"

32"

$9\frac{1}{4}$"

SIDE VIEW
BOTTOM SUPPORT

$9\frac{1}{4}$"

$7\frac{3}{4}$"

1" X $3\frac{1}{4}$" NOTCH
FOR BASEBOARD

E

B

C

BOTTOM VIEW
BOTTOM SUPPORT

Blanket Chest/Window Seat

This two level chest has a shallow top section with a pull-up door that serves as a window seat. The bottom section is a large full-width drawer. Since each level provides easy-to-reach storage, you don't have to dig through deep stacks of bedding to find what you want. The chest is designed without handles on either the drawer or the top door. There is no hardware to interfere with its function as a window seat. The floor of the top section is cedar-lined in such a way that the cedar aroma also permeates the contents of the drawer below.

The top of the chest is sized to accommodate a king-sized pillow with a sham as a pad, so that no special cushion is needed for the window seat.

Instructions For Blanket Chest/Window Seat

Cut all the pieces as described in the list of materials. All the pieces are rectangles with square corners except for the two Part B pieces that are the sides of the chest. Each of these pieces has a 1 ½" radius cut on the top front corner. Select the best face of each of the Part B pieces and put the two pieces surface to surface with the best face out. Carefully mark one board and then cut through both boards at the same time. Sand your cuts so that they blend smoothly into the top and front edges.

List of Materials

A	1	Lid	¾"X18 7/8"X34¼"	Hardwood Plywood
B	2	Sides	¾"X19"X21"	Hardwood Plywood
C	1	Front	¾"X10"X34½"	Hardwood Plywood
D	1	Back	¾"X19½"X34½"	Hardwood Plywood
E	3	Floor Supports	¾"X3"X17"	Hardwood Plywood
F	1	Drawer Front	¾"X7 1/8"X34¼"	Hardwood Plywood
G	2	Drawer Unit, Side	½"X5¾"X16"	Hardwood Plywood
H	2	Drawer, Bk/Frt	½"X5¾"X32½"	Hardwood Plywood
I	1	Drawer Bottom	¼"X16"X33½"	Hardwood Plywood
J	1	Lid Support	½"X¾"X24½"	Solid Hardwood
K	5	Floor	5/16"X3½"X34½"	Aromatic Cedar
L	1	Drawer Slide Set	16" Captive Roller	Blum or equal
M	2	European Hinges	Blum # 94M3650	Blum or equal
N	2	Mounting Plates	Blum # 195H7190	Blum or equal
O	33	Iron-on Veneer	13/16" or 7/8" wide	To match plywood

NOTE: Cut all pieces with the grain running in the direction of the longest dimension.

Iron on the veneer edging and then trim all the edges. File all the edges with a mill bastard file. You could sand these edges, but the file works faster. Glue build-up, which is common, can be removed from the file with a wire brush or a file card.

The surfaces to be covered with the veneer are as follows:

The top, front, and back of Parts B

The top of Part C

The top of Part D

All four edges of Part F

All four edges of Part A (If the lid is to remain in the same finish as the chest.)

Sand all components completely before you assemble the chest. This makes sanding much easier because you will not have to sand into corners as you would if you sanded after assembling the chest.

Assemble front and back panels with the floor supports as indicated in the drawing. It is essential that the top edge of the front be 2 ½" lower than the top edge of the back. Since the front is 10" high, this can be done by marking the back piece with a line the length of the back at 12 ½" from the top edge.

Assemble the sides onto the front and back assembly making certain that the top edge of the back is flush with the top and back edges of each side. The top edge of the front should be 2 ½" below the top edge of each side and recessed ½" from the front edge of each side.

Drill two 35mm (1 3/8") diameter holes exactly ½" deep in the back of the lid to accommodate the European hinges. The location of these holes relative to the edge of the door is critical but the distance from the sides can vary. If you center the holes 7/8" from the edge, the hinges will work fine. If the center of the hole is less than 13/16" or more than 15/16" from the edge, the hinges may not function correctly.

Insert and screw on hinges, and attach mounting plates to each hinge. If you don't know how to use these hinges, obtain a guide from your supplier or email me for details. Because you value precision fit in your projects, the time you take to become familiar with them is time well spent.

Fasten lid support to the inside back of the chest. Center it on the back panel exactly 2 5/16" from the top edge of the back.

Rest the lid on the front panel of the chest and on the rear lid support, making sure it is centered from side to side. Reach in from the bottom and drive the screws that came with the hinges into the mounting plate. Open and close the door, and make any necessary adjustments. You can install the lid easily by reaching in from the bottom. This is possible because the cedar bottom has not yet been installed.

Assemble the drawer by fastening the sides to the back and front pieces. Then fasten the bottom to square it up completely. Sides may be fastened with #4 finish nails, preferably galvanized. Bottom may be fastened with 1 ¼" nails with heads. The drawer is basically a simple butt joint box. The bottom is simply nailed on and is securely supported by the bottom mount drawer slides.

Install the drawer slides on the drawer and the chest, then slide the drawer into place. Install the drawer part of the slide by screwing it to the bottom of the drawer, flush to the front edge with the roller to the rear. Install the chest part of the slide 1 5/16" recessed from the front edge of each side and 2" from the bottom of each side. If you don't know how to use the European drawer slides, get details from your supplier.

Install the drawer front on the drawer unit. Drill four 3/16" holes, one in each corner of the front section of the drawer unit. Position them 3" in from the side edges and 7/8" in from the top and bottom edges. Drive two small nails centered between the holes on each side. Drive these nails from the inside of the drawer unit so that they protrude slightly on the outside. Close the drawer and align the drawer front to the front section of the drawer unit. There should be about 1/8" space at the top edge and at each side. Now press hard against the drawer unit with the drawer front so the protruding nails will pierce the back of the drawer front to preclude slippage. Now hold the drawer front in place with one hand. With the other hand open the lid and reach through the chest into the drawer unit and drive four 1" screws through the 3/16" holes in the drawer unit into the drawer front while maintaining pressure on the drawer front. Open and close the drawer to make certain that the clearances have been maintained.

Finish the chest with three coats of Deft Clear Wood Finish or any finish of your choice. Follow the instructions on the container. Sand with 400 grit sandpaper or #0000 steel wool after the second coat of clear finish. If you prefer, the chest can be stained before the clear finish is applied.

Install the aromatic cedar on the floor supports, and leave it unfinished. Place the first four boards so that the tongue and grooves are all tight and against one side. Measure and rip the fifth piece so that it will fit snugly, but not too tight. It should not be necessary to use a mallet to place this last board. These boards can be attached with 1" brads. One brad at each end should be sufficient since these boards serve no structural function in the chest.

Drawings on next page.

Contact me at bill@woodworkbusiness.com with any questions.

Blanket Chest Drawings

PROJECT DRAWINGS

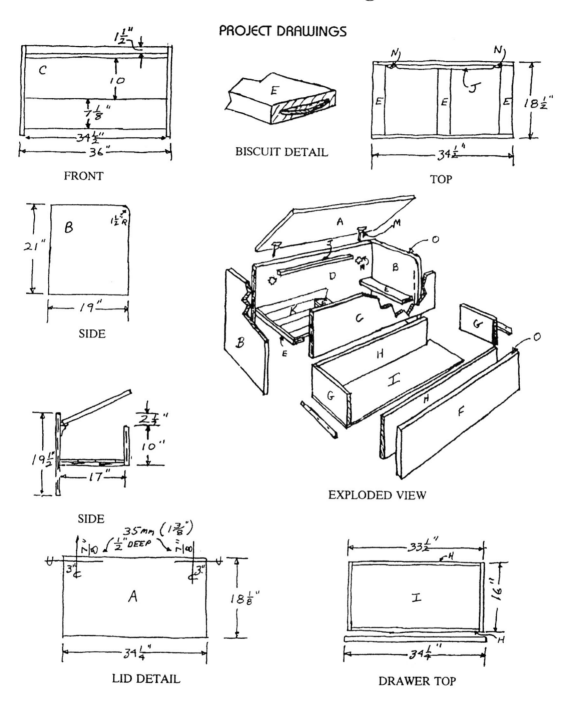

BISCUIT DETAIL

FRONT

TOP

SIDE

EXPLODED VIEW

SIDE

LID DETAIL

DRAWER TOP

End Table/Desk Combo

If you have a bedroom that sometimes doubles as an office, this project is for you. The end table is perfect for a telephone and lamp and the desk is ideal for handling personal bills and other mail. It also has space to store papers and books to read in bed. Filling a specific need is an excellent reason to develop unique projects.

This project differs from a regular end table in that it has much more storage space, a writing surface, and a place to sit. It differs from a small desk because it is lower in order to fit better next to the bed. One storage side is narrower than the other so that the foot space is away from the bed and the storage space is close to the bed.

It is a good project just as it is, but many variations are possible to adapt it to your situation. This one is 48" long, but it can be longer or shorter to fit your space. Other important variables are the edge molding and the finish. I did this one to match the headboard. Notice that the edge molding is a 1½" half round that is very close to the design of the headboard.

Materials List

A	1	Top	¾"X19"X46 ½"	Maple Plywood
B	4	Sides	¾"X18 ¾"X25 ½"	Maple Plywood
C	1	Left Top	¾"X14 ¼"X18 ½"	Maple Plywood
D	1	Right Top	¾"X9 ½"X18 ½"	Maple Plywood
E	1	Left Bottom	¾"X14 ¼"X18 ½"	Maple Plywood
F	1	Right Bottom	¾"X9 ½"X18 ½"	Maple Plywood
G	1	L. Back Panel	¼"X15 ¼"X24 ½"	Maple Plywood
H	1	R. Back Panel	¼"X10 ½"X24 ½"	Maple Plywood
I	1	L.Drawer Frt	¾"X14 1/16"X4 ¾"	Maple Plywood
J	1	R.Drawer Frt	¾"9 ¼"X4 ¾"	Maple Plywood
K	1	Left Door	¾"X14 1/16"X17 7/8"	Maple Plywood
L	1	Right Door	¾"X9 ¼"X17 7/8"	Maple Plywood
M	2	Top Edging	13/16"X1 ½"X46 ½"(SP)	Solid Maple
N	2	Top Edging	13/16"X1 ½"X19" (SP)	Solid Maple
O	2	L Drawer, F&B	½"X3 ½"X12 ¼"	Maple Plywood
P	2	R Drawer, F&B	½"X3 ½"X7 ½"	Maple Plywood
Q	4	Drawer Sides	½"X3 ½"X16"	Maple Plywood
R	1	R Drawer Bot.	¼"X8 ½"X16"	Maple Plywood
S	1	L. Drawer Bot.	¼"X13 ¼"X16"	Maple Plywood
T	1	Left Shelf	¾"X14"X17"	Maple Plywood
U	1	Right Shelf	¾"X9 ½"X17"	Maple Plywood
V	8	Shelf Pins	Blum or equal	5mm Nylonsteel
W	2	Drawer Slides	Captive Roller	16" length
X	4	Hinges	Blum or equal	110 degree
Y	4	Mount Plates	Blum or equal	Adjustable
Z	4	Knobs	1" Round Antique Brass	Amerock
1	2	Rubber Bump	Brainerd	Grey

Instructions For End Table/Desk

Cut the pieces described in the Materials List. Select the best faces of each Part B to be the outside, exposed surfaces. Use an appropriate blade for cutting your plywood. If you use the wrong blade there will be serious tear-out of the veneer that will require wood filler and will never look natural. A sharp hollow ground plywood blade or a carbide tipped, triple chip blade with at least sixty teeth will do a good job. Set the depth of the blade to exceed the thickness of the plywood by no more than ¼". These steps will ensure clean cuts that will improve the final appearance of your project and reduce filling and sanding.

Iron on the veneer edging and then trim the edges. You can file the edges after they are trimmed or you can sand them using a sanding block with 100 grit sandpaper. The file is faster and it can be easily cleaned when it gets clogged with glue. After filing, fine sand all the edges. Another good way to sand these edges is to use a sanding belt block, a block of wood with rounded ends that accommodates a regular sanding belt. This is a very useful tool because sanding belts are tough and long lasting. Since they are made to withstand the pressure and friction of belt sanding by machine, they last a very long time when used on a block by hand. The surfaces to be covered with the edge veneer are as follows:

The front edge of all Parts B.

The front edge of Parts C, D, E, and F.

The front edge of Parts T and U.

All four edges of Parts I, J, K, and L

Cut the rabbets on the back, inside edges of all four Parts B. This rabbet is ¼" deep by ½" wide to accommodate the thickness of the back panels (Parts G and H). You can cut these rabbets using a fluted or mortising router bit, dado blade, or with your regular table saw blade by making two passes. Make certain to cut the rabbet on the back edge and on the inside. You have already selected the outside surfaces for the Parts B, so this should not be a problem. Once the rabbet has been cut, the size of the Parts C, D, E, and F should match the depth of the inside of the Parts B measured from the front edge that has the veneer to the rabbet cut. The back panels will then fit over the rabbet cuts of the Parts B, and the entire back edges of the Parts C, D, E, and F.

Now cut the joinery. The sizes given for this project are based on using either biscuit joinery or nails and screws. You can also use dowels if you prefer. If you are using biscuit joinery, the handbook that came with your biscuit joiner should be very helpful in demonstrating how to make the necessary slots in the proper locations. To make the best possible use of your biscuit joiner I recommend The Biscuit Joiner Handbook.

Sand all the parts completely before you begin to assemble the project. Sanding in this manner is easy because all the surfaces are flat with no hard-to-reach corners or crevices. Sanding should be dependent on the finish. If you use Deft or some other brush-on product, sand only to 120 or 150 grit because the first coat of finish will raise the grain. If you use Bartley's Varnish or Stains, however, sand with 400 grit sandpaper until every piece is very smooth. Bartley's will not raise the grain, so further sanding will be unnecessary in most cases.

Before assembly you should drill the holes for the shelf pins that will hold the adjustable shelves. Make a hole template to be sure the shelf pin holes are properly spaced. I normally make the holes at 2" on center, but this can be done to your preference. Make the template by cutting a strip of ¼" thick plywood about 2" wide and 24" long, On the center (at the 1" line) of this strip draw a line completely across it. Next make a line across this line every two inches and mark the starting point at the bottom for future reference. Next, with an awl carefully punch each mark where it crosses the centerline. Then using a 5 mm drill bit, (preferably a brad point bit) drill every mark through the plywood. You now have a template. The holes will be drilled on the inside surface of all the sides (Parts B).

Set all the sides on your workbench with the bottoms facing each other and the fronts in the same direction. All the Parts B should now be on your bench with the inside surfaces facing up. Now clamp or tack the template in place for the first set of holes. Clamp the bottom edge of the template flush with the bottom edge of the Part B and flush with the back edge along the rabbet cut. Remember to purchase or make a stop for your drill bit to be sure that the holes will not go through to the outside surface. You can purchase a metal stop or make one from a piece of dowel. Now skip the first hole on the bottom and drill every hole until you reach about 6" from the top. (This is where the drawers go so you don't need shelf pinholes here). Once these hole are drilled, make two marks 2" back from the front edge of the Part B and clamp or tack your template in line with these marks and with the bottom of the template flush with the bottom of the Part B. Now drill the second row of shelf holes, again skipping the bottom hole and stopping at the same point as the back row. Now repeat these steps on the other three Parts B.

After the shelf pinholes are drilled the project can be assembled. You can use biscuit joinery for this project by simply cutting slots in the side edges on the cabinet tops and cabinet bottoms (Parts C, D, E, and F) and the inside top and bottom of all the Parts B. These slots must be in correct alignment and the proper depth to ensure a good assembly. Read your biscuit joiner handbook carefully or the basic instructions in this ebook for more details on biscuit joining. The easiest way to assemble this project is to nail it together, reinforce it with trim screws, and then fill all the holes. None of the nails will be on the front of the project. If you place it next to a bed as I did mine, none of the sides will be visible in any case. The top cabinet pieces are placed flush with the top edge of the sidepieces (Parts B) and nailed together with the front edges flush. The bottom cabinet pieces are recessed 1" from the bottom edge of the sides (Parts B) and nailed flush with the front edge. This is the basic assembly and it will be strengthened considerably when the back panel is attached later on. Your cabinet pieces are now ready to finish.

If you choose to laminate the top, now is the time to do it. Plastic laminate is an excellent surface for a desktop or any kind of table. It takes abuse very well and is easy to keep clean. Plastic laminate looks very good with a solid wood edging. Laminating this desk surface is quite simple. First, obtain a piece of plastic laminate slightly larger than the size of the top (Part A). A piece that is 24" by 48" would be ideal. Many plastic laminate distributors will sell small pieces like this. Others will sell laminate only in whole sheets or in the pieces that they may have in stock. Contact a company that handles plastic laminate and ask them how they sell it. You will have to select a color that will blend well with the finish on the end table/desk and with the decor in your room. You can also play it safe and use an almond or beige color that is quite neutral. You also need to buy at least a quart of contact cement, a cheap 2" brush, and a flush trim bit for your router or trimmer. Many other tools are appropriate for laminating, but these will do for a small job such as this. During the laminating you will also need a hammer and a wood block, but these you will probably already have in your shop.

Cut the laminate approximately 1" wider and 1" longer than the top (Part A). Next make certain that the top surface of the top (Part A) and the bottom surface of the laminate are clean and free of dust. Using the brush apply contact cement first to the bottom surface of the laminate and then to the top surface of the top, Part A. Allow the cement to dry until it is no longer tacky to the touch. This normally takes about ten minutes, but it can take more than thirty minutes if the weather is cold or damp.

Once the surfaces are ready you must place the laminate on the top in proper alignment because it will bond immediately. The simplest and most accurate way to ensure alignment is to use slip sticks. Just place four clean wood strips on the top surface of the top after the cement is dry. Then place the laminate on the strips and move it around until it is properly aligned. Now pull out the first strip and press the laminate down to bond this first section. Next pull the next stick until all the sticks have been pulled and the laminate is bonded to the top. Now get the flat wood block and lay it on the surface of the laminate. With the hammer, tap the wood block sharply as you move the wood block around the entire surface of the laminate. This will ensure a good bond all around. Finally, use the router with a flush trimmer bit to trim all the over hanging edges of the plastic laminate. Sand the edge of the top and the laminate with a sanding block and 80 grit sandpaper. If any excess glue got on the surface of the laminate, remove it easily with lacquer thinner.

After the top is laminated, install the edging. The edging is a 1 ½" wide, half round molding. I made this molding myself using a router table and making two passes on a 13/16"X1 ½" strip. This shape matches my bed. You can use a different shape to match your furniture. I used a ¾" round-over bit, carbide tipped. In order to use this large a bit you will need a router that will accept a bit with a ½" shank. If your router only accepts ¼" shank bits, I suggest you either purchase the half round molding or use some other design for the edging. Many designs would look good with this project. I used the half round because it matched the headboard. Your headboard may have an Ogee Classic edge, in which case you can easily match it with a ¼" shank router bit.

Whenever you are running strips through a router table or routering strips with a hand held router, remember to make two passes. Set the first pass too shallow to cut away a lot of the excess material. For the second pass you can set the bit to the proper depth and it will cut cleaner and smoother and create less friction. If you are not certain that the cut is even all the way, make a third pass with the bit set at the same depth. This will clean up any part of the cut that was not right. The simplest way to install the edging is to tape the individual pieces in place to check the miters. If the piece is too long you can easily trim it with your miter saw until it is perfect. Don't trim too much at once. Even if it takes two or three cuts before it fits, take your time so the miters will be tight.

Once all four pieces are taped in place and you can tell that all the miters are fine, fasten the edging to the top. The simplest way to do this is with glue and finish nails. However, you can use a biscuit joiner to avoid using wood filler. While the strips are still taped on the top, mark the location of the biscuits on the edging and on the plastic laminate. Adjust the fence on the biscuit joiner lower than the center of the blade on the edge of the top (Part A). This location is essential if you will be using a half round edging because the depth of the biscuit joiner slot may cut through the face of the half round if it is too close to the top.

Place the biscuit joiner fence on the laminate top and align the blade with the marks and cut the slots. Clamp the strips in place and use the biscuit joiner with the fence in the same position to cut the slots in the edging. Once all the slots are cut in the edging you are ready to assemble the top. You can start with any of the M or N parts. Put a small amount of glue in each slot, and then place a biscuit in the slot and tap it in gently. After all the biscuits have been put into the first piece of edging, put glue into the slots of the top on the side that corresponds with the piece you are working with. Now quickly align the biscuits with the slots and tap the piece in lightly with a rubber mallet. Make certain that the miters are properly aligned immediately because the glue will dry very fast as the biscuits swell. Follow this procedure all the way around with each M and N part until you have them all installed. Do this job quickly and then clamp all the edging to the top, checking the miters carefully as you tighten the clamps. It may be necessary to adjust the clamps so the miters will fit. Remember, this must be done promptly while the glue is still fresh. Allow the glue to set for at least two hours before releasing the clamps.

The drawers are simple butt joint boxes that are very easy to assemble. There are two drawers of different widths. Both drawers are the same height and depth. The assembly procedure is the same for both drawers. The sides are nailed to the fronts and backs with 1 ½" nails. The nails should be galvanized to grab better. These are normally called #4 finish or casing nails. Once you have nailed these together the bottoms are applied to the bottom edge of each drawer with 1" galvanized nails with heads. You may glue the bottom on if you choose, but it isn't necessary. Remember to use the bottom to square the drawer unit. Now use a belt sander with a 100 grit belt to sand the top edge of the drawers. Then use an orbital sander with 100 grit sand paper to final sand these surfaces, then soften the edges with a sanding block. To give your drawers a nice appearance you can router the inside of the top edges with a ¼" or 3/8" round over bit before final sanding. The drawers are now complete and ready to install after the project has been finished.

The first step for finishing is to decide what kind of finish to use to make the project fit in with the rest of the room. My project is next to a bed with a headboard that has a streaked looking dark and light base stain. I matched it with Bartley's Varnish. The first coat was Bartley's with some yellow and brown oil colors added to match the base color of the headboard. After this dried, I applied a second coat using Bartley's Varnish Stain in the Antique Oak color which Is quite dark. I applied it liberally and allowed it to set longer than normal before wiping it off; then I wiped lighter than normal to allow much more finish than usual to stay in a streaked effect to match the headboard. Once it looked right I stopped wiping and allowed it to dry. It matched almost perfectly.

At this point if you want more gloss you can apply another coat of Bartley's clear varnish. With Bartley's you do all your sanding before the first coat because it does not raise the grain. So sand everything with 400 grit sandpaper until it feels really slick. Then apply the Bartley's, or you can use some other finish. Deft Clear Wood Finish does an excellent job. Their stains are very good and dry in an hour. The Clear Finish can be recoated within two hours, making it possible to apply three coats to a project on the same day. Remember that with Deft it is not necessary to sand beyond 150 grit because it does raise the grain with the first coat. Apply the first coat and then sand the surfaces lightly with 220 or 400 grit sandpaper. Then apply the second coat and sand it with 400 or 600 grit sandpaper. The final coat will feel like glass. Remember to apply Deft sparingly after the first coat and especially the third coat. It has a tendency to run on vertical surfaces. Keep checking for runs as you proceed through the project.

After finishing the project, install the drawers and the doors. First install the drawers. The Blum drawer slides that are recommended are very easy to install, and they work smoothly. First, install the drawer section of the slide on the bottom of each drawer with the roller to the rear and the front edge flush with the front edge of the drawer unit. Use the 5/8" Blum 606 screws from the bottom. Use at least three screws on each section. Next install the cabinet section of the slide. First draw a line 4¾' from the top of each side of the project. Make this line on each Part B. Then measure in from the front and along this line 7/8". This measurement is necessary because the doors and drawers on this project are flush mounted. Now install the cabinet section of the drawer slides making certain that the bottom of the slide is on the top of the line, and the front of the slide is directly behind the 7/8" line. The easiest way to do this is to place each cabinet section on its side. Install the slide on one side and then flip the cabinet over and install the slide on the other side. After you do this on both units, the drawer will be ready to slide into place. Now slide the drawer into place, but do not install the drawer fronts until the doors are installed.

To install the doors, first drill the 35 mm holes on the back of them. This is a critical step that requires the right kind of bit. 35mm is 1 3/8", but you cannot use a standard bit to drill the holes in the doors. Most standard drill bits have points that could protrude through the face of the door when the hole is drilled deep enough to accommodate the hinges. A Forstner-type bit or the bits sold by Blum distributors especially to make the holes for the Blum hinges. These bits will make the holes perfectly. You should use a drill press or a euro hinge drill guide for these holes as it is critical that they be properly located and absolutely straight. You must carefully control the depth of the holes to be sure they are just deep enough to accommodate the hinges. This is usually a depth of ½", but I suggest that you make test holes in a scrap the same thickness as the door to make certain that the hinge fits properly in the hole before drilling any of the doom.

The center of each of the holes drilled on the back of the doors should be 2 ½" from the top and the bottom edge and 7/8" from the back edge. The 2 ½" dimension is not critical. You can place the hinge anywhere near the top and bottom. However, the 7/8" dimension is important. You have some latitude, but very little. If the hole is more than 15/16" in from the edge the door will not work properly. Set up a small table on your drill press and fasten a back fence to control the exact location of the hole from the back edge of the doors. Make several tests until the hole is located exactly where you want it. Once you have the location of the holes and the depth set, drill both doors. Then apply the hinges using the 5/8" Blum 606 screws and fasten the mounting plates to the hinges and tighten them in place.

Remember the two cabinet units are assembled completely except for the backs. The backs are left off to make the job of installing doors and drawers easier. To install the doors on this project, remove the drawers and place the first cabinet unit face down on your workbench. Now place some 1/16" shims in the space where the door will be. The shims can be any thin scraps of wood or laminate that you have around the shop as they are only temporary spacers. Now slide the door through the back of the cabinet unit and into its proper location, facing down with the hinges facing you and on the side to which they will be fastened. Space the door about 1/8" from the bottom and push the mounting plates against the side of the cabinet. Use an awl to punch the holes through the mounting plates into the side of the cabinet for the screws. Now drive the screws in. Place one of the rubber bumpers (Part Z1) on the opposite side of the hinges. This will serve as a bumper for the door. Use the awl to punch a hole for the screw, and screw the bumper in tight against the door. Lift the cabinet up, and the door is installed. Adjust the door after you install the back. Follow the same procedure with the other cabinet unit.

The next step is to install the drawer fronts. Put the drawer unit in its place. Drill two 3/16" holes through the face of the drawer unit (not the drawer front). Drill one hole close to each side of the drawer unit. Countersink the hole slightly on the inside of the drawer. Now ignore those holes and drive two small brads through the face of the drawer unit from the inside until the points protrude only about 1/16" on the outside of the drawer unit. Now place two shims slightly thicker than 1/16" on the top edge of the door. Next place the drawer front on these shims. The drawer front should fit well in the space. Divide the space on each side of the drawer front evenly. When the drawer front is in its proper place, press it firmly from the front; this will allow the nail points to pierce the back of the drawer front and hold it in place. Now reach behind the cabinet unit and push the drawer open while maintaining pressure on the front of the drawer front. Once the front has cleared the cabinet, use your hand as a clamp to hold the drawer front in place while you drive two 1" screws from inside the drawer into the drawer front.

Now install the two back panels (Parts G and H). These should fit into the rabbets of the two sides (Parts B) and flush with the cabinet top Pieces (Parts C and D). Once the panels are in place, make certain they are tight against one of the rabbets and nail along that line. Then make sure the top edge is square with the back panel and nail along the top edge. Now nail the rest of the back panel on both of the cabinet units. Use 1" nails with heads, spaced every eight inches. You can glue the back panels on if you choose.

Install the knobs on the drawers and doors. I centered the drawer knobs vertically and horizontally. Then I measured the same distance from the top of the door as the distance from the top of the drawer and centered the doorknob horizontally so the two knobs line up. This is a matter of preference. You can install the knobs you select in the location you choose. You may even choose to use a pull instead of a knob. Once you have located the position of the holes, punch them with an awl and then drill them with a 3/16" bit. The screws that come with the knobs will work on the doors.

You will need to buy longer screws for the drawers. The screw size is 8x32, and the length you will need is between 1 ½" and 1 ¾".

The last step is to install the top on your end table/desk. First drill 3/16" holes in the two cabinet top pieces (Parts C and D). Drill these holes close to the four corners. Position the two cabinet units and place the top on them. One top should touch the inside of the top edging. Once the top is in place, use 1¼" screws from the inside of the cabinet unit into the top. It may be necessary to countersink the screws slightly to get a good bite with the screws, but be careful to avoid having a screw pierce the laminate. For this purpose I find drywall screws work very well. If you want to make this connection stronger you can use six screws on each cabinet unit instead of four. Now your project is complete.

Drawings on next page.

Contact me at bill@woodworkbusiness.com with any questions.

End Table Desk Drawings

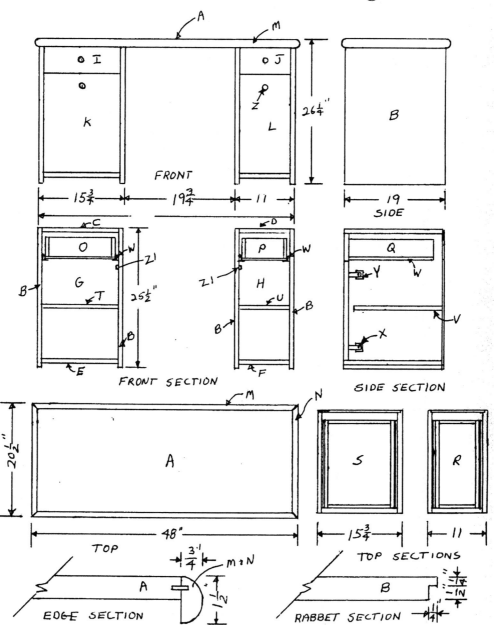

Entry Table

This entry table set can be a beautiful accent to a foyer or entry area in any home. To be creative, be open to options. The top can be done in several ways. The table edges can be profiled. Plus, you can even change the apron and the legs. Use these instructions as a guide, but when you see another way that appeals to you, by all means, try it. These changes will make it your design, a one-of-a-kind project created.

List of Materials

A	1	Top	¾"X9"X39"	Hdwd Plywood
B	2	Top Edges	¾"X1½"X42" Dbl Miter	Solid Hardwood
C	2	Top Edges	¾"X1½"X12" Dbl Miter	Solid Hardwood
D	2	Aprons	¾"X4"X37½"	Solid Hardwood
E	2	Aprons	¾"X4"X7½"	Solid Hardwood
F	4	Diags	¾"X3½"X3¾"	Solid Hardwood
G	4	Legs	1¾"X1¾"X29¼" Tapered	Solid Hardwood
H	107	Screws	1 5/8" and 2" X 6	Drywall Screws

Instructions For Foyer/Entry Table

Cut all the materials as described in the List of Materials. Read all instructions before cutting, as they contain details related to cutting various components of this project. When cutting various parts, watch for the best face, and try to blend the varying colors of the wood.

The solid edges for the tabletop are ripped from solid red oak planed to ¾" or 13/16". The edges for the table are ripped to 1½" strips. The next step is to sand the four sides of the strips. The faces are belt sanded carefully until the planer marks have disappeared. The edges are sanded lightly to remove any saw blade marks. Don't cut these strips to the proper length until they have been finished. The next step is to rout the edges to the desired profile. Many profiles are available but my choice for this project was the Ogee profile. The easiest and safest way to cut the profiles is with a router table. Make several tests on scrap wood before making the profiles on your strips.

Now decide how to fasten the table edges to the top (Part A). The simplest way is to use the biscuit joiner or a biscuit joiner kit with your router. Another way is to cut rabbets around the top edge of the table and on the bottom of the table edge strips. If you do this properly, you can then use short (¾") screws to fasten the table to the edge from the bottom where the screws will not be visible. You should also use glue on the joints between the top and the edge.

Once all the pieces are profiled, fine sand them with an orbital sander or by hand. Now you are ready to cut the miters. All the dimensions in the List of Materials are given long point to long point; that is, the longest point of the miter at the outside edge of each piece is the measuring point. Start by cutting each piece square and 1" or 2" longer than the specified dimension. This will make the pieces more manageable for the final mitering. Now, carefully cut one miter on the end of each piece. Next, measure each piece to the exact size and carefully cut the other miter. Whatever method you use to do the miters, cut a test from scraps first. Cut pieces for a small but complete square, and test the four miters. If the cuts are not tight, readjust your miter saw or jig, and try again. Take your time with this. Poorly cut miters will require wood filler and will never look good. Tight joints require patience, but they give a really professional look to your project.

The four legs (Parts G) are cut from 1¾" thick solid red oak. The first step is to rip the materials to 1¾" width. Check the thickness of your material. In most cases 8/4" hardwood that has been surfaced on the faces will be 1¾" thick, so you can use it as is. If it is thicker, flip your ripped piece and run it through the saw again so your piece will be 1¾"x1¾". Then cut four pieces 29¼" long. Next, cut the tapers. Make a simple jig for the tapers. You can make the tapers by using an adjustable metal taper jig purchased for this purpose. If you own one of these, by all means use it. If not, just make the jig described in the DRAWINGS on page 102. Once the tapers have been cut, sand the legs carefully on all four sides. Use the belt sander with a 100 or 120 grit belt. Do not over-sand. Sand just enough to remove planer and saw blade marks. The start of the tapers should be square and clearly delineated. Both tapers should be even. Fine sand all four legs with fine sandpaper in an orbital sander.

The top (Part A) is a simple 9"x39" piece of plywood. Choose the finish for the top before you apply the edging. The top of our project is covered with plastic laminate in a color called Fire Agate. You might choose a solid color laminate or a rough slate surface. Many marble-like colors are included in well over 100 laminate colors that are available. Once the top is cut to size, cut a piece of plastic laminate slightly larger. Apply the laminate to the wood surface, and then trim the laminate even with the edge of the wood. When this step is completed, the top is ready for edging. You might decide to use an attractive piece of hardwood plywood for the top and finish it with stain and clear finish, or with just clear finish.

Before assembling the table, sand all parts thoroughly. If you intend to use a clear wood finish such as Deft, sand all parts with an orbital sander up to 150-grit. Solid wood may be sanded to 220-grit. Using these finishes will raise the grain, so finer sanding will serve no purpose. It is important to sand between each coat. After the first coat you will feel the roughness. Before applying the second coat, hand sand with the grain using 220-grit sandpaper. After applying the second coat, hand sand with the grain again using 400-grit sandpaper. This procedure will produce a smooth, professional finish on your plywood.

If you decide to use Bartley's Clear Varnish or Bartley's Varnish/Stain, you should sand both the plywood and the solid wood to 400-grit with an orbital sander. Then do a final hand sanding using either 400-grit or 600-grit sandpaper. The surfaces should feel glass-smooth before you apply any finish. This initial sanding is necessary because, unlike other clear finishes, Bartley's does not raise the grain; therefore, sanding is not needed between coats.

The legs and the apron can be assembled in one of two ways. The simplest way requires using four apron diagonals (Parts F). These diagonals are attached on the inside of the aprons flush with the top edge and exactly 1" in from the edge as shown on the DRAWINGS. Placement is critical because it will control the positioning of the legs. Before assembly, drill six 3/16" holes in the apron diagonals (Parts F); see the DRAWINGS for the exact location of these holes on the long-point side of Parts F. Remember, Parts F are cut with a miter at each end; therefore, the short-point side and the long-point side are designated SP and LP, respectively, on the drawings. All measurements relating to the apron diagonals (Parts F) are taken on the long-point (LP) side. Use 1¼" drywall screws to attach Parts F to the inside of the apron parts. After all four Parts F are fastened with screws, your apron should look just like the drawing, except for the legs that have yet to be fastened to the apron.

Next, use a square to check the squareness of the apron. If your miter cuts are reasonably accurate and you fastened the Parts F in the right location on all four corners, the apron should be reasonably square. Perfection is not essential here, as a minor variation will not be noticeable, but it should be quite close to square. If it is too far off, one of your corners was not fastened in the proper place or your miters are inaccurate. You may have to check all Parts F for location before proceeding. If it isn't too far out of square, you can correct it with the installation of the legs. Position two of the legs in place, diagonally from each other. Do not fasten them. Use a sufficiently long clamp to span from the outside corner of one leg to the outside corner of the other. Remember, these legs must be placed on the diagonal that is longest according to your square. Pad your clamp surfaces so they will not mar the corners of the legs. Now tighten the clamp slowly while checking for squareness.

Once you have attained squareness, fasten all the legs tightly using 2" screws. Remember to predrill the legs with a bit slightly smaller than the diameter of your screws. Fasten all four legs tightly and then release the clamp. The apron should remain square. If it does not, retighten the clamp and leave it on until the apron is fastened to the tabletop. In most cases the apron will remain square after this step and you can proceed to the top without reclamping. Flip the apron upright. Drill ten holes as shown in the drawing of the apron. These are 3/16" holes drilled from the top edge of the apron approximately ¼" from the outside and at approximately a 60 degree angle toward the inside of the apron. Four holes are drilled on each long apron side and one hole in the center of each short apron end. Flip the apron over again and use a countersink bit to countersink the holes on the inside of the apron. These holes will facilitate the attachment of the apron to the top.

Another way to assemble the apron is to use my favorite tool, a biscuit joiner. Start by marking the end of each apron (Parts D and E) at 2" that is the center. Set the fence on your biscuit joiner for a cut at exactly 3/8" to the center. This will make the biscuit slot exactly centered on both ends of both Parts D and both Parts E. Now readjust the fence on your biscuit joiner to make a cut at exactly 5/8" to the center. Always test your cuts on scrap wood whenever you readjust the fence or the blade depth. Never take anything for granted. Mark 2" from the top of each leg (Parts G) on the outside surface and the corner that will be facing the apron ends (Parts D and E). Using these lines as a guide, cut the biscuit slots in the legs. Each leg requires two biscuit slots to accommodate two apron ends. Next, put a little glue in each leg slot and insert a #20 biscuit wafer. Follow through promptly by putting glue in each end slot of the apron pieces and attaching them to the appropriate leg.

Once all four legs have been positioned and the tops of the aprons and legs are flush, use clamps on all four sides to tighten the joints. Check for squareness promptly because glue dries rapidly on biscuit wafer joints. You can attain squareness by adjusting the clamps in one direction or another. If all else falls, use a clamp across the diagonal as with the previous method until squareness is attained. Finally, measure the distance between the legs at the ends. These distances should be the same or very close to those at the apron. If they aren't, either clamp them together or cut a thin piece of scrap to use as a spreader to separate them. Once the glue is dry, the spreaders can be removed along with the rest of the clamps. Using either of these methods, the legs should protrude beyond the apron by ¼" on all sides.

The tabletop can be assembled in two ways. The simplest way involves using nails and wood filler. Test fit the pieces of table edging that you have cut to each end of the table. Place both pieces of Parts B and both pieces of Parts C on the outside of the tabletop (Part A) and check the miters for fit. Mark any cut necessary to ensure a good fit. Now put some glue on the inside edge of both Parts B and clamp them tightly to the table top with the miters in the proper location. Make sure that the top edges of the Parts B and the tabletop (Part A) are flush all along the top. Use a small bit on your drill, a size slightly smaller in diameter than a #8 finish nail. Drill four holes spaced across the Parts B from the outside edge toward the tabletop. Drill only through the Part B. Now insert a #8 finish nail in each hole and drive it carefully. Finish the driving with a nail set to avoid damaging the edging; set the nail approximately 1/8". Do the same thing to the other Part B. Then glue and clamp on the Parts C, following the procedure above using only two nails. Next, check each joint for flushness and use a #4 finish nail in each corner to keep the miters tight and even. Be sure to drill a hole for the nail first, or you may crack the wood. To insure a tight fit, make certain the drill hole is slightly smaller than the nail itself.

You can fasten the table edge without nails by using a biscuit joiner. Set the fence of your joiner at the 3/8" center location as before. Position your Parts B and C around Part A and check your miters. Mark the location on both the tabletop and the edging for the biscuit slot. Use five biscuits for each side of Part B and two biscuits for each side of Part C. Cut all the biscuit slots. Finally, use the short-point of the miters as your center mark and cut a half biscuit slot on each miter end. Put glue and biscuits in each slot on the tabletop. Cut two biscuits in half and place a half biscuit on each end of the Parts C. Now put glue in the slots of the first Part B and put it in place. Follow with both Parts C and then with the final Part B. Promptly clamp all the pieces tight, making certain that all joints are neat and tight. Remember to use glue sparingly in biscuit joints. If you get a little ooze-out, do not spread it around. Let it dry a little and then remove it easily with a pocket knife, taking care not to mar any surfaces.

Before any further assembly, apply the finish to your project. This makes the finishing job much easier. Decide now how you want to finish your project. I like natural wood, so I seldom use stains. However, if your project has been made of maple, birch or some other light-colored wood with little figuring, staining may enhance its appearance. The two finishes that I recommend are Deft Clear Wood Finish with or without Deft Stains, and Bartley's Clear Varnish or Varnish and Stains.

If you decide to finish with Deft, remember the sanding instructions outlined above. Deft Stain and Deft Clear Wood Finish will raise the grain and so require sanding between coats of finish; however, do not sand after using Deft Stain or any other stain. If you sand stain, some of it will be removed, causing discoloration and a splotchy look. After staining, apply the first coat of Clear Wood Finish, and then sand lightly by hand with fine sandpaper of a grit no more than #220. Take special care when sanding near corners. Sand flat surfaces only. If you sand the edges of the corners, you will wear through the finish and stain to the original wood color. When using Deft, you need three coats of Clear Wood Finish for a good job, but four coats ensures excellence. Be careful after the second coat because Deft has a tendency to run on smooth vertical surfaces. Apply it thin and avoid over brushing, as this may leave brush marks.

Every few moments, check back to finished areas to correct any runs while the finish is still wet. Deft dries extremely fast. In warm weather it will dry to the touch in fifteen to twenty minutes. Once drying starts it is unwise to try to brush out runs. It will leave unattractive brush marks on a finish that is normally self-leveling.

Bartley's Clear Varnish is easier to use than Deft because it does not run. It is applied with a rag, although it will also apply well with a fine, soft brush. Staining can be done with Bartley's Varnish Stain standard colors, or you can mix your own colors by adding Bartley's Stain or oil colors to the Clear Varnish. The important thing with Bartley's is to complete all your fine sanding before you start finishing. Sanding between coats is not required because Bartley's does not raise the grain. Apply the first coat liberally, wiping a medium sized area of four to six square feet. Then use another rag to wipe off the excess and lightly buff the surface. Wipe and buff with the grain. After the first coat is done, wait at least six hours before applying the next coat. Apply the second coat in the same way as the first, but give it more final buffing. Two coats produces a smooth surface and are usually sufficient. For additional sheen and protection you can apply a third coat. Remember, always read and follow the label instructions when using any finishing product.

The next step is to fasten the table top to the apron and legs, using 2" drywall screws in the 3/16" holes that you previously drilled through the apron. Make sure that 2" screws are not too long by inserting them into several of the holes and checking how far they stick out. If the holes were drilled at approximately a 60 degree angle, the screws will protrude ½" to 5/8", and this will work fine. If they protrude more, use the next shorter size drywall screw, 1 5/8". Once you have the proper screws, place the top on the apron and center it all around by measuring at each end of all four sides. The best place to measure is at the legs. At this point the overhang should be ¾" at each side of all four legs. When the top is centered, put a couple of scrap pieces on the tabletop and clamp the top in place at two points. This is best done at the two ends. Next, reach underneath and drive the screws into each hole. Tighten them snugly, but do not break or strip a screw by over-tightening them. Your table is now complete.

Drawings on the next page.

Contact me at bill@woodworkbusiness.com with questions. Thanks.

Foyer Table Drawings

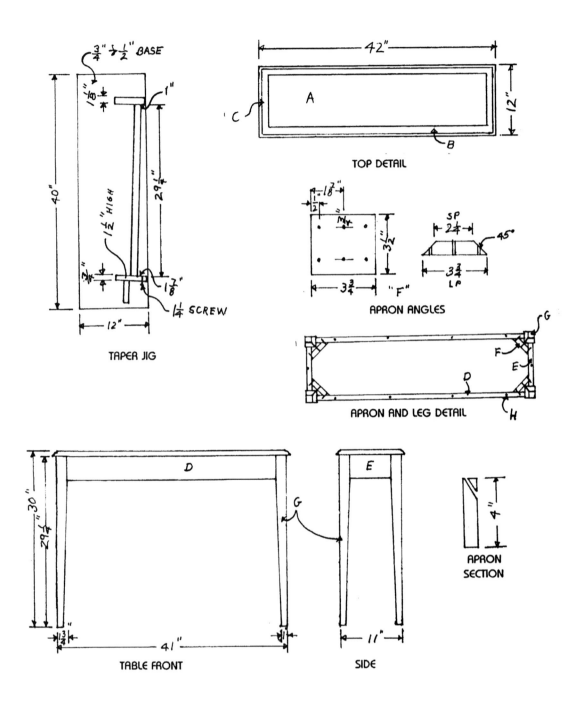

Kitchen Range Shelf

The Kitchen Range Shelf can be easily installed on most ranges, but these instructions are for a shelf to fit a standard 30" range. The dimensions can be easily altered to accommodate any range. This very functional project makes excellent use of space atop the range back that is often wasted. In this position it can accommodate both useful and decorative kitchen things.

This range shelf is made of red oak hardwood but it can be built of other materials and finishes to match or blend well with the cabinets. On this project I used a beaded edge to match the doors on the cabinets. Edge treatments for you to choose from include the bead, cove, round over, Ogee and classical. You can also choose the joinery method for assembly. I suggest biscuit joints as it is my favorite assembly method, but I also provide instructions for assembly with screws.

All the information you need to build the project just as I did is included; you can simply follow the instructions to the letter. However, you can exercise design options to make the project your own. Don't be afraid to experiment. You will probably be pleasantly surprised at the result.

Instructions For Kitchen Range Shelf

List of Materials

A	1	Shelf	6"X30"	Solid Hardwood
B	1	Back	8 ¼"X30 ¾"	Solid Hardwood
C	2	Shelves	3"X8"	Solid Hardwood

First, cut to length and width all the pieces described in the List of Materials. Select the most attractive parts of your boards. Watch for knots; you don't need to avoid them completely if they look attractive, but avoid them if they have holes or cracks. Make certain that there are no knots on the edges because this could create problems when you rout the profile.

Cutting these pieces from hardwood will involve several steps. The first two steps are straight lining and ripping. The next step, cross cutting, can be done in many ways depending upon the tools you have. I do most of my cross cutting on a sliding miter saw and recommend it for the cuts required on this shelf. If you do not have one, you can use a table saw or a radial arm saw.

On a table saw, since the pieces for this project are small, you can make all cross cuts using the bevel guide. Attach a board to your bevel guide to give it a larger surface contact with the material being ripped. This board can be used in one of two ways. You can attach a 2"x18" board that reaches just short of the blade path or you can attach a 3"x24" to 30" board that goes beyond the blade path. If you attach this piece, make sure to cut through the board before making your first crosscut. With this board your cuts will be more stable and much safer.

If your bevel guide has a clamp for the material, by all means use it. Never use your rip fence as a guide for cross cutting pieces. Cross cutting always poses the threat of kickback if you twist the material to one side or another. That is why the bevel guide is so important and why it must be held steady and fed into the blade slowly. If you use the rip fence to size the pieces, you will most certainly have a kickback. The piece between the blade and the fence will be thrown back at high speed, and it can hurt you seriously. Kickbacks can be frightening, even if they don't hurt you; A piece of hardwood thrown at high speed into your chest will cause you great pain if not serious injury.

The importance of safety when using any shop machine cannot be overemphasized. This is especially true when using the table saw. It is the most commonly used shop machine, and it is involved in the largest number of shop injuries. The potential for injury, if you are careless, is extremely high. Give your cutting 100% attention. Analyze each cut from start to finish to make certain it is safe and check the location of both your hands before starting the machine. Never use a machine when you are very tired or when you have been drinking alcohol. One mistake is all it takes to change your entire life.

Once you have cut all the pieces to size, use your band saw to cut the radiuses. If you don't have a band saw, the cuts can be made with a jigsaw. Cuts made in this manner will probably require extra sanding. Remember that you can make changes to personalize this project. Perhaps you like larger or smaller radiuses or you prefer small cove or scallop cuts on the corners. Maybe you like the project with square corners and a straight back. Whatever shape you select, your shelf will perform its function. Go ahead and experiment. The more you do the more you will enjoy it and the more you will learn about designing your own projects for other functions. Remember, instructions like these are based on one person's idea of how a project should be built. It is definitely not the only way and not necessarily the best way since there is no "best way."

Once all the parts have been cut you are ready to sand. The easiest way to sand the edges of this project is with a combination belt/disc sander. These units come in several sizes, but the most common are either a 6"x48" belt with an 8" or 9" disc or a 4"x36" belt with a 5" or 6" disc. Their advantage is that they allow you to sand the inside radiuses on the end of the belt sander by placing the radius of the project gently against the radius of the sander. The outside radiuses can be sanded on the disc by placing the surface of the project pieces on the sanding table and slowly sanding the edges. Or you can hold the pieces vertically over the belt sander and sand the radiuses with the flat surface of the sander. Remember to apply pressure very gently and to keep the project moving. The idea is to gently shape the radiuses to smoothness without losing the proper shape. Too much pressure will quickly alter the shape of the radius and ruin your project.

When doing the outside radius, if you have a disc with a table, set the table square with the disc. This will make the job easier and it will keep the edges square. After the radiuses are sanded, sand all the flat surfaces lightly. If you are using good sharp blades on your table and radial saws, very little rough sanding will be required. Once you have sanded all the flat surfaces, check the radiuses one last time to make certain that the flat sanding has not affected the transition from straight to radius. You can avoid this step if you prefer by sanding the flat surfaces first.

The cutout on the back (Part B) cannot be sanded completely with the belt sander. It will have to be sanded by hand or with a drum sander. If you are doing it by hand, use 80-grit sandpaper on a small block of wood, until the saw marks have been removed. Then sand it again using 120-grit sandpaper.

If you don't have a belt/disc sander, you can sand this project with a regular hand held belt sander and a small drum sander attachment for your drill press or a hand held drill. Clamp the project pieces and carefully sand all the flat edges and the outside radiuses. Remember, let the weight of the belt sander do the work; do not apply pressure. If your sander is not sanding with its own weight, it is time for a new belt. Applying pressure will not only create excessive wear for your sander, it could cause you to ruin the shape of your project because it is difficult to control a belt sender under heavy pressure. Once the flat edges and the outside radiuses have been sanded, you can sand the inside radiuses with the drum sander. The ideal drum size for this project is 3", but a 1½" or 2" will do the job.

After sanding all the edges, sand the faces of all the pieces. This is a very important step because if it is not done properly planer marks will show through your finish. The degree of sanding required here will depend on the roughness of the surfaces. Wood distributors do their planing in different ways. Some will provide a surface with mild planer marks that are easily removed with light sanding. Others will send their lumber out with deep planer marks that require serious effort to smooth out. Still others will plane their lumber with an abrasive sander, using a very rough grit sanding drum. These are the worst. It takes a great deal of sanding to get through the deep scratches inflicted by this kind of planing/sanding. Avoid this kind of surface if you can.

If you have a thickness planer and maintain sharp blades on it, a quick and light pass through your planer will measurably reduce the amount of sanding required. If you work a lot with hardwoods investing in a small thickness planer can save you a lot of work. It can also save you money since you can purchase rough sawn lumber that is always cheaper than lumber that has already been planed.

To determine when you have sanded enough to remove all planer marks, you will need adequate lighting. If your shop doesn't have good lighting, set up a light over your sanding work so you can clearly see if any planer marks remain.

Once you have completed sanding the planer marks off the faces, do your final sanding with an orbital sander. Start with a 100-grit sandpaper and sand the entire project including all edges and faces of all the pieces. Then switch to 150-grit and repeat the process. By now you should know what finish you will use. If you are going to use a brush-on finish such as Deft, your sanding is complete for now. If you are going to use Bartley's Gel Varnish, two more steps are required. Switch to 220-grit paper and sand all the pieces again. Finally, switch to 400-grit and repeat the process. This is an important step, so sand thoroughly and feel the surfaces to make certain the sanding is complete. Look at all the surfaces to be sure that no planer marks or other defects remain.

By this time you should have made a decision about the kind of profiles you want to use. Again, the choice is yours. I chose a beaded edge, but you have many options. For this design it is important to choose a profile in the ¼" size for proper assembly, but beyond this requirement any choice is acceptable. Once you choose, place the appropriate router bit on your router or router table. For a small project such as this a router table is a blessing. It is much easier to move small pieces past the machine rather than trying to move the machine past small pieces. If you don't have a router table you may find it difficult to cut the profiles on the two small shelves (Parts C).

For those without a router table two suggestions will make the job of cutting these two small pieces easier and safer. First, consider buying a special pad advertised in many woodworker's catalogs. If you are a regular woodworker and have purchased anything, you probably have several of these catalogs. This small, inexpensive pad holds small pieces in place while you rout their edges. They work well and eliminate the need for clamping.

An alternative is to clamp your router to a table upside down and then run the small piece through the router. This may be easier with some routers than with others. If you do this, remember that the router must be clamped securely to keep it from working loose and perhaps injuring you seriously. Once the router has been clamped and before you turn it on, try to shake it loose. Make a genuine effort to dislodge it to be sure that it is securely clamped. A large powerful router has tremendous torque and could easily twist loose during startup if it is poorly clamped.

But the safest way to make these profiles and the way I recommend is to use a router table. If you don't have one, buy one or, better yet, make one. There are many router table plans available from catalogs and in Woodworking magazines. Or design one for yourself that will meet your needs and fit your shop. Some companies even have router table kits that include a removable piece for the router to be attached to and other useful parts. These are helpful but not essential for a router table.

Once you have cut the profiles it is back to sanding. If you are using Deft or some other brush-on finish, sand all the profiles lightly with 150-grit sandpaper. If your router bit is really sharp, very little sanding will be necessary, just enough to soften the corners. Don't round over the corners; just knock off the sharp edges. If you are using Bartley's, you need the two extra steps of sanding with 220 grit and 400 grit sandpaper. Do all this sanding gently by hand. The profile should remain distinctive and not lose its character.

At this point you can finish the pieces or proceed to the assembly steps before doing your finishing. Once again you need to make a decision. Either method will work well. It seems easier to me to finish the project prior to final assembly, but this is simply a preference. You may think assembling the project first and then finishing it is easier and simpler.

If you are finishing with Deft Clear Wood Finish, Defthane, or Deft Wood Armor, apply the finish according to the instructions on the can. Remember that when instructions say apply liberally it doesn't mean to overdo. It still requires some brushing to smooth out the finish. I like the Deft Clear Wood finish because it is a self-leveling brushing lacquer. It also dries to the touch in less than thirty minutes and can be recoated in two hours. This makes it possible to apply three coats in one day. I have used Deft Clear Wood finish for over twenty years with great results, and I recommend it to you. However one problem with it is the strong fumes. The vapors can be overwhelming, so it must be used in a well-ventilated area. Use a fan to blow the vapors out through a window or door, and get yourself a respirator that works for lacquer fumes. It will make working with this product much more enjoyable.

One final rule with Deft, do not go back to areas previously brushed. Deft begins to dry in minutes. If you are careful it will not run. If you do notice a run after it begins to dry, leave it along. After it dries, remove the excess carefully with a razor blade and sand the surface until it is smooth. If you go back with the brush you will lose the self-leveling benefit and the brush marks will be quite obvious and unattractive.

Remember that you will need to sand between coats for best results. The label says that sanding is necessary only if the surface feels rough. At the very least you should sand with 400-grit sandpaper after the second coat before applying the third coat. And if you want a really glass-like finish, try sanding the third coat with 600 grit sandpaper and then apply a fourth coat. Deft Clear Wood Finish comes in Gloss or Semi-gloss. I like the Semi-gloss because I simply don't care for high gloss on anything. But the choice is yours. Either one will do a great job for you.

If you use Bartley's Gel Varnish it is still important to work in a well-ventilated area, but this product does not have a strong odor. Apply Bartley's with soft cloth such as a T-shirt remnant. You will need three pieces of cloth. One is relatively small for applying the finish liberally. Rub it into the grain. You can apply it across the grain initially, but make your final pass with the grain. Allow it to set for two to five minutes, wipe off the excess with another larger cloth. The last step is to buff the finish with the third clean soft cloth. Do not allow large areas to dry before buffing them. The job should be complete before the finish is dry. Bartley's dries slowly, so wait six hours before applying a second coat. Two coats do a good job. A third coat gives you a beautiful finish.

If you intend to stain (and I prefer not to), use either Bartley's Gel Varnish Stain for the first coat followed by Bartley's Clear Varnish, or use Deft Stains that dry completely for recoating in one hour. They go on easily, and you can clean your brush with soap and water.

You can assemble the range shelf unit using either of two methods. The simplest way, requiring the fewest tools, is to screw it together. Since the screws will enter from the back of the unit, none of them will be visible. To use screws the first step is to drill 3/16" holes through the back (Part B) in the appropriate locations. The hole locations are marked on the drawings. For the bottom shelf all the holes must be on a centerline 3/8" from the bottom edge of the Part B. There are five holes. Once you have the center line, measure 2" from each side for the end holes and mark them, Then measure 8 ½" from each end for the second hole and 15 ¼" from either end for the center hole. The holes for the top shelves are drilled on a centerline at 1 ½" from the top edge of the Part B.

Placement of the holes starts at 1½" from either side with the second hole for each of the small shelves (Parts C) at 6¾" from each end. Once you have marked all nine of the holes, punch them lightly with an awl and drill them with a 3/16" brad point bit. Mark these holes on the face side of the Part B. Once all the holes are drilled, turn the Part B face down and slightly countersink or ream the holes to be sure the screws won't protrude and cause problems during installation of your unit. The next step is to clamp Part A in place on Part B and then drive in the screws when everything is correctly aligned. Next clamp each of the Parts C onto the appropriate location on the Part B and drive in the screws. Your project is now ready for installation.

The second method for assembly is also simple but it requires a biscuit joiner. I suggest you use either #10 or #20 biscuits. To cut the biscuit slots use the fence on your biscuit joiner. For the first cuts set the fence so the blade will cut at 3/8" to the center. Next mark the center location of each cut on all the parts. On the bottom edge of Part B, mark for five biscuits. The simplest way to do this is to clamp the Part A to the Part B in proper alignment. Then, from the bottom, mark for five biscuit slots. Make your marks so they cross both pieces. This will be the center mark of the biscuit slot, so make certain that the end slots are not too close to the ends. If they are too close the biscuit slot could extend beyond the end of the board and be visible. Now take the clamps off and clamp down the Part B, making certain that the back edge is clear of the bench so that the biscuit joiner can be used. Align the biscuit joiner with the line and with the fence flat against the bottom edge of the Part B. Keeping the biscuit joiner flat on the surface and properly aligned, cut all five slots.

Now clamp the Part A face down with the back edge hanging over your bench. This time align your biscuit joiner with the line and the fence flat on the bottom surface of the Part A. Making certain that the biscuit joiner is flat on the edge and properly aligned, cut all five slots. With the biscuit joiner fence unchanged, cut the slots on the back edges of the Parts C. To find the location of these slots, clamp the shelves in place on the Part B and mark for two slots on each shelf. Mark on the bottom of the Parts C and lightly on the face of Part B just below the location of the Parts C. Now unclamp the Parts C and clamp them on the workbench with the back edge hanging over your bench and the face up. Cut the two slots on each shelf.

Now readjust the fence on your biscuit joiner, Up to now it has been set to cut at 3/8" center. Reset it to cut the slots at a 1½" center. Clamp the Part B so that the top edge is free to accommodate the biscuit joiner fence. Place the fence on the top edge of the Part B and align the biscuit joiner with the marks. Make certain that the biscuit joiner is flat against the surface and cut all four slots. To assemble, place a little glue in the slots on the Parts C and the Part A and insert biscuits. Next place the Part B face up on your bench and put a little glue in each slot. Align the Parts C and the Part A and tap them into place gently. Check for proper alignment and then clamp them in place making certain that the clamps have not pulled them out of square. Allow the glue to set, remove the clamps and you are ready to install the unit. Remember to use glue sparingly in these biscuit joints. It does not take much for strong joints and excess glue will be forced out onto the face of your project and make a mess that will be hard to clean.

To install your shelf, first find a couple of studs behind your range, measure their location, and transfer these dimensions to the back (Part B). Drill your holes about 1" from the bottom so they will be easily covered by the things on the shelf. Either use a finish washer or ream the hole precisely to the size of an attractive brass screw and screw the unit to the wall. Two-inch screws should be sufficiently long for this purpose, since the shelf unit should rest on the back of the range. On some ranges the top of the back will be wide enough that it will not be necessary to screw the range shelf to the wall.

Drawings on next page.

Contact me at bill@woodworkbusiness.com with questions. Thanks.

Stove Shelf Drawings

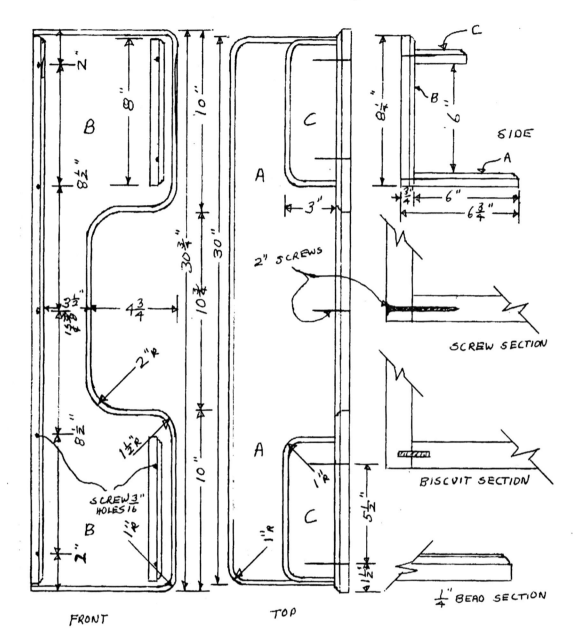

FRONT

TOP

SIDE

SCREW SECTION

BISCUIT SECTION

$\frac{1}{4}$" BEAD SECTION

Laundry Room Cabinet

List of Materials

A	2	Top and Bottom	¾"X8 ¼"X66 ¼"	Maple Plywood
B	3	Sides and Center	¾"X8 ¼"X31 ¾"	Maple Plywood
C	2	Scribe Strips	¾"X1 3/8"X33 5/8"	Maple Plywood
D	4	Doors	¾"X16"X33 5/8"	Maple Plywood
E	4	Shelves	¾"X8"X32"	Maple Plywood
F	4	Hangrails	¾"X2"X32"	Maple Plywood
G	1	Back	¼"X33 ¼"X66 ¼"	Plywood
H	88lf	Iron-on Veneer	13/16" wide	Maple
I	8	Mounting Plates	#195H7100	Blum or equal
J	4	Hinges	#91M2750	Blum or equal
J1	4	Hinges	#91M2650	Blum or equal
K	16	Shelf Pins	Plastic over metal	Blum or equal

Instructions For Laundry Room Cabinet

First, choose and buy the material you will be using. I used maple plywood for my project. There are several grades of maple plywood including shop grade, cabinet grade and furniture grade. Any of these can be very good or very bad depending on the batch. Sometimes they have a pleasing, clear grain pattern with few if any knots. Other times they have many knotholes that have been filled. Look carefully at the material to make certain it is what you want. If you plan to paint the project instead of using a clear finish, filled knots in maple plywood will not be a problem. However, if you are going to stain or clear coat, filled knots can be quite unattractive. I suggest that you purchase a better grade or purchase your material elsewhere. Naturally you may decide to use oak or ash or some other hardwood plywood, but this will increase the price of your project and may be unnecessary for a laundry room. For this project you will need to purchase two sheets of 3/4" plywood and one sheet of ¼" plywood in addition to the iron-on veneer and the hardware.

Cut your pieces as described in the List of Materials. All the pieces are rectangles with the grain of the plywood running along the longest dimension. On paper lay out the most effective way to cut the plywood to get the best possible use out of each sheet. You will have more plywood than you need, so the better your layout the more plywood you will have left for your next project. Rip all the pieces first and then crosscut using a safe method for crosscutting. Do not crosscut using the table saw rip fence; this can cause dangerous kickbacks.

Iron on the veneer edging, then trim all the edges. File or sand all the edges until they are smooth and look good. As you sand watch the corners and feel them to be sure you leave a clean, smooth edge. If you use a file, you can clean the glue build up with a file card. The surfaces to be covered with veneer are as follows:

The front edge of Parts A
The front edge of Parts B
The inside and bottom edges of Parts C

All four edges of Parts D

The front edge of Parts E

The exposed edge of Parts F

Sand all components completely before you do any assembly. This makes sanding easier and faster because you will not be sanding into corners. Use a small orbital sander starting with 120-grit sandpaper. Then go over it again with 180 or 220 grit sandpaper. By now you should have decided what finish you going to use. If you use a Deft Clear Wood finish or a polycrylic finish that will there is no need to sand beyond 220-grit. If you plan to use a finish such as Bartley's Gel Varnish, sand the entire project again using 400-grit sandpaper.

Before the actual assembly, drill the holes for the shelf pins. I drilled mine 2" apart using an aluminum jig that I made. You can make yourself a small one-time-use jig from a narrow strip of ¼" plywood. Drill the holes 2" apart or closer if you choose. The size of the holes depends on the pins you will be using. I use the 5mm shelf pins, but you can also get them in ¼". You will need to install a stop on your drill bit to keep it from accidentally drilling through the sides of your project. I use a 5mm carbide bit especially made for drilling shelf pinholes. However, any bit of the proper size will do. I suggest that you use a brad point bit for a neater hole. As an alternative you can use metal shelf standard and clips to support your shelves. If you decide to do this, they can be installed after you apply the finish.

If you use shelf pins, drill the rear row of holes about 1" from the back of the cabinet and the front row about 1" from the front edge of the cabinet. If you use the metal shelf standards, install the rear standard about 1" from the back of the cabinet and install the front standard directly behind the hinge mounting plate. Install these metal shelf standards after the cabinet is assembled.

Before starting to assemble the cabinet components you must decide on the method you will use for fastening them together. For this project I used nails. In my shop I had pneumatic finish nailers that nail pieces together rapidly. If you own a compressor, a new or used pneumatic finish nailer can be a good investment. If not, I suggest you assemble your project using #6 casing galvanized nails. The galvanizing on the nails helps them to hold better than bright nails. If you prefer you can use screws, biscuits, or dowels for the assembly. The first step is to attach the top and bottom (Parts A) to the Parts B that are the right and left side and the center divider. Mark the location of the center divider on the Parts A, then fasten the top to the two sides and the center. Fasten the bottom in the same manner.

Now install the hang rails on the top and the bottom. Place the first hang rail and nail it through the side and then through the center. Now place the second hang rail (Part F) and nail it through the other side and then toe nail it to the center divider. Make certain that the hang rails (Parts F) are flush with the back of the cabinet. Follow the same procedure with the other two hang rails. Then nail the hang rails through the bottom and the top.

The last step is to install the back. Place the cabinet face down on your workbench or on the floor. Apply the back, turning the best face into the inside of the cabinet. Nail the back on, using 1" galvanized nails about 4" apart Use the back to square up the cabinet. To do this, nail the back flush with the edge of one side and then straighten it to flush along the top or bottom while nailing. Then nail the rest of the back. For now the assembly is complete. The scribe strips must still be attached to the cabinet, but we will attach them as part of the installation process in order to make the job easier. The doors are also a part of the assembly and these should be installed as described in these instructions and then removed for finishing and installation. You install them at this point just to be sure that they fit correctly before you apply finish to them.

Now the holes for the hinges can be drilled into the doors. I used Blum concealed, self-closing hinges. In order to accommodate them, you drill holes into the back of the doors at the proper location. The holes are 35mm diameter and approximately ½" deep. For this project I used the Blum Module 100 hinges. They swing open 100 degrees. The instructions for these hinges indicate that the edge of the 35mm hole should be between 3mm (1/8") and 6mm (¼") from the edge of the door. The best way to ensure that these holes are drilled correctly is to make a table jig for your drill press. Unless you have one of those new portable jigs for European hinge holes, a drill press is essential because the hole must the correctly located and straight.

My drill press table jig is simply a 10"x24" piece of plywood that I have fastened to the drill press table with screws and washers. I clamped a fence on top of the drill press table to complete the jig. After I chuck in the 35mm bit I measure 7/8" back from the center point of the bit to the location of the fence and clamp it tight with two C-clamps. Keep the fence as straight as possible with the table. Now check the depth that the bit will drill. First do this with the drill off to set the height of the table close to correct. Then using a scrap of plywood the same thickness as the door, drill one hole. Check that the distance from the edge of the hole to the edge of the board is close to 3/16". Then check the depth of the hole by placing the hinge in the hole. If the hole is too shallow, the hinge plate will not reach the door and the hinge cannot be properly installed. If the hole is too deep, the hinge will dance in the hole. Adjust the depth of the hole and then test again.

When you have the depth set and the fence in the right location, you are ready to drill the holes in the doors. The remaining dimension is the distance of the hinge center from the top and bottom of the door. This distance is not critical. I usually use a 2 ½"' center for this purpose. The easiest way is to mark the drill press table 2 ½" on each side of the bit center. This way it is only necessary to place the door inside up on the drill press table. Push the back edge against the fence and align the top or bottom of the table with the 2 ½" line and drill the first hole. Now slide the door across so that the opposite edge is on the opposite 2 ½" mark and drill the second hole. The door is now ready to have the hinge screwed on after the finish is applied to it.

The next step is to apply the finish. For my cabinet I chose Deft Clear Wood finish. Since I wanted the light color of the natural maple, I did not apply a stain. You may wish to stain your cabinet to match some other piece in your home or simply to select a color that you prefer. In finishing, first make certain that everything is properly sanded. Since the sanding was done prior to assembly, very little sanding should be needed at this point. Before any finishing product is applied, the surfaces to be finished should be dry and clean. Take the time necessary to clean all surfaces and every crevice and to fill all the nail holes with wood filler. If you have a shop vac, use it to dust the cabinet thoroughly.

Once the cabinet is clean, it is ready for the first coat of clear finish or stain. If you are staining, wipe the stain with the grain, removing all excess stain to avoid streaks. Once the stain is applied you are ready for the first coat of clear. The stain will raise the grain a little, but don't be tempted to sand the surface smooth. If you sand the stained surface it may become splotched since the sandpaper may wear through the stain in some places, especially corners. Just be sure that all surfaces are clean, then apply the first coat of clear.

If you use Deft stains, the project will be ready for the first coat of clear in about an hour in good weather. After applying the first coat of clear, wait about two hours and then lightly sand all surfaces by hand using 220-grit sandpaper. This will leave the surface quite smooth and ready for the second coat. Apply the second coat and once again allow it to dry for two hours. Remember that the second coat will be applied on a very smooth, non-porous surface. Be sure to comb out the clear coat carefully with the grain in order to avoid runs. Allow the second coat to dry for two hours, then sand once more using 400-grit sandpaper. Two coats are sufficient for the inside of the cabinet, so I suggest you sand only the front edge of the cabinet, the scribe strips and the front and edges of the doors. After applying the third coat to the outside surfaces wait for two hours before installing the cabinet. Using Deft Clear Wood Finish or some other rapid drying clear finish you can apply the stain and three coats of clear within one eight hour day. Then you are ready to install the cabinet the next day or even that same evening.

You may also choose to paint your cabinet a color of your own choice. If so, use a good grade of oil base paint and apply it according to the instructions on the can.

When the finish is dry, you are ready to install the doors. The simplest way to install doors with European hinges is to use special jigs that the hinge manufacturers sell. These jigs are very expensive and are only cost-effective if you do commercial work on a reasonably large scale. I still install European doors without using these jigs, and you can do the same and avoid that expense. First, install the hinges on the doors. Start by placing the hinge in the 35mm hole with the part of the hinge with the adjustment screw facing toward the center of the door. Making certain that the screw plate is aligned with the edge of the door, use a VixBit to drill for the screws. This is a simple self-centering bit that automatically controls the depth of the hole. It is inexpensive and readily available locally or through woodworker catalogs. As an alternative, you can simply punch a starter hole with an awl, being careful to center the hole. Next, drive the screws into the holes. Use only the proper screws for this purpose.

Once this hinge is installed, install the mounting plate onto the hinge by sliding the mounting plate into the grooves on the hinge arm. The mounting plate will fit properly only in one direction, so make certain that it slides in correctly. Slide it all the way in until it stops and back it off slightly (less than 1/16'). Next, tighten the retainer screw that keeps the hinge and mounting plate together. Now follow this same step on every hinge hole. Remember that the hinges to be fastened to the center partition of the cabinet are not exactly the same as the ones that will be installed on the doors to be fastened to the sides. The ones on the sides (called full inset hinges) are easily recognizable by the angled hinge arm. The hinges that go in the center (called half overlay hinges) have an arm with a slight crook in it. Both of the hinges on a door must be the same kind. Since the doors are identical, there is no need to identify them or separate them.

After the hinges and plates are installed on all the doors, install the doors on the cabinet. First place the cabinet face up on a pair of saw horses or a worktable. Now take the first door with full inset hinges and place it on the cabinet with the hinge mounting plates against the side of the cabinet. Make certain the top of the door is flush with the top of the cabinet and the hinge mounting plates are against the side. Reach in through the opening next to the door and install screws in the mounting plates, taking care not to move the door. Now do the same thing with the door for the other side of the cabinet. This door also has full inset hinges. Now open these two doors and grab the first door with the half overlay hinges and place it flush with the top of the cabinet and mounting plates against the center partition. Reach in through the opening and drive the screws into the mounting plates without moving the door. Do the same thing with the last door. Now the doors are completely installed. Adjusting the doors at this time would be a waste of time. They will be adjusted as part of the installation procedure.

Installing your cabinet is the next step. This laundry room cabinet is installed in the same way that upper kitchen cabinets are installed; therefore, these instructions will cover steps to consider if you are installing upper kitchen cabinets.

With upper kitchen cabinets you must consider the wall on which they will be installed. Does it have a soffit at the top? If it does, the cabinets should be installed tight against the soffit. Or, if you intend to install some kind of large decorative molding at the top of the cabinet, you may want to install the cabinets below the soffit in order to allow space for the molding. If there is no soffit, the cabinet should be installed at 54" from the floor unless it is a cabinet over a range, sink, or refrigerator. Such cabinets should be installed so that the top of each cabinet is flush with the top of the standard height cabinets.

The first step for a standard cabinet (which is usually 30" high) is to mark the wall at 54". Measuring up from the floor, make two marks some distance apart, then check the level between them. If the line between them is not level, raise the low side of the level before you draw the line. If there is only a minor difference you probably won't have any serious difficulties with the installation. If the difference is significant, however, check some other things before continuing with the installation. The decisions you make will depend on the number of cabinets involved, the length of the wall and other considerations that will determine the final look of the installation. You want the installation to look right; it will do little good to level your cabinet if looks out of level because the walls are not square. Sometimes it is impossible to make a cabinet look level, but often you can get a good-looking job by making certain compromises. For example, after measuring from the floor at two points, if the level indicates that using the two points will give you an unlevel line, check the squareness of the wall to the level line. If your level line is not square with the wall, check the squareness with a line made between the two points measured from the floor.

You can make this squareness check with a framing square or any large piece of plywood that you know is square. If the wall is square with this line and you are installing only one cabinet such as the laundry room cabinet, the wise choice is to follow the line between the two points. The finished job will look level because the cabinet lines up with the wall and the floor. In this situation leveling the cabinet might be "right", but it would look wrong; most people would assume that the cabinet rather than the wall was not level. Large kitchen jobs require a much more intensive review of the wall conditions before you install cabinets.

Another thing to remember is that the 54" is merely a standard distance. It is not carved in granite. You may wish to place your cabinets a little lower or a little higher for special conditions. For example, because my laundry room cabinet was only 9" deep, I could install it lower than normal and still clear the door of the washing machine when it opens. I installed it lower so it would be easier to reach into it. You are not stuck with standard dimensions if some other size suits you better.

The next step is to locate the studs so you can put the installation screws in the right place. To find the studs easily, use a stud finder that measures density. Remember to check your findings and make your marks on the wall section that will be covered by the cabinet. Once you have located all the studs, measure the distance from the wall and write the number next to each mark. Now transfer the sizes to the back of the cabinet. Take into consideration that, because of the scribes, the cabinet is smaller than the wall space. I suggest you cut a small scrap of wood the size of the scribe space and just hold it in place for your tape as you take the measurements.

Mark the back of the cabinet at each stud location, then make a cross mark at 1¾' from the top and bottom of the cabinet. This will place the screw in the center of the hang rail. Now drill each mark with a 3/16" bit. Now you are ready to fasten the cabinet to the wall. This is easier if you have someone help you. If you have help, the doors can remain on the cabinet during the installation. I use pipe clamps to help hold up the cabinet while I drive the screws into the wall.

Simply unscrew and remove the turn screw from two clamps of over 5' and then slide the other part of the clamp attachment on to the pipe until it is approximately the right height to accommodate the cabinet. Place the clamps where they will be accessible while holding the cabinet up. Raise the cabinet into its approximate position and then open the door on each end. Quickly put the clamps in place with a slight angle away from the wall. Now check your lines. If the cabinet is too low, slowly push up one side at a time and raise the clamp. If it is too high, release the clamp and allow it to drop slowly until the cabinet reaches the line. Once the cabinet is aligned with the line, get on the stepladder or stool and drive 2 ½" drywall screws into each stud.

When the cabinet is installed, nail on the scribe strips. If these strips fit tight to the wall when properly aligned with the doors, no other molding or strip is needed. However, if there is a gap between the wall and the scribe strip install a small molding such as a quarter round or a ¼"x ¾" decorative strip to cover the gap. This should be finished to match the cabinet. Now your project is finished except for installing the shelf clips and shelves at the level you select.

Drawings on next page.

Contact me at bill@woodworkbusiness.com with any questions.

Laundry Cabinet Drawings

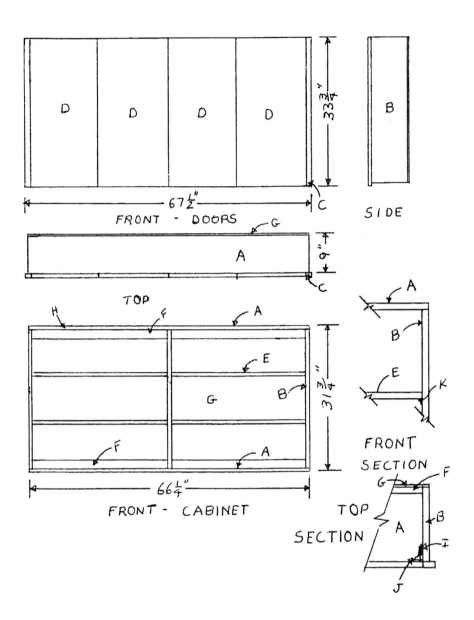

Foyer or Bathroom Mirror Frame

List of Materials

A	2	Frames	¾"X2"X27 ½" Dbl Miter & Rabbet	Solid Hardwood
B	2	Frames	¾"X2"X21 ½" Dbl Miter & Rabbet	Solid Hardwood
C	4	Strips	5/16"X5/16"X28" Cut to Fit	Solid Hardwood
D	12	Screws	5/8"X5	Blum # 606
E	1	Mirror	18"X24"	Precut Mirror

Mirror Frame Instructions

This mirror frame was built of solid red oak. You can use any hardwood you prefer and get the same results. Start by obtaining all the necessary materials as listed above. Use solid hardwood that has been planed and straight lined unless you have a thickness planer. Rip 2" wide strips of sufficient length to make the two Parts A and the two Parts B. Rip a 5/16" strip half the length necessary for the Parts A and B. Sand the 5/16"X3/4" strip with a belt sander and then rip it into two 5/16"X5/16" strips to hold the mirror in place

Sand all the 2" wide strips with a belt sander. The 2" faces should be sanded until all the planer marks have been removed. This is important because it is common to assume that materials that have been planed are ready for fine sanding and finishing. This is inaccurate and a good smooth finish requires the removal of all planer marks. The simplest tool to use for this purpose is the belt sander. The edges must also be belt sanded. In this case the sanding should remove all saw marks and any friction burns.

Next, cut the rabbet for the mirror with a router or your table saw. If you use a router, it is best to have it on a router table and move the material past the router bit. You can use a fluted router bit with a fence or guide on the table. Or you can use a rabbeting router bit with a ball bearing pilot Either way, make the rabbet in two passes to avoid over-heating the router bit. If you decide to use the table saw for the rabbet, there are two ways to do it. The first, which is done with a Dado blade, re-quires only one pass. The second, done in two passes, uses a regular blade. To use a Dado blade, set the depth carefully. If you use a standard Dado blade, assemble it so it will cut at least 3/8" wide. Clamp a board to the inside surface of the rip fence on your table saw—a ¾" thick board about the size of the rip fence should be fine. Now set the depth of the Dado blade as close as possible. Then measure from the outside edge of the Dado to the rip fence 5/16" plus the thickness of the board. If your board is ¾" thick, the distance from the outside edge of the Dado blade to the rip fence should be 1 1/16".

Put the board at the top edge of the rip fence with hands well away from the blade. Slowly lower the board onto the Dado blade. The blade will barely cut the board 1/16". Now turn off the saw and clamp the board to the rip fence. Make certain the clamps will clear the path of the cut Use a scrap to test the cut It should be exactly

5/16" wide and 9/16" deep. If the scrap is correct, run the 2" strip through to make the rabbet cut. If the scrap is off, make appropriate adjustments and try again. Do not cut the frame strips until you have cut a scrap piece correctly. Remember, Dado blades can be extremely dangerous. Think through every step, and keep your hands well clear of the blade. Avoid pieces with knots, dados have a tendency to kickback knots. Take the time to be safe. Notice in the drawings how the rabbet can be cut in various ways.

NOTE: Rabbets can also be cut with an electric hand planer. Most of these planers are built to accommodate rabbeting. If you choose this tool for the job, read the planer's instruction book carefully. It will describe how the planer can be used for rabbeting.

The next step is to router the edges to the desired profile. Many profiles are available. Choose the one that best suits your decor. Maybe a simple round over will serve your purpose, or a nice Ogee. The easiest and safest way to cut the profiles is with a router table. You can purchase a router table, but for the most part they have work surfaces that are inconveniently small.

To cut profiles, it is best to use a carbide-tipped router bit with a ball bearing pilot This makes the job quick and easy without the need for a fence. Avoid using high-speed steel router bits for hardwoods as they will dull quickly and then begin chipping and burning the wood. A high quality carbide tipped bit is an excellent investment and will give you smooth, clean cuts for many years. With such a bit, even an inexpensive router will perform well. With a steel bit, even a very expensive router will not do a good job.

Once all the pieces have been profiled and rabbeted, fine sand all of them with an orbital sander or by hand. Now you are ready to cut the miters. All the dimensions for the mitered pieces in the List of Materials are given long point to long point That is, the longest point of the miter at the outside edge of the piece is the measuring point Start by cutting all the pieces square and 1" or 2" longer than the actual measurement. This will make them more manageable for the final mitering. Now carefully cut one miter on one end of each piece. Next, measure each piece to the exact size, remembering to measure the long points at the outside edge. Carefully cut the second miter on each piece. Whatever method you choose to cut the miters, cut test pieces from scraps first.

One way to test is to cut pieces for a small, but complete square and test-fit the four miters If the cuts do not fit tightly when the frame is put together against a square, you must readjust your miter saw or jig and try again. Take your time with this and make reference marks on your miter saw or permanent adjustments to your jig so that this testing will not be necessary in the future. Poorly cut miters require wood filler and seldom look good. Because tight joints give a professional appearance they are worth the patience they require.

Once all the miters are cut, you are ready to assemble the frame. Assembling can be done in at least two different ways. The simplest is to use nails and glue. Hold your pieces in place with miter clamps. These come in various styles and are readily available in woodworking stores, home improvement stores, department stores such as Sears, and from woodworker's catalogs. These clamps make assembly easy, especially when you are using nails. They hold the joints tightly together while you are nailing them.

To use nails and glue, first apply a little glue on one miter surface of a PartA and place it at 90 degrees to the appropriate miter on a Part B. If you use individual corner clamps, clamp the joint tightly, making certain that all surfaces are flush and even. If you use a miter clamp system that clamps all four corners of the frame at once, repeat the process on all four miter joints until you have a complete frame. Then clamp it tight, making sure that all the joints are flush and even. Miter clamps should assure squareness, but always check the squareness of your frame anyway. Now put into your drill a drill bit that is slightly smaller than the nails you plan to use. The size of your nails should be related to the bulk of the frame. In this case use a #6 finish nail. If you don't have a proper sized drill bit, cut the head off one of the nails and chuck it into your drill. You can use this nail to drill the holes the right size. Drill from one outside corner through a Part A and only slightly into the Part B.

Repeat this step on the other side of the same corner, drilling through the outside edge of the Part B and only slightly into the Part A. Align the two holes so they do not cross into each other, otherwise, the second nail may not go in or it may bend. Hammer the two nails partially in, then, to avoid damaging the wood surface, use a nail set to set them into the wood. Follow the same steps with all four corners of the frame.

You can assemble the frame without nails by using a biscuit joiner in one of two ways. The three sizes of biscuits available are #0, #10, and #20. I prefer, when possible, to use the #20 because it is the largest so it has the most glue surface. If you use #0 biscuits you can use the center of the miter cut as a guide for making the biscuit slot. Measure along the miter cut itself from the long point to the short paint, and mark the exact center. Use this center mark to guide the cutting of the biscuit slots on all eight miter cuts. Set the depth of the cut by setting the fence on your biscuit joiner so that the blade is exactly 3/8" to the center.

Remember to clamp each piece down tightly before making your cuts. Move carefully, making sure that the fence is completely flat against the face of the frame, and the cutting surface is tight against the miter cut. This will ensure a good straight, square slot and proper alignment of the miters.

If you use #20 biscuits, instead of marking the center of the miter cut, clamp each piece as before. Use the short point of each piece as the center mark for your cut. This will give you half the size of a #20 slot. Simply cut two #20 biscuits in half and use one half piece for each corner

With either biscuit method, place a small amount of glue in one biscuit slot and insert the biscuit. If you use a full #0 biscuit, insert it as close to the center of the slot as possible. If you use #20 biscuits, insert them with the square end, even with the short point of the miters. Put glue in the second miter biscuit slot and quickly fit the pieces together. Do this on all four corners; then clamp the frame together using miter clamps as described above. Check all the joints, making certain they are neat and tight. Also check the frame for squareness. Use glue sparingly in biscuit joints. If you do get a little glue ooze, don't spread it around. Let it dry a little, and then remove it with a pocketknife being careful not to mar the surface. When the glue is completely dry you can sand off any glue that might create problems with the finish.

After the glue has set and the clamps have been removed, it is time for final sanding. The degree of final sanding depends upon the finish to be used. In any case, first check all the joints to make sure they are flush and even. If they are not, you will need to do some significant sanding to fix them. If you have taken your time in the assembly process, however, extensive sanding should not be needed.

If you intend to use a regular stain along with clear wood finish such as Deft products, sand all parts with an orbital sander and by hand with 150 to 220 grit paper. Finer sanding now serves no purpose because these finishes raise the grain, but you will need to fine sand between coats of finish. If you use stain, do not sand after the stain is applied. Apply the first coat of clear wood finish before doing any further sanding. Sanding a stained surface can cause blotches, and corners can lose their color.

If you intend to use Bartley's Clear Varnish or Bartley's Varnish Stain, sand the mirror frame with 400-grit sandpaper. The surfaces should feel glass smooth before you apply the finish. Since Bartley's does not raise the grain, your fine sanding is done first, and no additional sanding is needed between coats.

Now you are ready for the finishing. As you can see by the previous instructions, you make many decisions based upon your preferences and the tools you have available. By now you should have decided about the finish for your frame because you had to choose which sanding procedure was appropriate. I choose to avoid stains if I can because I like the look of natural wood. However, some woods such as maple, birch and other light colored woods often have little figuring. In this case, staining may well enhance the beauty of your project, or you may want to stain your frame to match the color of other pieces of furniture in your home.

The two finishing systems that I recommend most often are Deft Clear Wood Finish with or without Deft Stains and Bartley's Clear Varnish or Varnish Stains. If you decide to finish with Deft, remember the sanding instructions outlined above. The process I use for Deft Clear Wood Finish involves sanding with 220-grit sandpaper after the first coat has dried. Then I sand with 400-grit sandpaper after the second and third coats. For those projects in which I use a fourth coat, I sometimes sand with 600-grit sandpaper before applying the fourth coat. Feel the finish, and judge for yourself. You want the surface to feel almost glass smooth.

Be especially careful when sanding near corners. Even after one or more coats of clear have been applied, it is easy to sand too far on a corner. This is especially true when stain is used. Remember, too, that as more coats are applied the surfaces become slicker, and runs are more likely. Deft has a tendency to run more when it's applied on the third or fourth coat. This is not a serious problem on horizontal surfaces, but vertical surfaces can be difficult if too much material is applied. After the first coat, use Deft sparingly, and comb it out to avoid runs. Check back to previously finished areas every few minutes so that you can comb out any runs while they are still wet. Deft dries extremely fast. In warm weather, it will dry to the touch in minutes. Once drying starts, it is unwise to brush out runs or to add more finish. Attempting this will just leave unsightly brush marks on the surface.

Deft is self-leveling, so when it is properly applied it will leave a finish that looks sprayed on. The main advantage of Deft products is their quick drying. Stains can be clear coated in one hour. Clear can be recoated after two hours. So if you get an early start and the weather is reasonably dry, you can stain your frame and apply three coats of clear finish all in the same day. With some projects this may be important to you.

Bartley's Clear Varnish is easier than Deft to use because it does not run. You can apply it with either a rag or a brush. You can stain with Bartley's premixed varnish stains, or you can mix your own colors by mixing Bartley's Varnish Stain with Bartley's Clear Varnish. Or you can add oil colors to the Bartley's Clear Varnish. Remember that with Bartley's all the sanding is completed before you start the finishing because it does not raise the grain.

Next I will describe the steps I follow when I use Bartley's; they are the same whether or not I use stain. Apply the first coat liberally with a rag over the entire frame. Now use a clean soft (T-shirt) rag to wipe off excess and to lightly buff the surface. Move with the grain when wiping and buffing. Wipe until the finish is smooth and even, with all excess finish removed. Allow the first coat to dry for at least six hours before you apply the second coat. Apply the second coat in the same way, but use a completely clean cloth for the buffing. Two coats produce a nice smooth finish and are usually sufficient. For additional sheen and protection, you can apply a third and fourth coat.

With the frame finished, it is time to install the mirror. You can order the mirror from a glass company that will cut it to size for you, or you can shop local home improvement stores. I bought an 18"x24' beveled glass mirror for my frame from a home improvement store for about $15. It probably isn't the same quality you would get from a glass shop, but it certainly looks good.

The first step in installing the mirror into the frame is to place the frame face down on a pad or cloth on your workbench. Make certain there are no small tools or wood scraps under the cloth. Now place the mirror face down in the rabbet. Measure the mirror strips (Parts C) and cut them to the proper length. Drill three 3/16" holes evenly spaced in each strip. The first and last holes should be about 2' from the ends with the other holes evenly spaced between them. Put the strips in place behind the mirror and drive 5/8" Blum 606 screws carefully through the holes and into the sides of the rabbet in the frame. Before putting on the strips, place a piece of paper or, better yet, some thin cardboard, over the mirror back. This will protect the mirror while you are driving the screws and protect the back of the mirror during any future transit. Cut the cardboard the correct size, and then screw on the strips.

This protection serves an important purpose because the back of a mirror is very sensitive and easily scratched. Such scratches will show through and ruin the appearance of the mirror. Do not over tighten the screws, as they are short and can strip easily. Also do not apply excessive pressure to the mirror strip against the back of the mirror. Only slight pressure is needed to hold the mirror in place. The last step is to install a picture wire or serrated hanger clip so you can hang your mirror on the wall. I prefer to install two of the 5/8" Blum 606 screws 6" down from the top of the mirror and in the center of the frame member Parts A. Drive these screws until 3/16" is sticking out. Now tie a picture wire of at least 20-pound test from one screw to the other, allowing a little slack. Tie this wire well enough so that it cannot come loose under stress. Check it by pulling on it with a pressure well in excess of the weight of the mirror.

If you decide to use serrated picture clips instead of wire, do not use the little nails provided with the clips. They will come loose, and your mirror will wind up broken on the floor. Instead, use a small drill bit to drill holes large enough for at least 5/8"X4 screws, or use 5/8" Blum 606 screws to insure that the clip will hold on to the back of the mirror frame. Center this clip on the top Part B at the back of the mirror.

Drawings on next page.

Contact me at bill@woodworkbusiness.com with questions. Thanks.

Mirror Frame Drawings

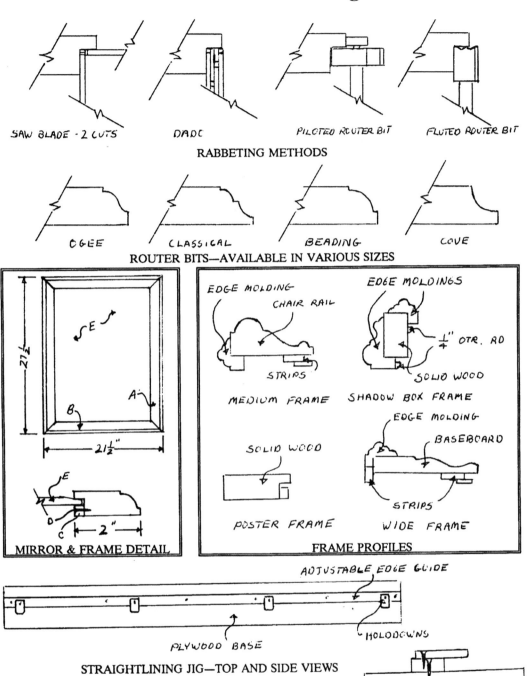

RABBETING METHODS

ROUTER BITS—AVAILABLE IN VARIOUS SIZES

MIRROR & FRAME DETAIL

FRAME PROFILES

STRAIGHTLINING JIG—TOP AND SIDE VIEWS

123

Study Desk

List of Materials

A	2	Sides	¾"X23"X29 ¼"	Hdwd Plywood
B	1	Back Support	¾"X12"X45 ½"	Hdwd Plywood
C	1	Front Support	¾"X6"X45 ½"	Hdwd Plywood
D	1	Divider	¾"X3 ¾"X21"	Hdwd Plywood
E	2	Drawer Front	¾"X4 ¾"X22 ½"	Hdwd Plywood
F	2	Drawer Unit, Bk/Frt	½"X2 ½"X20 3/8"	Hdwd Plywood
G	2	Drawer Unit, Sides	½"X2 ½"X18"	Hdwd Plywood
H	1	Drawer Unit Bottom	¼"X18"X21 3/8"	Hdwd Plywood
I	10sf	Plastic Laminate	30"X48"	Wilsonart/Equal
J	25lf	Iron-on Veneer Edge	13/16"	To match plywood
K	2	Drawer Slides	½" spacing	Blum or Equal

Instructions For Study Desk

Cut all the pieces as described in the List of Materials. All the pieces for this project are rectangles with square corners. Cut them with the grain running in the direction of the longest dimension. Always select the best faces of your plywood for the exposed sides. For example, there are two parts A that comprise the sides and legs of the desk. The sides of these parts that face out should be the ones with the most attractive grain patterns. Since Part B is exposed to the back of the desk, this should be the best side. The two Parts E are the drawer fronts; the front side of these should be the most attractive. If you are using plywood with a strong grain pattern, cut both Parts E from the same piece. Make this piece long enough for both parts and then cut it in two, making certain that you install each piece to expose the continuity of the grain pattern. This is easy to do and contributes a great deal to the appearance of your desk.

Iron on the veneer edging and then trim all the edges. There are various ways to trim the veneer. You can do it with a sharp utility knife if you work carefully. You can also file all the edges with a mill bastard file. And, you can sand these edges, but the file or the knife works faster. Glue build-up, which is common, can be removed with a wire brush or a file card. The edges to be covered with the veneer are as follows:

The front and back of Parts A
The bottom of Part B
The front of Part C
The front edge of Part D
All four edges of Parts E

Sand all components completely before you assemble the desk. This makes sanding much easier because you will not have to sand into corners as you would if you sanded after assembly.

Assemble Part D onto the top of Part C. Part D must be in the center of Part C and flush with the front of Part C. Be certain that Part D is square with Part C. Then assemble Parts A (the two side panels) onto the ends of Part B and Part C. Be certain that the front edge of Part C is recessed 1" back from the front edge of Parts A. Part C should be fastened exactly 3 ¾" down from the top edge of Parts A. The back edge of Part D should be fastened to the inside surface of Part B, flush with the top edge of Part B, and in the exact center. Part B should be installed flush with the top edge of Parts A and recessed ¼" from the back edge of Parts A. Once you have completed this, the desk assembly is finished except for the drawers and the drawer fronts.

Assemble the drawers by fastening the sides to the back and front pieces. Then fasten the bottom to square it up completely. Sides may be fastened with #4 finish nails, preferably galvanized. Bottom may be fastened with 1¼" nails with heads. The drawers are basically simple butt joint boxes. The bottoms are simply nailed on and are securely supported by the bottom mount drawer slides.

Finish the desk before final assembly of the drawer and fronts. This makes the finishing job easier and keeps the finish material off the drawer slides. I recommend either of two methods for finishing this desk quickly and easily and still getting a really good finish. To finish the project as quickly as possible, use Deft Clear Wood Finish or Deft Wood Armor. Both dry to the touch in less than thirty minutes and may be recoated after two hours. This means you can apply three coats in the same day. It does take three coats of these products to ensure a good strong finish. The main shortcoming of Deft Clear Wood Finish is its excessively strong odor and vapors. It is essential to use it in a well-ventilated area or wear a respirator. Read and follow the directions carefully.

Deft Wood Armor cleans up with water. It works very well in spite of its milky look in the can. It will provide a very attractive and strong finish when properly applied. Wood Armor does not have the strong odor or vapors of Deft Clear Wood Finish. However, it does not work well in temperatures below 65 degrees, whereas Deft Clear Wood Finish has performed well for me in temperatures as low as 40 degrees. If your shop is neither cooled nor heated, Deft Clear Wood Finish is a great year round product, but remember that many finishing products are highly flammable. Take care when heating your shop with any kind of flame.

When using Deft products you need to sand between coats. This is especially true on plywood because the grain is easily raised. Sand your project parts using 220-grit sandpaper on an orbital sander. When loading your orbital sander take care that the sand paper has no sharp edges. Check this with your hands, and bend all the edges up slightly. A sharp paper edge will leave a repetitive orbital pattern on the wood. This will look very unattractive under the finish.

Your parts should have been sanded before assembly and no further sanding is necessary before applying the first coat. After applying the first coat of Deft Clear Wood Finish or Wood Armor, sand the entire project by hand using 400-grit sandpaper. Apply the second coat after making certain you have wiped the surface clean of all dust. I suggest using a tack cloth. After the second coat has dried for two hours, sand all surfaces lightly by hand using 400-grit sandpaper. Always sand in the direction of the grain. Feel all the surfaces as you sand, making certain they are silky smooth. Once again, dust off the entire project and wipe it with a fresh tack rag. This will leave it ready for the final coat. Apply the final coat carefully, making certain to comb it out carefully to avoid runs. Keep checking for runs as you work and comb them out promptly. If you walk away for a few minutes and then find a run, don't comb it out. This finish will be too dry at this point and you will have terrible brush marks. The best thing to do is to allow it to dry almost completely and then carefully remove the run with a blade. Then sand the entire surface and apply another coat. Do not apply additional finish in an attempt to get rid of a run. This will not work well with Deft.

When the finish is completely dry, install the drawer slides. The drawer sections of the slide set are installed by screwing them to the bottom of the drawer flush to the front edge with the roller to the rear. The desk section of the slide should be installed directly on top of Part C and recessed 1\16" back from the front edge of Part C. These sections should be installed on the inside of both Parts A and on both sides of Part D. It is essential not to install these sections upside down. Make sure the manufacturers name is right side up when installing them. If you don't know how to install these drawer slides, get details from your supplier. Blum has a highly instructive catalog that provides valuable details on all their products.

After the slides are installed, put the drawers into the desk to make certain they work well and ride solidly on the rollers. If one side or the other is springy, you will need to correct this before the drawer front is installed. Leave one side screw in place on the cabinet section of the slide and remove the other two. Adjust the slide section up or down to compensate for the problem. To avoid this problem completely, take care to install the cabinet section of the slide square with the front edge of the desk.

Install the drawer front on the drawer unit. Drill two 3/16" holes in each side of the front section of the drawer unit. Position them 1" in from the sides; center them from the top and bottom. Drive two small nails next to each of the holes. Drive these nails from the inside of the drawer unit so the protrude slightly (about 1/16") on the outside. Close the drawer. Lightly mark the exact center point of the desk where the drawers will meet. Align the left drawer front to the front section of the drawer unit. There should be a 1/8" space from the top edge of Part A This can be checked by placing a level across from one Part A to the other. This will take the place of the desktop. You should also have a 1/8" space to the left side of the drawer front from Part A and a 1/16" space from the centerline. These spaces are approximate, but they should not be too tight as they may rub and cause the finish to wear.

Once the drawer front is properly aligned, press firmly against the drawer unit so that the protruding nails pierce the drawer front and keep it from sliding around while you are fastening it. Maintain pressure on the drawer front while you reach into the drawer and drive two 1" screws into the holes. For additional strength you may use 1 ¼" screws with washers to avoid piercing the face of the drawer front. Follow the same procedure for the right hand drawer fronts. This will leave a 1/8" space between the drawers. Once both fronts are installed, operate the drawers to be sure that the clearances are maintained.

The final piece needed to complete your study desk is the top or Part L. There are various ways to complete and finish this desktop. I like plastic laminate over plywood because it provides such a smooth, easy to clean surface. You can also leave the desktop natural using iron-on veneer edging or, better yet, solid wood edging. A solid edging could be left square or could be rounded. You can also purchase a ¾" wood molding to apply to the edge. Or even use a combination of laminate and solid wood edges.

I opted for plastic laminate and instructions for installing this laminate product are included in this book. To laminate the top, first laminate the edges on all four sides. These edges must be trimmed and sanded before applying the top piece.

After the edge laminate is complete, fasten the top to the desk. The simplest way to do this is with screws. I use 2" drywall screws. Place the top on the desk, making sure it is centered all around. There should be a ¼" overlap on all four sides. Measure this overlap from the front, back, and sides of Parts A. Once the top is in place, drill six 3/16" holes so that there are two holes over each Part A and Part D. The holes should be approximately 1½" from the front and back edges of these parts. Reach under the top and lightly mark all four corners with a pencil. Remove the top and apply a thin line of glue along the top edge of Part B, Part D and both Parts A Replace the top making certain to align the pencil marks in each corner. Drive the six screws until they are slightly countersunk into the surface. It is important that the heads of these screws be below the surface of the wood to avoid interfering with the laminate. Immediately after driving the screws, check for any glue ooze and clean it with a damp cloth. Now laminate the top. This will cover all the screws and complete your project.

Drawings on next page.

Contact me at bill@woodworkbusiness.com with questions. Thanks.

Study Desk Drawings

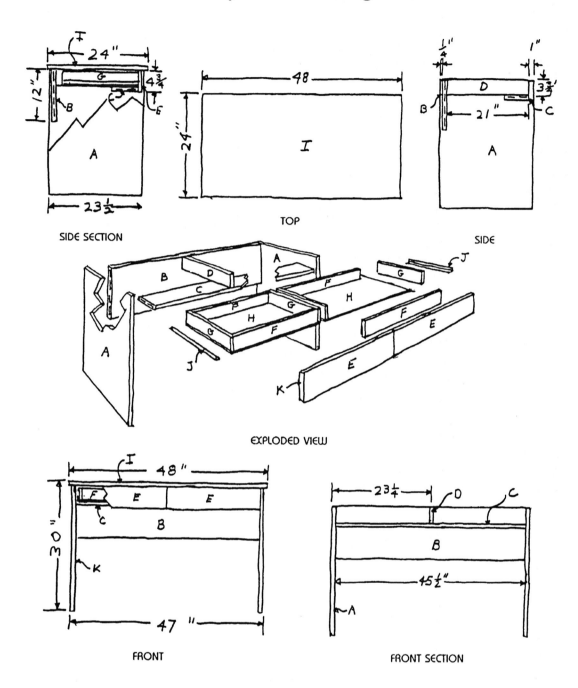

SIDE SECTION

TOP

SIDE

EXPLODED VIEW

FRONT

FRONT SECTION

Bonus 1
Twenty-Seven

Find photos and additional information on podiums at:
http://www.woodworkingbusinessbook.com/projects/podium.html

The Podium Business Project

Podium/Lectern Instructions

The instructions for these podiums were written during the actual construction of twelve podiums. Since it was my intent to duplicate this design for other customers, the construction methods were developed for ease of repeatability.

Even though this is a custom made product, consistency of design is essential. The only differences among units should be the material and color selected by the customer. In every other respect these units must be identical as is normally the case with manufactured items. Care must be taken in the cutting and milling process to ensure this consistency.

If you expect to be involved in building podiums for various customers, a commitment to this high level of product consistency is essential. The second requirement is for all work to be of high quality, reflected by clean, square cuts and smooth, accurate millwork. Payment for your work is dependent on meeting these standards, as is repeat business.

Even though a lot of time was spent developing this construction process, it is subject to improvement. While building these units, don't hesitate to develop ideas and methods of your own that may make the job easier or better. It is critical to remain open to new ideas. Don't be locked into this design if a better idea surfaces.

I suggest that you read this section carefully and completely before starting the project. This will give you the complete picture and help you follow the process from beginning to end.

Podium Cutting Notes

Cutting plywood requires some specific steps to assure clean edges without tear out. It is also essential to have the best face of the plywood exposed. Remember the following:

The Plywood should be a good plain sliced grade instead of rotary cut. This will allow for a much better finish and improve the appearance of the units. Usually an AB or A2 grade will give the best results.

The Table saw blade should have 60 to 80 carbide-tipped teeth and be of high quality.

The table saw should have a freshly-cut throat plate that fits snugly around the blade to preclude bottom tear out. This step is critical unless you own a table saw with a scoring blade. Run a test piece cutting against the grain to make certain there is no tear out.

Cut all the panels to rectangles first. Use the measurements in the cutting list since the drawings are not to scale. Once the panels are cut, stack them separately, preferably on dollies for easy movement.

Separate the side panels and then place them in pairs with the best face out. With most plain sliced plywood, both faces should be good so take a moment to pick the best.

Use an angle-cutting guide on your table saw to cut the top angles. Or use a sliding table if your table saw has one. Make certain to maintain the side panels in pairs after you cut them so you will be certain to maintain the best surfaces out.

Always move slowly through the cuts to give the blade time to cut without tearing out.

The materials list below includes everything except the finishing products, sandpaper and sanding belts.

Podium List of Materials

ID	Qty	Description	Size or Info	Material
A	1	Front Panel	23"X42"	Hdwd Plywood
B	2	Side Panels	23"X42"	Hdwd Plywood
C	1	Bottom Panel	23"X23"	Hdwd Plywood
D	1	Tabletop Panel	23"X23"	Hdwd Plywood
E	1	Cover Bot. Panel	22 ¼"X23"	Hdwd Plywood
F	1	Cover Top Panel	22 13/16X23"	Hdwd Plywood
G	1	Cover Box Door	9"X21 ¼"	Hdwd Plywood
H	1	Top Panel	5"X23"	Hdwd Plywood
I	2	Cover Side Panels	8 ½"X22 1/8"	Hdwd Plywood
J	1	Cover Rear Panel	8 ½"X23"	Hdwd Plywood
K	2	Toe Space 1	3 ½"X20"	Hdwd Plywood
L	2	Toe Space 2	3 ½"X16 ¾"	Hdwd Plywood
M	16lf	Edging	¾"X ¾"	Hdwd Plywood
N	32f	Edging	1 ¼"X1 ¼"	Hdwd Plywood
O	1	Front Edging	¾"X1 ¼"	Hdwd Plywood
P	2 lf	Piano Hinge	1 ½"	Brass
Q	1	Magnetic Catch	Standard	Metal
R	2	Casters	3 ¼"	Metal/Plastic
S	101	Biscuit/Plates	#20	Comp. Beech
T	1	Tabletop Laminate	Standard	Plastic Laminate
U	18	Drywall Screws	1 ¼"	Metal
V	1	Podium Lamp	Standard	Metal

Preparing for glue up - Start by gluing small ¼" plywood pads to clamp surfaces with epoxy glue. This will save time and make the clamping process easier. It will virtually eliminate clamp marks that would later require sanding. This is just one time saving step. As you prepare for assembly, make certain that you keep things as simple as possible.

Apply laminate to the "D" panels and trim with a flush trimmer bit on your trimmer or router. Set your table saw blade bevel to 9 degrees and the rip fence so you can cut the angle along the back edge of the "D" panel. The laminate side should be the long point of the angle. Do not remove more than 1/16" of material at the long point.

The next step is to apply the ¾ " X ¾ " solid edging to all the center panels of the podium. It is important to apply this edging before assembling the podiums when it will be much more difficult. Use biscuit joinery to apply the edging. Set the fence of the biscuit joiner so the cut will be centered in a ¾ " plywood edge.

Make a marking jig for the biscuit locations. This jig should be 23" long, preferably a ¾ " X ¾ " piece. Mark the locations of the biscuits as follows:

     1 ¾ ", 6 5/8 ", 11 ½ ", 16 3/8 ", 21 ¼ "

Use a square to carry the marks to all four sides of the marking jig. Notice that the dimensions are the same from either end of the jig. This will simplify the process, making it difficult to cut the slots backwards.

Panels "H" and "C" require ¾ " X ¾ " solid wood edging on the front and back edges. This edging should be milled to within 1/32" thicker than the plywood. Here again, you can save a lot of time during the final sanding if you check this closely. Even though the wood edging is referred to as ¾ " X ¾ ", remember that plywood is often manufactured to metric dimensions. Chances are the plywood you use will be a little less than ¾ " thick. Mill the edging to match the plywood plus 1/32".

With the "H" and "C" panels face up on your worktable, use the jig to mark the biscuit locations on the front and back edges. Now clamp each piece, one at a time, to your worktable and cut the biscuit slots.

Precision is essential for this step if the edging is to fit flush with the plywood. Make certain the fence is properly adjusted and secure. Always test your cut on a scrap piece. The biscuit joiner should be set up for # 20 biscuits. Make certain to keep the biscuit joiner fence flat on the panel surface. This is essential for accuracy.

Once all the biscuit slots are cut on the "H" and "C" panels, you can cut the slots on the edging. Small pieces like this edging are difficult to slot accurately. By making a simple bench jig you can improve the accuracy significantly. The jig is made by attaching a ½ " X 3" wide piece of plywood to a piece of 3/4" plywood that is 4 3/8" wide. Both pieces should be at least 30" long. Nail the ½ " piece to the ¾ " piece, flush on one edge. This will leave a ½ " X 1 3/8 " space on one edge to accommodate the edging. Clamp the jig to your worktable and place two pieces of the edging on the jig. This will allow the front edge of the outside piece to extend 1/8 " beyond the edge of the jig. The ½ " piece will serve as a stop but is lower than the top of the edging so it will not interfere with the biscuit joiner fence. By using two pieces together, a 1 ½ " flat surface is created making it easier to keep the biscuit joiner fence flat on the surface.

Now use the marking jig to mark all the 23" edge pieces and then cut the biscuit slots using the table jig. If you have milled the edging correctly and accurately measured your marking jig, it won't matter which edge of the edging you cut the slots on. They will fit properly as long as you place the marks on both the edging and the plywood on the same side.

Next use #20 biscuits to glue the edging onto the panels. Use glue only in the biscuit slots and apply sparingly. If possible, use one of those glue tips designed especially to put glue into biscuit slots. Never apply glue to the edge of the panel or the edging. This will ooze out and make a mess that will be extremely difficult to clean. The biscuits alone will provide an extremely strong bond. Clamp the pieces together and allow the glue to dry for at least 2 hours.

After the glue is dry, unclamp the pieces. Before proceeding, use a ¼ " carbide tipped, round over router bit to round over the top and bottom of the front edge and one side of the back edge of the "H" and "C" panels. The front edge will be whichever one you select. It is essential to rout these round overs now because it will not be possible after the podium is assembled.

Now the biscuit slots must be cut in the top and bottom edge on the "A" panels. This is done in the same manner as the "H" and "C" panels.

The next step is to cut the slots on the inside of the edging that you attached at the back of the "H" and "C" panels. To do this accurately, place a 3/4" piece of plywood with a good straight edge on your worktable. This piece should be a least 24" X 24". The size of this piece is not critical since it only serves as a work surface. Place it on the worktable so the edge overhangs. Now place the first "H" or "C" panel on this plywood, face down and back edge, with the hardwood edging, flush with the plywood edge. Clamp both pieces together to the table. Make certain the clamp is far enough back to clear the biscuit joiner. Mark the back edge of the panels using the marking jig. Place the mark where it will be visible when the biscuit joiner is placed for the cut. Use the biscuit joiner upright, with the fence against the double edge formed by the panel and the work surface piece of plywood on your worktable. This 1 ½ " flat surface will help you keep the biscuit joiner flat for accurate cuts. Cut each slot on the back edging of all the "H" and "C" panels.

The next step is to cut the biscuit slots on the side edges of the "A", "C", "D" and "H" panels. These are the biscuit slots that will be used to assemble the podium sides to the center sections. Do these now while the panels can be laid flat on your bench.

So that every inside panel will fit any of the side panels, use a biscuit slot location template to maintain a consistent pattern. Even though each podium will be assembled individually, using a template will make things easier. Just lay panels "A" and "H" on your bench with the best face down and mark the biscuit slots on each side. The "H" panel will only take two biscuits because it is so narrow. The "C" panel should be placed on the bench with the good surface up because it is the bottom piece and the good surface should be inside instead of on the bottom of the podium. Set the biscuit joiner fence so the blade cuts at the center mark of the plywood thickness. This will place the cut at 5/16" from each surface. Once all the biscuit locations are marked, place each panel on a raised surface with the marks visible. Place the biscuit joiner fence flat on the panel surface, line up the biscuit joiner with the slot location marks and cut all the biscuit slots.

Now you can proceed to glue up the center sections of the podiums. Gluing up the center sections makes the final assembly of the podiums much easier because it allows you to control three panels as one piece during the final assembly.

NOTE: These instructions apply to both the Standup and the Tabletop podiums.

The center sections to be assembled consist only of the "H", "A", and "C" panels. The "H" panel forms the top of the podium and the "C" panel is the bottom. Place the "A" panel on your workbench with the bottom and top sticking out beyond the bench. Put glue in each of the biscuit slots and then insert a #20 biscuit in each slot. Next put glue in each slot of the back edge of panel "H" and slide the slots over the biscuits on one end of panel "A". Follow the same procedure with panel "C" and put it on the other end of panel "A". Flip this unit over carefully and then apply the clamps tightly making certain that the edges are flush with each other. After the glue is dry, remove the clamps and make certain that all the round overs have been done.

Remember, the "H" panel must have a round over on the corner where it meets panel "A" and a double round over on the other edges. Panel "C" should have the same round over pattern. If you have not completed this, you have one more chance. You will not be able to round the corners after the podium is assembled. The next step is to assemble the side panels.

As with most woodworking projects, there is more than one way to do this. You can use the method described here since it has worked for me. During the process you may well come up with a better or simpler method to accomplish the same thing. Obviously you should take advantage of those methods.

The steps are as follows:

Create a tabletop surface that is about 26" X 44" to work on. This can be a piece of plywood over a couple of sawhorses or any other table arrangement of a comfortable height.

Place a piece of ½" plywood cut to a size smaller than the side panels you will be working with. You will need one size of the upright podiums and another for the tabletops.

Keep your side panels as pairs with the best side out. The initial process of pairing must be done before the angles are cut on the side panels to make certain the best surfaces will show after the podiums are assembled.

Place a panel flat on the ½" plywood so it overhangs on all sides making certain that the good surface is down. Now you are ready to cut the biscuit slots for the 1 ¼" edging. There is no need to create a slot cutting pattern for this task. Simply mark the slot locations freehand. Start by placing a mark approximately 1 ¾" - 2" from every corner. Then place a series of marks approximately 4" - 5" apart all the way around the edge of the panel. These marks should be made on the inside face of the panels. Do this to every one of the side panels. Cut all the biscuit slots by first clamping the panel to the table. Change the clamp position as necessary. Cut the slots using the fence on the biscuit joiner and set to cut a slot centered in the ¾" thickness. The fence should be set at about 5/16" from the blade. Once all the slots are cut in the side panels, you are ready to start applying the 1 ¼" edging.

Before beginning the application of the 1 ¼" edging, all the pieces should be belt sanded using 100 or 120 grit belts. Do this carefully to remove all the planer marks and make certain that the pieces remain square by avoiding excessive sanding. Then make a simple bench setup and use your router with a 1/4" round over bit to round one corner of every piece. It is best to use a handheld router for this task because slight bows in the edging will make it difficult to maintain an even round over on a bench mounted router. This step is essential because this rounded edge will serve as the edge that goes against the outside of the panel and it will not be possible to round it after the edging is applied to the panel.

NOTE: When cutting the 1 ¼" edging to fit the side panels, make adjustments to the angles of your miter saw while cutting the pieces for the first side panel. Miter saw gauges are not always accurate and you should strive to make these angle cuts as tight as possible. Tight joints look better and save you time and avoid unsightly wood filler. The following steps will make the job easier.

Place the first side panel on the ½" plywood with the good face down. Place the first piece of edging, preferably the longest piece, down with the rounded over corner down and toward the edge of panel. This is critical because you will not be able to cut this round over after assembly.

Cut all the angles as described in the drawings and make certain the pieces fit around the panel. Check every joint to make certain it is a tight fit.

After all the edging has been cut and placed around the side panels, transfer the biscuit slot location marks to the edging.

Remove the edging to your bench. Use the jig that you previously made to cut the slots on the ¾ " X ¾ " edging to support this edging while you cut the biscuit slots. The biscuit joiner should still be at the same setting. Cut all the slots on the edging, making certain that the biscuit joiner fence is flat with the top of the edging.

Insert the biscuits into the slots in the panel after applying glue. Remember to apply the glue sparingly and into the slot making certain glue is applied to both surfaces. It is essential not to apply too much glue because it will ooze out and make a mess that will be difficult to clean. I suggest using one of those glue dispenser tips made especially for use with biscuit joinery. Once the biscuits are inserted into the panels, apply glue to the individual slots in the edging pieces and quickly put them in place. If necessary tap them with a rubber mallet and make certain all the joints fit tightly. This step should be done rapidly to be certain that you are within the open time of the glue.

Clamp in all directions with as many clamps as necessary to ensure a tight joint between the panels and the edging. Make one final check of all the joints and then put the panel aside for at least two hours to dry.

Attaching the side panels - Once the side panels are dry, you can remove the clamps and you are ready to start the final assembly of the podiums. Before starting, use a random orbit sander with 100 or 120 grit sandpaper to remove pencil marks. Also you should make certain that the edging pieces are even with the panel surfaces. Use the sander to smooth out any problems. Remember that you can sand quite a bit on the solid wood edging but very little on the plywood. Excessive sanding of the plywood can cause you to go through the veneer and into the core surfaces that will not finish well.

All the surfaces should be almost completely even if you took the time to handle the biscuit joinery carefully. Once all the surfaces are sanded you have to complete the rounding over on all the side panels. Using the router with the same ¼" round over bit, round over the bottom corner and the last top corner. Then, using a finishing sander, soften the corners on the top and top front of the 1 ¼" edging.

Finally, sand the round over with a finishing sander. It is much easier to finish all of this before beginning the actual assembly. Once this is completed, you are ready to assemble the sides to the center section. During this final assembly process it is easy to have messy glue run out if care is not taken. This is the procedure that has worked well for me and if you follow it carefully, none of the glue will run out and make a difficult to clean mess:

Place one of the complete side panels from a pair on the worktable with the inside surface up.

Place the center section on top of this side panel in its proper orientation. The inside of the center section should follow the joint between the side panel and the edging. Once this is properly located, transfer the biscuit slot marks to the side panel. The biscuit slot marks will be on the inside of the center section and will easily transfer to the correct location for cutting the biscuit slots on the side panels.

Adjust the setting on your biscuit joiner at this time. To get the correct setting, measure the distance that the 1 ¼" edging sticks up past the plywood panel on the outside of the side panels. In most cases this will be ½" or slightly more. Increase the distance between the blade of the biscuit joiner and the biscuit joiner fence by exactly this amount. For example, if your biscuit joiner blade was set at 5/16" from the fence, it will now be set to 13/16" above the fence. This will compensate for the additional ½" and allow the center section to be located correctly.

NOTE: Do not take this dimension for granted. Every time you make a change to the biscuit joiner, the router, or any power tool, you must test. This is time consuming but not as bad as making a mistake that will require you to disassemble and remake a project. Make certain you will get the result you want. Once you have tested that the cut is the correct distance, cut the slots in the side panels.

Cutting the slots in the side panels can be tricky. I suggest that you clamp the side panel in place while cutting the slots. Clamp the side with two edges overhanging the bench. This is important because the overhang will allow you to use the biscuit joiner fence. Cut the slots on those two overhanging edges and then loosen the clamps and move the side panel so the other two edges are hanging over the bench. Now complete these last biscuit slots.

For the next step it is helpful to have a second biscuit joiner. This step takes two forms. The first is based on having a second biscuit joiner. This biscuit joiner is setup without a fence so that it can be used to cut biscuit slots on a flat surface. At this point you must cut the slots for the laminated podium tabletop. This tabletop will not be installed during this assembly process, but the slots must be cut now because they will be much more difficult to cut after the assembly. For this step you will need to make another slot cutting pattern. Use a board about 30 inches long and two or three inches wide. Make a mark close to one end and mark it either End or Start. Now measure 4 inches and make another mark and continue until you have a total of 7 marks. Call the 7th mark Start or End, the opposite of your first mark. Now use a square to transfer these marks across the face and edge of the board and then also mark them across the other surface. On the other side also transfer the Start and End marks. Now your pattern is ready.

NOTE: If you only have one biscuit joiner, you should first complete step 4 above on all the side panels. Do not change the fence setting until all the side panels have been completed. Then you can remove the fence from your biscuit joiner and prepare to make these cuts.

With the side panel on your bench, measure from the front top edge of the panel down 2 3/16 inches. At the top back of the side panel, measure down 6 1/8 inches. These measurements must be taken from the panel edge, not from the edge of the 1 ¼" edging. Now place the pattern on the side panel on the two lines you have marked with the pattern board on the bottom side of the marks. This means toward the bottom of the podium. Line the pattern up with the two lines and then line up either the Start or End line with the front edge of the panel. Once again remember to line up with the plywood edge and not with the 1 ¼" edge. Now clamp the pattern board in place and to the bench.

Hold the biscuit joiner upright and place the face of the biscuit joiner against the side panel surface and the bottom of the biscuit joiner against the pattern board. Now line up the biscuit joiner center with the first 4" mark and cut the slot. Repeat the process for all five holes.

NOTE: Even though there are 7 marks, two of them are Start and End marks for alignment with the side panel and not for cutting slots. Once you have made these slot cuts in the side panels they are ready for assembly. I suggest you use a finish sander and give the surface a quick pass to take the sharpness and splinters off the slot cuts.

Repeat these same steps with the other side from the same pair. Keep the pairs together to make certain the biscuits will line up.

Clean all the parts and blow out all the dust from the biscuit slots.

Next, put one of the side panels back on the bench and then put the appropriate center section on top of the side panel properly oriented. The next few steps must be done quickly to take advantage of the glue's open time. Start by gluing biscuits into the top edge of the center section. This should be easy to do because the glue goes into the slot by gravity. Once all the biscuits are inserted, remove the center section and glue biscuits into the slots in the side panel that remained on the bench.

For the next step, remove the side panel with the biscuits and put the side panel without the biscuits on the bench with the inside face up. Now put glue into all of the biscuit slots on the side panel without the biscuits. Now carefully place the center section on top of the side panel with the biscuits down and line the biscuits up with the slots in the side panel. Once they line up, use a rubber mallet or dead blow hammer to drive the biscuits evenly into the slots.

Quickly begin putting glue into the slots at the top edge of the center section. Once again you will have gravity on your side so the glue should run into the slots easily. Now place the side with the biscuits on top of the center section and line up the biscuits with the slots. Use the mallet to tap this side panel into place on the center section. Once the biscuits have been inserted, you can raise the podium so it is sitting on its bottom and then clamp the sides to the center section. Use as many clamps as you need to ensure a tight joint between the sides and the center section. You will need to use eight to ten clamps for this procedure.

Once the clamping is completed, check every joint carefully because once the glue dries you will not be able to do anything about an open joint.

CAUTION: Ease of assembly is directly related to the care taken in cutting the biscuit slots. Precision is critical. Biscuit joiners are seldom the cause of a lack of precision. The problem is most often carelessness. It is essential to maintain correct alignment for every cut. Take your time and make certain that the fence is totally flat on the work. Carelessly rushing through this process will ensure a difficult assembly and most likely serious misalignment problems that may be irreparable.

Once the podiums are assembled to this stage, there are still three parts that must be completed. They are listed below.

The Cover Box that goes in the center of the podium with a door facing the back. The box is used to store the podium cover. This box is optional and can be replaced with a single shelf as an alternative design.

The toe space is the small box that raises the podium to its full height and provides the space for the casters.

The laminated tabletop has an edging that is raised to serve as a pencil stop. This panel also has a 1" hole drilled close to the back edge of the left corner for the cord from the podium lamp.

The first step is to finish the tabletop. Start by covering the panel with the laminate. Cut a piece of laminate about one inch larger all around than the panel. Apply contact adhesive with a brush to both the top surface of the panel and the back surface of the laminate. Allow the glue to dry for five to ten minutes. The glue should be dry enough that it does not stick to your hands when you touch it. Don't let it dry too long or it won't bond. Next, line the laminate up with the panel making certain that it overlaps all four sides. If you lack experience with laminate, it is best to use a slip-sheet for the alignment process. Once the laminate has been placed, roll the surface with a laminate roller. The last step is to use a trimmer or router with a laminate trimming bit to trim off the excess laminate.

Set your table saw blade to 9 degrees and cut the back angle of the tabletop. The laminate should be the long point of the angle and it should be cut with the laminate surface up to avoid tear out by the blade. You may have to create a fence on the left side of the blade to cut this angle on your table saw. Once the angle is cut you can apply the front edge piece. Use the biscuit joiner and mark the biscuit locations on the bottom side of the tabletop and the edge piece. The piece is then installed flush with the bottom edge of the tabletop and sticks up ½" to form a pencil stop. Clamp this as you did the other panels and allow the glue to dry. I suggest you apply the finish to this edging before assembling it to the podium because it is much easier. Actually, the best bet is to apply the finish to these pieces before applying them to the laminated tabletop. This will preclude the need for taping.

The final step is to use the biscuit joiner to cut a continuous slot along both side edges of the tabletop. This slot should start immediately behind the edging and run all the way back through the end of the tabletop. Clamp the tabletops to your bench and cut the slots with the biscuit joiner. Instead of just making a cut and then pulling out the biscuit joiner, make six or eight cuts and then start at the beginning and leave the blade in the cut by maintaining pressure on the biscuit joiner and sliding it slowly towards the back edge of the tabletop. It is essential to maintain the pressure on the biscuit joiner throughout the cut. The biscuit joiner is spring-loaded and will give you continuous resistance. By maintaining the pressure you will have the entire slot the correct depth. Do this to both sides of the tabletop. The tabletop is now ready to install later.

Next assemble the Cover Box that is comprised of panels "J", two panels "I", panel "E" and panel "F". This box is not a structural element in the podium so it can be assembled with nails or screws and without biscuits. Panel "F" is visible and therefore must be cut from the same material as the rest of the podium. The same goes for panel "G" which is the door panel. The other panels can be cut from some other material since they will not be visible except when the Cover Box door is open. For example, I have made these podiums out of oak and mahogany and the boxes were always made from maple or birch plywood that is less costly in my area. I suggest sticking with hardwood plywood because construction plywood such as pine is somewhat unstable for this purpose.

Build the box by nailing or screwing Panel "J" to the back edges of panels "I". Next, nail or screw panel "F" on top of the U shaped by panels "J" and "I". Notice that panel F has an unfinished edge. This is because it will be covered by the piano hinge for the Cover Box door. Panel "E" should have a ¾" X ¾" edge in front. It is nailed to the bottom of the U shaped by panels "J" and "I". This forms the Cover Box. Panel "E" and "F" should be nailed flush with the back edge of the U shape. Panel "E" sticks out 3/16" beyond panel "F". This thickness accommodates the piano hinge making the door fit properly.

The door must be edged on all four sides. Follow the same procedure as before for applying the edging. Apply the two 21 ¼" pieces first. Once these can be unclamped, apply the two short pieces. Once the door is assembled, sand all the surfaces smooth and remove all the biscuit joiner location marks. Use the round over bit to round over the top and bottom front edge of the door. Do not round the short ends.

Cut the piano hinge to size and install on the door with the knuckle sticking up slightly (1/8") beyond the edge. Drill for the screws and then apply the hinge. Center the door on the box again placing the hinge slightly above the top edge of the box. Screw the hinge to the box keeping it as aligned as possible. The slight rise will allow the door to swing open a little more than normal for better access to the cover. The last step is to drill two 1" holes at the left rear of the cover box. These holes should be 2" from the back and 2" from the side to match the hole in the tabletop. All of these holes will accommodate the electrical cord from the lamp. The Cover Box is now ready to install.

The procedure for installation is simple but should not take place until after all the finishing work is done. If you install the Cover Box before finishing the podium, it will just be in the way. So, take note of the following procedure but do not install until later. Make two pieces of plywood that are 16 inches high and about 20 inches long. Place these in the podium with one of the long edges on the bottom of the podium. The Cover box is then rested on these 16 inch pieces. Over the door and reach inside of the box and screw it in place. Use 1 ¼" drywall screws because they are self-tapping and drilling is unnecessary. Place six screws on each side and four screws to the back.

The last item to be built before the finish is the toe space. The toe space is much wider than it is deep in order to accommodate the casters. The casters are installed to clear the floor by ¼" when the podium is upright. By tilting the podium to the rear, the casters will touch the floor and facilitate rolling the podiums to various locations.

To make the toe space cut four 3 ½" long pieces of the 1 ¼" edging for each standup podium. On one corner make the mark for the biscuit slot at 1 3/4 inches. Using the jig you previous made, cut the biscuit slots. Then use the ¼" round over bit on your router to round over three corners of the edging pieces. The only corner not to be rounded is the one with the biscuit slot marks. On panels "K" (2 pieces) and "L" (2 pieces) mark the biscuit slot locations at 1 3/4 inches on the inside surface of the panels. Once all the biscuit slots are cut you are ready to assemble the toe spaces. Assemble two of the edging pieces onto each of the "K" panels gluing in the biscuits as before. Clamp these together and allow them to dry.

Change the setting on the router to the same setting you used for cutting the biscuits on the side panels. This is ½" more space between the fence and the blade than before. The ideal thing is to cut all the biscuit slots necessary, including the toe space, with the first biscuit joiner setting. Then once the setting is changed you can leave it that way for all the slots using this spacing. Otherwise you will have to be changing the router setting several times. Use the new setting to cut the biscuit slots in the edging pieces that are glued to the "K" panels. Place the biscuit joiner fence on the outside edge of the edging and the face of the biscuit joiner against the inside edge of the panel. It is essential to clamp the piece down for this operation. Once you have cut the two biscuit slots on each of the panels units, use glue to assemble and clamp them together. Cut two pieces of ¾" plywood from any material and make two support nailers the same size as panel "L". This is then nailed in place to serve as a nailer to attach the toe space to the bottom of the podium. These support pieces will also serve to square up the toe space. The exact location of the toe space on the podium should be determined by the size of the caster. You should leave enough space behind the toe space to accommodate the casters bolted to the bottom of the podium. Measure the caster mounting plate and add about ½ inch. The toe space is then attached to the bottom of the podium using 1 ¼" drywall screws.

The podium is now complete except for the installation of the Cover Box, tabletop, casters and the podium light. All of these will be installed after the finishing process is completed.

Staining the podiums - The first step to finishing the podiums is the staining. The ideal situation would be to leave the wood natural and simply apply a clear finish coat. Unfortunately, staining will be required for most podiums. Most people have a concept of how certain wood should look and it is seldom the natural color.

Staining seems like a simple process but it can be very troublesome and a poor stain job will ruin the appearance of an otherwise good piece of furniture. There are many ways to apply stain. My favorite is to spray it. This gives very even results and the stain can be sprayed very sparingly making the wipe off much easier. Spraying gives much more control than brushing. Brushing can do a good job also but uses more material and it takes more time to wipe off the excess stain.

There are some stains that do not require wiping but they are rare. Usually wiping is the most critical element in the process. When you see a poor staining job it can be attributed to poor wipe off technique. The biggest mistake people make is trying to get the color darker by allowing the stain to dry longer. The only thing you will get from longer drying times is a more difficult wipe off. If a darker shade is needed, apply a second coat and wipe off as before.

The reason this causes so many problems is that drying times vary with weather conditions. With extreme heat and humidity, stain will dry fast and you should apply it in sections and then wipe off each section before proceeding to the next. In colder weather or in an air-conditioned space, you can often stain the entire podium and then wipe it all off. The stain should be wiped off thoroughly making certain that no streaks are left. The grain of the wood should be clearly visible through the stain. To do this successfully you need plenty of light and rags. Use two rags at a time, the first to remove the excess stain and the second, cleaner rag to remove any remaining streaks. The best procedure is to discard the first rag when saturated. Then start using the second rag as the first rag and get a new rag to replace the second rag. If in doubt, discard the rag and replace it with a clean one. The best rags for this purpose are old white tee shirts. Tee shirt rags are often available in large boxes for a very reasonable price.

If the stain does get too dark you can promptly lighten it by wiping the surface with mineral spirits. If it dries overnight before you realize that it is too dark, you can lighten it somewhat by using a rag wet with lacquer thinner or Acetone. When doing this, use protective gloves and glasses, keep the rag moving and use lots of rags or splotches will form and be difficult to remove.

Once the stain has been applied to all the surfaces and properly wiped, it should be allowed to dry overnight before applying the final finish. Once the stain is dry you are ready to proceed. Do not sand the stained surface. The stain may well raise the grain and it will appear to be too rough for the finish coat. Certainly it would be better if the surface was smoother but sanding the stained surface can also create splotching that is difficult to control. Best to apply the first coat of clear before sanding the surface.

There are many finishes available. I prefer to use lacquer for my podiums because it dries fast, but you can use polyurethane or varnish. If you are spraying, then lacquer is definitely the easiest to control. If you are not already experienced with spraying lacquer it is essential to practice on several scrap pieces before beginning the actual job. It is easy to make a mess with lacquer.

The first step is to apply the lacquer sanding sealer. Don't use the finish lacquer itself for the first coat. The sanding sealer has more pigment and it sands very easily and smoothly. With both the sanding sealer and the finish lacquer, weather conditions are important. If you are spraying in an air-conditioned area, everything should work well. If your shop is not air-conditioned, then you must deal with the heat, cold and humidity. All of these can cause you problems. Do not spray if the temperature is less than 50 degrees. If the temperature is high and conditions are humid, a retarder is essential. Without a retarder the lacquer product will dry too fast and there are two potential consequences. One is that the lacquer will dry before it hits the surface and be applied as a powder. This will leave a very rough surface that will be difficult to sand out. The second problem is blushing. This is when the surface you are spraying turns white. Retarder can be used to correct both of these problems. The lacquer manufacturers usually recommend no more than 5% retarder. My experience has been that as much as 15% may be needed to spray in very humid conditions.

Retarder alone is not the answer. You must also spray from much closer which means that the spray fan will be narrower. This can be adjusted to some extent. I set my spray gun to spray as much liquid as possible together with as little air as is necessary to spray the liquid. By using this combination, retarder, and spraying from about six inches from the surface, the lacquer will flow out smoothly.

I strongly recommend a high-volume, low-pressure (HVLP) sprayer for this kind of work. It is much simpler to learn to use and does a very good job with a degree of care.

One of the most common mistakes made while spraying is to move the spray gun in a slightly circular motion. This creates many problems. With this method the spray gun is closer to the work at the center of the circle than it is at the two ends. What usually happens under humid conditions is that the center section will be smooth and toward the ends the surface will be rough because the lacquer dried too rapidly before having a chance to flow out. The spray gun should be moved parallel to the work surface and no more than eight inches away. Most of the time, under these conditions, I would spray at six inches away. This should give an excellent finish. I suggest one coat of sanding sealer and at least two coats of lacquer and preferably four coats of lacquer.

After the sanding sealer is applied, sand all the surfaces using 320 or 400 grit sandpaper. The surface should feel smooth as glass before applying the lacquer. Once the sanding is complete, clean all the surfaces with a rag and then follow that cleaning with a good wiping using a tack cloth. This will remove all the dust that can cause rough surfaces. Then apply the first coat of lacquer.

At the risk of being repetitious, I think it is necessary to repeat the cautions about applying lacquer. There are many things that can go wrong. The lacquer can dry before hitting the work surface causing a very rough and difficult to sand surface. The lacquer can blush leaving a white haze over everything. The lacquer can run if you spray it on too heavily or simply hesitate in one spot as you spray. Practice is the one thing that can avoid these hassles. This doesn't mean a quick practice on a small spot before you start. That is enough for someone who is highly experience in spraying lacquer. If you lack that experience, practice on several large pieces. Watch the flow out and then wait for the surface to dry and see how it looks and feels. Lacquer properly applied will feel smooth as glass and have no orange peel effect. Follow the instructions previously described and then practice over and over until you get great results. Then you are ready to tackle a furniture spray job.

Even when things go well, you may wind up with a run. Perhaps someone interrupted you and broke your concentration for a moment. If you hesitated with the spray gun on one spot for just a moment, you will have a run. Having experienced this I know it is no fun. There is no simple way to correct the problem. It will not sand out well and if you cut it the surface will always have a blemish. The best thing to do is remove the lacquer from that particular section using Acetone. Use protective gloves and glasses. Soak a rag with acetone and wipe the surface evenly and the lacquer will come off promptly. Keep the rag wet and moving and it remove all the lacquer. When you finish this it may be necessary to apply a little stain with a rag before spraying the surface. This procedure will ensure a very smooth and even job.

While I believe that sprayed lacquer is the best product to finish commercial units such as these podiums, there are options. Personally I would not use a brush with any finish with the possible exception of Deft Clear Wood Finish. Brushed on varnish or polyurethane will almost always show some brush marks and that is almost always unacceptable in a product of this caliber. Deft can be brushed on and it will look like it was sprayed. However, you must adhere to the instructions to the letter. One deviation and brush marks will appear. The Deft product is self-leveling if handled correctly. It is the only brush-on product that I would recommend for projects of this kind.

If spraying is not an option, you can get an excellent job using Bartley's Gel Varnish. This product does have some disadvantages. It costs much more than lacquer and has a six-hour drying time. It is also much more labor intensive than lacquer. On the other hand, it has many advantages including that it is more forgiving of mistakes and does not raise the grain as do most other finishes. You can sand your project until it is as smooth as glass and the application of the Gel finish will leave it as smooth as before. You can apply several coats without sanding between them.

Another advantage is that Bartley's Gel Varnish comes with the stain color of your choice already in the finish. This precludes the first staining step.

My preference when using Bartley's Gel Varnish is to apply one or two coats with the color I have selected. The first coat should give it the color I want. If I want it to be darker, I apply another coat of the color gel. Once the color is correct I then apply Bartley's Clear Gel Varnish for all additional coats. I suggest a minimum of three coats of this product and prefer four or five.

Even though the gel varnish is thick, it can be applied with a brush to get into all the cracks and corners. After the gel is applied, allow it to dry for a very short time and then wipe off the excess until the surface is very smooth. Then allow it to dry before applying the next coat.

Once the finish is applied, you can install the cover box as previously described. The 16" height is not critical. You can adjust that up or down depending on customer preferences. You can even make the cover box larger or smaller in height depending on preferences or simply replace the cover box with a shelf. In that case you should install the shelf using the same instructions as the tabletop.

Installing the tabletop - Remember that you cut a long slot on both sides of the tabletop, the "D" panel. The matching slots for this panel are on the inside of the side "B" panels. Before starting the installation of the tabletop, drill a 1" hole close to the back edge of it. This hole should be about 2" from the back and side of the tabletop "D" panel. The next step is to install the biscuits in the slots on the inside of the "B" panels. Place a pad on a worktable and lay the podium on one side. Then put glue in the slots and insert the biscuits. Tap them in tightly, flip the podium over so the other side is on the bench and repeat this process. Allow the glue to dry for about ten minutes because you want to be certain that these biscuits do not move while installing the tabletop "D" panel.

Apply glue in the long slots on both sides of the tabletop. Do not run glue the entire length of the slot. Instead, start at the back edge and apply glue about two thirds of the way up the slot. Then align the tabletop with the first two biscuits on the two "B" side panels and begin sliding in the tabletop. You may need to pad the front of the podium and place it against the wall or some other immovable object. You can also put the pad on the floor and place the podium front down on the pad. This will allow you to apply pressure against the floor as you slide the tabletop "D" panel over the biscuits and all the way to the front "A" panel. The 9-degree cut on the back edge of the tabletop "D" panel will fit perfectly against the front "A" panel. Make certain that the joint is tightly closed against the "A" panel. Then use four clamps to tightly clamp the "B" sides to the "D" panel. Once the glue dries your podium is completed except for the toe space, casters and podium lamp.

Installing the toe space, casters and lamp - Place the podium with the front face down on a padded worktable. I can't emphasize enough how important it is to use pads once the finish has been applied to your podiums. You want to deliver the podiums in perfect condition and pads will help you do that. Next, place the toe space on the worktable at the bottom of the podium in the correct orientation. It will only fit one way and still accommodate the casters. Don't attach the toe space, just use it as a guide to install the casters.

The casters are installed by placing the caster base almost flush with the back edge of the podium and even with the outside edge of the toe space that is still unattached.

While holding the casters in place, use a pencil to mark the location of the holes. Do this for both casters and then drill the holes. I suggest that you use ¼" X 1 ¼" carriage bolts and drill ¼" holes for them. Place the bolts in the holes from inside the podium to the bottom. Use a flat piece of steel with a clamp to embed the carriage bolt properly into the wood. Place the caster over the bolts and then install the nuts and washers tightly to hold them in place. Once the nuts are very tight, coat them with a product such as LockTite to make certain they will never come loose.

After the casters are installed, move the toe space up against the base of the caster make certain that they clear the wheels and then fasten the toe space to the bottom of the podium with 1 ¼" drywall screws. Use at least 8 screws for a strong fit. Now you can stand the podium up on the floor.

The last step is to install the podium lamp directly under the "H" panel and run the electrical wire through the holes and into the bottom part of the podium. The lamp you purchase will have instructions for installation but they normally take only two small screws.

The podium is now ready for delivery to your customer. Remember to pad them carefully and tie them down tightly during delivery.

On the next page are drawings for the podiums that will help you to better understand the cutting and assembly instructions. The rear cover has some photos of the completed podiums. You can also find additional photos and information at: http://www.woodworkingbusinessbook.com/projects/podium.html .

SAFETY NOTE ON SPRAYING LACQUER: Lacquer is an excellent finish but it poses serious dangers for anyone using it. It is not for the inexperienced or for those with inadequate spraying facilities. In addition to the strong and dangerous fumes and vapors, for which a good respirator is essential, you must also consider the flammability of lacquer. Electrical equipment used in areas used for spraying must be designed to preclude sparks or a flash fire could result. **DO NOT USE LACQUER UNLESS YOU KNOW ALL THE RULES TO ENSURE SAFETY.**

Contact me at bill@woodworkbusiness.com with questions or comments.

A. William Benitez Woodwork Services

JOB DRAWINGS

Table Top Podium, Lectern

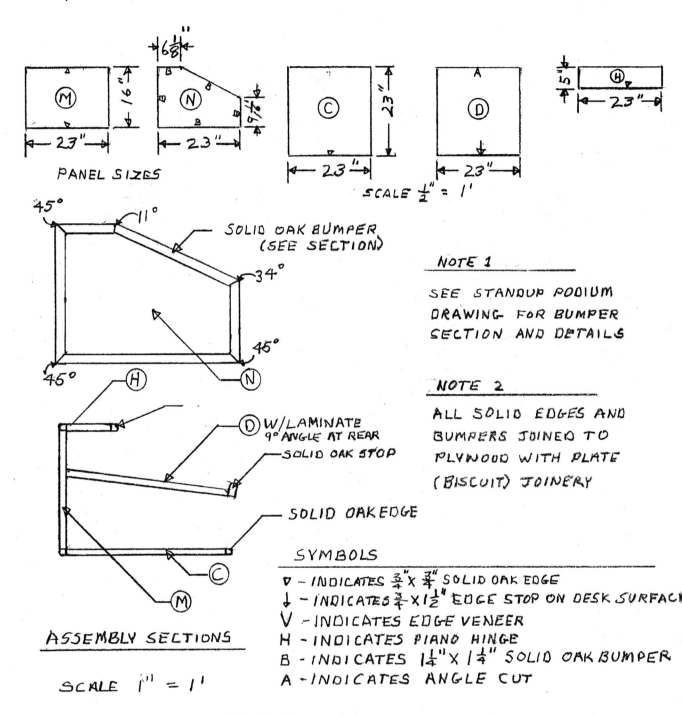

PANEL SIZES

SCALE ½" = 1'

NOTE 1

SEE STANDUP PODIUM DRAWING FOR BUMPER SECTION AND DETAILS

NOTE 2

ALL SOLID EDGES AND BUMPERS JOINED TO PLYWOOD WITH PLATE (BISCUIT) JOINERY

SOLID OAK BUMPER (SEE SECTION)

W/LAMINATE 9° ANGLE AT REAR

SOLID OAK STOP

SOLID OAK EDGE

ASSEMBLY SECTIONS

SCALE 1" = 1'

SYMBOLS

▽ - INDICATES ¾"× ¾" SOLID OAK EDGE
↓ - INDICATES ¾"×1½" EDGE STOP ON DESK SURFACE
V - INDICATES EDGE VENEER
H - INDICATES PIANO HINGE
B - INDICATES 1¼"× 1¼" SOLID OAK BUMPER
A - INDICATES ANGLE CUT

NOTE 3

WHERE LETTER ARE THE SAME FOR TABLE TOP AND STANDUP PODIUMS IT INDICATES INTERCHANGABLE PIECES

A. William Benitez Woodwork Services
Standup Podium. Lectern

JOB DRAWINGS

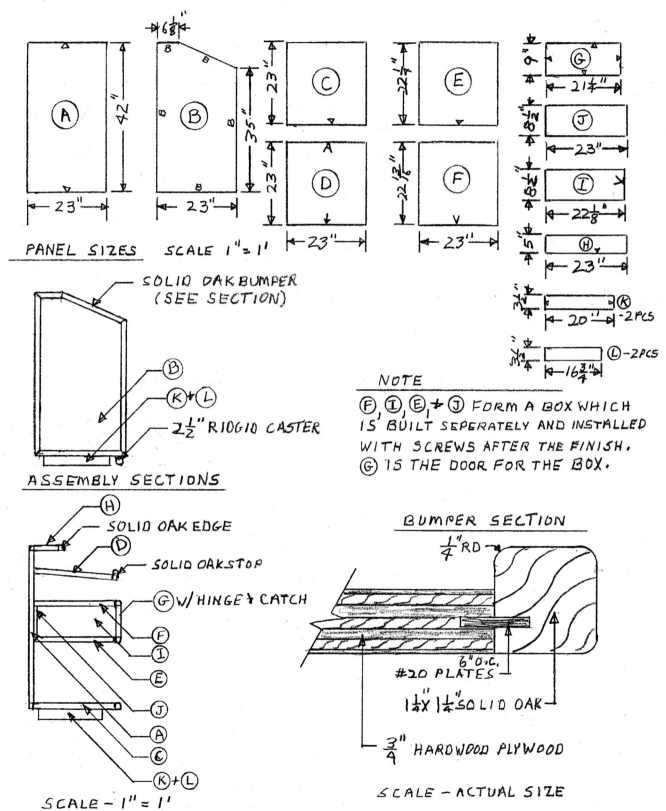

PANEL SIZES   SCALE 1" = 1'

SOLID OAK BUMPER
(SEE SECTION)

Ⓑ

Ⓚ+Ⓛ

2½" RIGID CASTER

ASSEMBLY SECTIONS

Ⓗ
SOLID OAK EDGE
Ⓓ
SOLID OAK STOP
Ⓖ W/ HINGE & CATCH
Ⓕ
Ⓘ
Ⓔ
Ⓙ
Ⓐ
Ⓒ
Ⓚ+Ⓛ

SCALE - 1" = 1'

NOTE
Ⓕ, Ⓘ, Ⓔ, & Ⓙ FORM A BOX WHICH
IS BUILT SEPERATELY AND INSTALLED
WITH SCREWS AFTER THE FINISH.
Ⓖ IS THE DOOR FOR THE BOX.

BUMPER SECTION
¼" RD

6" O.C.
#20 PLATES
1¼" X 1¼" SOLID OAK
¾" HARDWOOD PLYWOOD

SCALE - ACTUAL SIZE

Bonus Two

Twenty-Eight

Laminating Countertops

Instructions For Laminating Tops

Laminate-clad tops are used in kitchens and bathrooms as well as for desks and tables. Laminate is a strong and easy to clean plastic composite surface material. The product is sometimes referred to as mica a word adopted by the cabinet industry because it is short for FORMICA (Registered Trademark), the company that introduced the plastic laminate.

There are two basic kinds of laminate-clad tops. The first is called post-form and is easily recognized by its rounded corners and the fact that there are no seams in the top. The backsplash, the surface and the front edge are all molded from one piece of laminate. This kind of top is built in a specialized shop using a special post-form grade of laminate and costly equipment to heat and form it to fit a shaped top. The second kind is called square edge and, as the name implies, it has square edges. In addition, the top has seams where the various pieces of laminate are joined together to cover the top. For many years the post-form tops were the most popular, but now square edge tops can be found in many of the newest homes and condos. Part of this popularity is due to the lack of miters (surface corner joints) in the corners of many L shaped tops using the square edge system. These miters are prime areas of water leakage in the surface of a countertop.

This guide is devoted to the construction of square edge laminate-clad tops. The methods of construction and laminating described have been used to make tops of all shapes and sizes. To develop the simple procedures described in this guide, the various methods normally used to manufacture countertops were reviewed, simplified, and improved. The changes help to avoid material waste and build a stronger and longer lasting top. Plus, these modifications make it possible for a small shop with limited equipment to construct quality tops of all shapes and sizes.

Materials needed for most tops - Most countertops that are manufactured by top shops are constructed with laminate over particleboard. The reason for this is basic economics, particleboard is cheaper than plywood and it does the job. It also stays very straight and flat, this is important when making tops. Unfortunately, particleboard is very susceptible to water and one good soaking can begin an irreversible deterioration process. Obviously this can create serious problems when particleboard is used in kitchens and bathrooms. In addition to this shortcoming, it has little structural strength and doesn't hold nails and screws well.

In spite of all its shortcomings, particleboard is very popular and can be found in most manufactured cabinets and even in most kitchen and bath cabinets built by small cabinet shops. One reason is that particleboard is available to cabinet shops and manufacturers in precut sizes common to cabinet construction. For example, particleboard for countertops comes in the 25 ¼" width in lengths up to 12' to accommodate kitchen counters. It is also available in 11" width for use in constructing upper cabinets. Large material suppliers will precut to specification and also sell particleboard laminated with shelf liner. All this saves the manufacturer or cabinet shop a tremendous amount of labor thereby reducing costs and speeding up the cabinet construction process. All these advantages do little to overcome the basic deficiencies of particleboard and it remains inferior to plywood for the construction of laminate-clad tops.

The methods described in this guide are based on using plywood that comes in 4' by 8' sheets and of varying thickness. Countertops are built from ¾" thick plywood of fir or pine. Either AC or AD grade can be used and either interior or exterior plywood may be used. The letters indicate the quality of the face veneer of the plywood.

With both AC and AD plywood, both faces are sanded reasonably smooth. The A face has no knotholes because they have all been plugged or filled. The C or D face does have knotholes. The basic difference between the exterior and interior plywood is the glue. The exterior plywood is laminated with glue that is resistant to moisture. This glue also tends to cause the plywood to bow and cup once the bundles are untied. Interior plywood bows less and is preferred if available. Do not use CDX plywood even if it is a bargain. This plywood is intended for sheathing large areas such as roofs. It has a very rough surface and often bows and cups badly. In addition, it often has only 3 plys (layers) of wood as opposed to the five plys found in most AC and AD plywood. This makes CDX plywood much weaker.

Besides the plywood, you will need other materials. A small amount of ¾" thick white pine or spruce lumber, wood glue, nails, caulking, screws, contact cement, vaseline, and of course, laminate. These items will be described further in the section covering construction. Most of them can be found at local home improvement stores or lumber companies. Wholesalers maintain a fairly complete selection of laminate colors and styles. You should be able to get a display chain with color chips to show your customer.

Tools needed to build tops - Laminate-clad tops can be built with just a few workshop tools, but some specialty tools make the job easier. As a minimum you will need the following tools:

Measuring tape	Electric Circular Saw
Hammer	Rip guide for circular saw
Saber saw	Electric drill and bits
Router and laminate trim bit	Jack or block plane
Sanding block	Screwdrivers
Saw horse or other work support	8 foot straight edge
Mill bastard file (large)	Square

The following tools will make the job much easier:

Table saw or radial saw	Belt sander
Electric screw gun (or drill attachment)	J roller (to press laminate)
Laminate trimmer (small one hand router)	Framing Square
Rubber mallet	

In addition you will need a roller pan, a roller handle, a short nap paint roller cover, and a small brush for spreading contact cement.

If you plan to do a great deal of laminate work, I strongly encourage you to invest in a Slitter. This is a tool made by various European manufacturers including Holz and sold by many laminate wholesalers. This tool makes it easy to cut strips of laminate with a very smooth edge without a power tool. It will cut strips ranging in width from 3/8" to 3 ¼". Without this tool you will have to use a table saw to rip the laminate. Since the laminate is so flexible, ripping in this manner is more difficult.

Description of laminate-clad tops - Laminate-clad tops come in various sizes and shapes. Kitchen countertops are usually 25¼" wide. This width includes the backsplash that is 1¼" thick and rises 4" above the surface of the countertop.

NOTE: Beginning here I will mention various drawings that will be used to illustrate various things about building tops and using laminate. These drawings are numbered and begin at the end of these instructions. The drawings begin with number 1 and continue in numerical order.

Drawing # 1 illustrates a section of a kitchen countertop. The countertop is made up of several elements. The surface of the countertop is ¾" thick but it is made to look thicker by the plywood buildup that is nailed and glued to the underside of the top before the laminate is applied (See drawing # 15). The buildup is made of either 5/8" or ¾" thick plywood depending on the thickness of top you desire. A 5/8" buildup will give you a thickness of 1 3/8" and is standard. However, it is not necessary to purchase a sheet of 5/8" plywood just to cut the buildup strips. It would be much less wasteful if the strips were ripped from the ¾" plywood left over from cutting out the surface and backsplashes. This will only make a 1/8" difference in the thickness of the top and could save a lot of money when making only one small top.

The backsplash can be made in one of two ways. The most common is to use ¾" plywood and a ½" thick strip of pine or spruce for the buildup. However, it can also be made from 5/8" plywood and a thin strip of 5/8" plywood used as the buildup. Both of these methods will provide a 1¼ " thickness for the backsplash. The strip on the back of the backsplash is called a scribe strip because it facilitates easy scribing of the top to a less than straight wall. Drawing # 2 illustrates a section of a backsplash and this construction is also used for side splashes

Kitchen and bath countertops have buildups along all outside edges. The edges are then covered with laminate. The parts of a top that face a rear or sidewall normally have splashes. These splashes keep the water off the wall. They are normally 4" above the surface of the top. The splash at the back of the surface is called the backsplash and the splashes at the ends where the top runs into a wall are called the side splashes. Both are constructed in the same manner. The ends of tops that are not against a wall are covered with laminate and this laminate is called a cap (See drawing # 16).

All tops are constructed in basically the same manner. Bath tops are exactly the same except for the width. Instead of 25¼" wide, they are only 22½" wide. Bar tops are also similar except that in most cases they do not require a splash. Sometimes a bar top that comes straight out from a wall will have a splash but it isn't necessary. Bar tops have the standard buildup all the way around the exposed edges. And, in those cases where a bar top overhangs the cabinet by several inches to form a space for bar stools, a second build up directly over the cabinet wall may be necessary for adequate support (See drawing # 3).

There is no prescribed thickness for desk and tabletops. These range from ¾" to 2" but in most cases should be limited to 1½". Desk and tabletops have the buildup installed completely around the top and this is then covered with laminate. Sometimes a desktop will be laminated in its original ¾" thickness, without a buildup.

Measuring the top to ensure a good fit - The first and most important step in making a top of any kind is the measurement. When the top merely overhangs and is capped at the end, a small error in the measurement may go unnoticed. But if a top fits between two walls or between a pantry or oven cabinet and a wall, the measurements become critical. If the measurements are too short, some form of unattractive trim will be necessary to cover the gap. If the measurement is too long, the top will not fit. It may be possible to sand down the excess to make it fit, but if it is a significant error, you may have to cut the top and this can be difficult after the laminate has been applied. Therefore take all measurements carefully and then check each one. Drawing # 4 illustrates a basic kitchen space and the measurements that are necessary.

If there is an existing top that is being replaced, check it for fit. If it fits well, measure it carefully and use these measurements for the new top. If the existing top does not fit well, measure the space so the new top will fit properly. It should fit close enough to the wall to accommodate a thin bead of caulking. A top should overhang ½" to 1" over the side of a cabinet, however, there is no hard and fast rule. If you have the room, you may wish to overhang several inches to accommodate a radius instead of a square corner. Or you may wish to overhang up to 12" to add a foot of counter space even though your cabinets are smaller. You have flexibility here depending on the size of your kitchen. Even the width of the cabinet can be adjusted if you desire. The standard width of a kitchen countertop is 25¼". This is wide enough to accommodate a standard size sink or built in range top.

You may already have narrow cabinets without a sink. Or, you may wish to build narrow cabinets because your kitchen is too small to accommodate the standard size. In this case simply build the countertop in the same manner but make it narrower. Measure the depth of your cabinet from the wall to the front edge and add 1¼" to this size and you have the width of the top. To simplify the measurement process, use the depth measurement of your cabinet to measure the size of the countertop surface. Once the splash is fastened to the back of the surface, the top will then be 1¼" wider and facilitate a 1¼" overhang over the cabinet.

When measuring a countertop, the squareness of the wall is of critical importance. With a straight top, an off square wall may create some difficulty. But with an L shaped or U shaped top it can ruin the fit of your top. In most cases the walls will be adequately square so that a square top may be fitted. But you may run into a non-square wall and a top can be built to accommodate the actual angle instead of the normal 90 degree corner. A large framing square is helpful in determining squareness, but not absolutely necessary. You can determine the squareness of the corner using a measuring tape. Drawing # 5 illustrates how this is done. Basically you use a 3,4,5, formula or any multiples of these numbers depending on the size of the corner to be measured. For example, measure 3" from the corner along one wall and then 4" from the corner along the other wall, Then measure diagonally from the 3" mark to the 4" mark. This should give a measurement of 5" if the corner is square. You can use a multiple of these numbers such as 6, 8,10 or 12,16,20. As long as they are multiples of 3,4,5, they will always work. If the measurement indicates that the corner is square or very close, you will be able to fit a square top with little difficulty. However, if there is a major discrepancy the top should be cut to fit the wall. In this case write down the numbers and use them to make the cut for your top instead of a square cut. For example, if the measurement is 6,8,10¼, you would transfer that measurement when marking the top. It is best to check the top against the corner before applying the laminate or the backsplash. In this way, if it is slightly off, you can correct it. In most cases you will find that this method will facilitate a good fit on the wall.

Building the top - Once the measurements are taken you are ready to start building the top. To simplify the instructions for building we will assume the size of various tops. Construction of kitchen countertops, bar tops, and vanity tops will be covered. These instructions can be applied to the construction of tops of any shape or size.

Drawing # 6 illustrates 4 different tops. The upper two are kitchen countertops. The top on the left is a desktop and has no splashes. The fourth top is a bathroom vanity top. The dotted lines indicate the location of the buildups

As with all projects the first step is to purchase the materials. Prepare a list of materials for every project. The materials list for a straight 8' kitchen counter-top would include the following items:

1 sheet of 3/4 " plywood AC or AD (4 X 8)

1 sheet of standard grade laminate in selected color. This sheet may be a standard 4' X 8' size.

1 package or pound of #3 or #4 box nails (if available, cement coated nails are preferred because of added grip) The ideal is to use a pneumatic nailer if one is available.

1 container of wood glue

1 gallon of contact cement

1 roller handle and cover

1 roller pan

1 small throwaway brush

1 – 12' long piece of parting strip (½" X ¾") or 1 – 6' long piece of 1 x 2 pine for ripping backsplash buildups

15 - 1½" to 1 ¾" x 6 screws (preferably self tapping drywall screws)

1 caulking gun and tube of caulking

After obtaining all the materials you can build the top by following these steps:

Cut the plywood to the proper sizes. Use a straight edge to ensure that the top will be straight and even. Remember to deduct the thickness of splashes from the overall measurements. Place the plywood on sawhorses or some other steady work support on which you can cut with your electric circular saw. Place the straightedge so that the saw blade will cut exactly down the center of the plywood sheet. This cut should be at the 24" mark. Depending on the kerf of the blade being used, this should leave you with two pieces approximately 23 15/16" wide and 8' long. One of these pieces will be the surface of your top. The other will be cut for the backsplash and the build-ups for the top. Put one of the 8' pieces aside and leave the other one on the saw-horses. Place the rip guide on your circular saw and set it at 5½". Rip two strips 5½ X 8 feet long and put them aside.

NOTE: This 5½" strip will give you a 4" backsplash above the surface of the top. This is a standard size backsplash, however, you can make it higher or lower if you prefer. If your kitchen has tile on the wall between the backsplash and the upper cabinets, it is essential that you measure the size of the existing backsplash and make the new one 1/8" smaller. Go to the capped end of the existing top and measure from the bottom edge of the top to the top edge of the backsplash. Deduct 1/8" from this size and use this measurement in place of the 5½" size. In this way the new backsplash will fit under the tile and leave room for caulking.

Now rip two pieces 1½" wide by 8' long and then rip two ½" strips from the 1 X 2 pine unless you have purchased precut parting strips. For this top we are assuming that the countertop will fit against a wall on the right side and overhang the cabinet on the left side.

To assemble the components of the top, place the 2' by 8' piece on the sawhorses with the C or D side facing up. Cut 1¼" off one end of this piece making it 94 ¾" long. It will be 8 feet long when the side splash is attached. Cut a piece of buildup to fit along the front edge of the surface bottom. Glue and nail the 1½" buildup strips flat to the edge of the plywood. Keep the two edges as even as possible to reduce the necessity for sanding. Use the #3 or #4 box nails for this task or a pneumatic nailer with 1 ¼" nails or staples. Also nail a buildup strip on the side of the top that will overhang the cabinet (see drawing # 7). It is not necessary to install buildups on the edges of the top that will have splashes. In this design the splashes will support the top on the cabinet without buildups of any kind.

Next place one of the 5½" by 8' plywood pieces on the sawhorses. Cut to size and nail and glue the ½" buildup strip to the back and even with the top edge of the splash. On the end of the splash that will overhang the cabinet, cut, nail and glue a piece of the ½ " strip as shown in drawing # 8. Now cut a piece 25¼" long from the other piece of 5½" splash. Install the ½" strips on this splash in the same manner as the other one. Install one piece along the top edge and the other small piece on the end that will face the front edge of the top. When fastening buildups place the strip even with the edge of the splash to reduce the necessity for sanding.

Once you have completed the buildups, the top is ready to be covered with plastic laminate. However, it is best to sand the edge lightly to make certain that they are even. This is best done with a belt sander, but a sanding block with 80-grit sandpaper will do the job. If any of the edges are uneven, the belt sander will quickly correct this, however, use the sander carefully because it can easily cut too deep and make your edges irregular. If a belt sander is not available and the edges are not even, a block or jackplane can be used to even up the edges. Once the edges of the top surface and the splashes have been sanded, you are ready to apply the laminate.

Laminate is best applied to tops in a certain order. The edges of the top surface and the face of the splashes are applied first. Cut the laminate to size using a circular saw, table saw, or radial arm saw. With a circular saw or radial arm saw, cut the laminate face down, with a table saw cut it face up and cut the pieces slightly larger than necessary. For example, the strips for the edges of the top should be ripped 2" wide even though the edge of the top is only 1½" wide. The face piece for the splashes should be cut 6 " wide even though the face is only 5½" wide. The length should also be a little longer than the plywood. This additional length and width allows the overhang necessary to accommodate trimming.

During the job of cutting the narrow strips, a laminate slitter is very handy. If laminate work is going to be a large part of your work, the laminate slitter is an excellent investment.

Begin the laminate application by applying a coat of contact glue to the plywood edges of the tops with the throwaway brush. Then place the laminate pieces you have cut on top of the counter surface and use the throw away brush to spread contact cement on the back of the laminate. Spread it as evenly as possible but do not stretch it thin. Now apply contact cement to the faces of the splashes. Then return to the edges of the top surface and apply a second coat of contact cement. This second coat is important because plywood edges have a tendency to absorb a great deal of the cement and one coat may not provide a good bond. Now wait for the contact cement to set. Depending on weather conditions and the work area, this will take from 5 to 20 minutes, but the cement will be workable for about an hour. Test contact cement by touching it. If it does not stick to your fingers it is ready for bonding.

The next step is critical. Contact cement is so named because it bonds on contact and it attains more than 70% of its bonding power immediately upon contact with the other cement surface. Therefore it is essential that the laminate be placed exactly where it belongs because adjustment is not possible after the two surfaces have touched. For the edges, alignment is reasonably easy. You merely start at one end by placing the laminate end flush with the end of the top and allow it to stick up and down about ¼" past the surface and the buildup. This excess will be trimmed later. Slowly press the laminate strip against the edge until you have reached the end of the strip. Next place the second piece of edge banding. This piece is placed against the front edge piece where it overhangs the end of the top. Press it with your hands along its full length keeping it approximately ¼" above and below the surface and the buildup. Do not slide your hand along the edge of the plastic laminate as it is very sharp. This piece will also be a little long but it will be trimmed off later.

Now apply the laminate to the faces of the splashes. This is a little more difficult. To make certain that it is applied in the right position, use some short sticks. Place one stick across the face of the splash every 16" to 24" (See drawing # 9). Be certain that the sticks are clean to avoid getting dust on the contact cement surfaces. Place the laminate on the sticks and align it to the correct position. Remove the first stick on one end and press the laminate down to the wood (See drawing # 10). Proceed across the length of the splash removing one stick at a time and pressing down the laminate. The laminate should fit correctly on the face. It is important to press the laminate tightly against the wood to attain a good bond. Hand pressure is not sufficient for this. In addition, attempting to apply this pressure by hand can result in serious cuts as the laminate edges are very sharp before they are filed. A J-roller is ideal for pressing the laminate against the wood. Or, you can apply sufficient pressure by using a flat piece of wood and beating on it with a hammer. The edges can be pressed tight by using a rubber mallet, but do not beat the surface of the laminate with a steel hammer at any time. If you are using a steel hammer, use a flat wood block. When pressing the laminate against the face of the splash, merely move the wood block around as you beat it with the hammer. This will create sufficient pressure to ensure a good bond.

NOTE: As with any glue, all surfaces should be clean and free of dust and grease before applying the contact cement. This is critical with laminate surfaces because small pieces of debris can cause bumps in the face of the laminate and eventually damage it.

The next step is to trim the excess laminate. On the edge of the top surface you will notice that one place requiring trimming is against a laminate face. This is at the corner of the top. It is critical to rub this laminate surface with Vaseline or a wax stick to lubricate it. The Vaseline serves as a lubricant for the trimmer bit pilot that is spinning at 22,000 to 28,000 rpm and would otherwise burn the laminate surface. Wax sticks can also be used for this purpose. Burn marks caused by the trimmer bit's solid pilot are permanent so it is essential to be careful when running a trimmer bit along a laminate surface.

NOTE: There are three basic types of trimmer bits. One has a ball bearing pilot that does not require the use of Vaseline as a lubricant because the pilot remains stationary while the bit is turning. These bits have two disadvantages: 1) they do not cut as close as the solid pilot bits therefore more filing is required after the cut and 2) when contact cement builds up on the bearing it sometimes freezes in place. If you do not notice this it will burn the laminate surface in the same manner as a solid pilot. The second type of trimmer bit has no pilot. The router or trimmer itself has the pilot or pin that guides the bit along the edge of the work. The disadvantage of this kind of bit is that perfect alignment between the router or trimmer body and the bit is critical and must be maintained at all times. This kind of bit can easily damage laminate edges with even the slightest misalignment. The third and recommended type of trimmer bit is the solid pilot bit. This bit and its pilot are all one unit and therefore alignment is limited to setting the proper depth. However, the laminate edges upon which the pilot will pass must be lubricated.

Solid pilot bits come in two types. One is the bevel edge. This bit has a pilot that is smaller than the shaft of the bit and the cutting edge is at a bevel. This is a popular bit but it can damage laminate if the depth setting of your router or trimmer slips while using it. The cut for this kind of bit is set so that the bevel edge cuts very close to the edge of the other laminate surface. Since the pilot is smaller than the shaft, a drop could cause the cutting edge to cut too far and damage the laminate surface. The pilot and the shaft of the flush edge trimmer bit are the same size and a drop would merely stop the cutting action.

After trimming off the excess laminate, the edges of the splashes and the surface of the countertop should be sanded lightly with a belt sander. Also sand the bottom edge of the surface. If a belt sander is not available use an orbital sander or a sanding block with 80-grit sandpaper. The purpose of this sanding is to get the edge of the laminate even with the wood surfaces prior to the application of the rest of the laminate. This will also make the bottom smooth to the touch. The trimmer bit will trim very close but there is still a slight bit of laminate passing the edge of the wood. Instead of sandpaper, this excess can also be removed with the flat mill bastard file. Whether sanding or filing, it is essential to keep the surfaces flat and perpendicular to the laminate. Avoid too much sanding or gouging the edge as this will create a void that the laminate surface will not follow. These voids are very unattractive and a sure sign of an unprofessional job. Take a little time to make certain that the edges are adequately sanded. Feel the edge of the laminate to make certain there is no excess, however, do not feel the edge immediately after belt sanding as this could burn your fingers. Continue sanding or filing until the laminate is even with the wood.

After cleaning off all wood surfaces you are ready to apply the rest of the laminate surfaces. Apply glue to the laminate strip that you have cut for the edges of the splashes and apply two coats to the edges of the splashes to ensure a good bond. You may apply contact cement to the laminate for the surface and the surface itself with a brush, however, a roller will do a faster and better job on large surfaces. One good coat on the back of the laminate and the surface is adequate for a good bond. Allow the contact cement to set. After the cement is set, apply the strip to the top and side edges of the splashes in the same manner that the strips were applied to the edges of the top. Then use the stick method previously described to apply the surface laminate. Some experts recommend using slip-sheets instead of sticks for placing the laminate and they work well.

With a lot of practice, you can apply large sheets of laminate to wood and particleboard surfaces without the use of sticks or slip-sheets. Until you acquire this level of skill, the stick method is quick and easy to use and ensures that every piece of laminate will be lined up for bonding.

Once the laminate has been placed, roll or press it tightly using either a J-roller, a rubber mallet or a hammer with impact block. Make certain that you have a good bond by pulling up lightly on the laminate to see if it separates from the wood. If it separates, press it harder. A slight separation is not uncommon immediately after the pieces are bonded together, but if the laminate simply pulls up from the wood, you do not have a bond. Either the contact cement was allowed to dry too long, or weather conditions have precluded a good bond. Read the label on the contact cement to determine ideal conditions and repeat the process at a later time under better conditions. In most cases you will get a good bond.

If the laminate is not properly placed, it can be removed promptly by using lacquer thinner or contact cleaner in a small squeeze bottle. Squeeze lacquer thinner along the edge and begin to separate the laminate from the wood slowly. Continue to pour in the liquid as the laminate separates from the wood. Pull the laminate slowly or it will break. Once the laminate is removed it can be repositioned without reapplying any additional glue. Simply allow the lacquer thinner to dry and then reapply the laminate in the proper position.

Once the laminate has been applied, the excess must be trimmed off. This time, as before, you must be certain to apply Vaseline or a wax stick to all the laminate surfaces upon which the trimmer pilot will run. The Vaseline can be applied easily with a small rag or piece of cotton. Do not apply sparingly. Make certain that you can see the Vaseline on the surface of the laminate. However, there is no need to put it on thick. After the Vaseline is applied proceed to trim off the excess. Always keep the router or trimmer moving smoothly. It is not necessary to move fast, but do not stop in one place as this can burn the surface of the laminate even with the Vaseline.

The next step is filing the trimmed edges. This requires great care because it is easy to go too far and damage the laminate surface. The purpose of the filing is to remove the tiny excess left by the trimmer bit and the sharp edge of the laminate. You can feel the excess with your finger. It is a minor amount and very little filing is necessary. The action of the file should be forward and across the edge at the same time. Always file across the edge and into the perpendicular laminate surface. If you file towards the outside edge, it is possible to chip the laminate. Watching the glue line is the simplest way to know when the filing is complete. The contact cement flows over the laminate joint and is visible if the filing job is done in good light. Place the file at approximately a 10-degree angle as shown in drawing # 11. Proceed to file forward and across toward the other laminate surface. As the file reaches the proper point, the excess glue will disappear from the glue line. The line will then cleanly divide the two laminate surfaces. When the glue disappears stop filing on that area and proceed along the glue line until all the excess glue is gone from the line. After this filing is complete, change the angle of the file to approximately 45 degrees and gently file off the sharp corner of the laminate (See drawing # 12). Proceed carefully as the file will quickly remove material. Be sure to keep your file clean with a file card or wire brush.

After the filing is complete, clean all of the contact cement and dust off all the laminate surfaces by wiping it with lacquer thinner, contact cleaner, mineral spirits, or acetone. Your top is now ready for final assembly.

The top is assembled with screws and caulking. Start this step by drilling 3/16" holes every 12" along the bottom edge of the splashes. The holes should be located 1" from the bottom edge of the splash. Also drill a hole 7/8" in from the edge where it will meet a side splash (See drawing # 13). Drill the holes from the laminate side into the wood to avoid chipping. Apply caulking in a bead along the center of the wood edge of the top surface where the splashes will be attached. Use 2 or 3 of the #4 or #3 nails to carefully nail the splash in place. This nailing is only temporary to make installation of the splash screws easier. Make certain that the splash is the proper length and that it is even with the bottom of the buildup. Use a small block of plywood the same thickness as the buildup as a guide to make certain the splash is in the proper location. After nailing in place, install the screws one at a time from the back of the splash into the edge of the top surface. Tighten the screws until the caulking oozes out and a very thin line remains (See drawing #14). After all the splashes have been installed in this manner, clean off the excess caulking with a plastic putty knife or a square piece of laminate. Wipe the joint clean with a damp cloth. The joint should be very tight so that water cannot pass through it.

NOTE: If your top requires a cutout for a sink, lavatory, or range, this cutout should be done before the components of the top are assembled. It is possible to make these cutouts after assembly, but it is much more difficult. In same cases it may be necessary to make the cutout from the bottom of the top. In any case, it is almost always best to make the cutouts prior to installing the top. Cutouts are best made with a saber saw having a fine to medium blade. It is necessary to drill a hole in the top to start the cut for the saber saw. The actual size of the cutout should be obtained from the sink, lavatory, or range. Most will bring instructions or a template (pattern) or both. Be sure to center it in the location you want. Once the hole is cut it cannot be changed.

Fitting the top - Place the top on the cabinet to make certain that it fits properly. Many times the walls will be crooked and the splash will not fit tightly along its entire length. If this is the case, mark those areas of the splash that are touching the wall by running a pencil held upright directly against the wall. This will mark the areas that will need planing or sanding for a better fit. A belt sander is the best tool for this job, but it can be done with a plane if the nails are removed. Sand the back of the splash to the line and until it fits reasonably tight against the wall. Within 1/8" is close enough since this area will be filled with caulking after the top has been fastened in place.

Installing the top - This is the final step in the process. It is difficult to cover this step completely because the installation method will depend on how the cabinets were built and prepared to accommodate the top. First you must remove the existing top if there is one. To do this the sink and other appliances in the top must be removed. The top should be attached with screws, but in some kitchens you may find that the top was nailed in place. Unfortunately this is not rare. Once the existing top has been removed you must make certain that the cabinet has adequate attachment locations. If the existing top was screwed in place in an adequate manner, there should be no difficulty in using these same components for fastening the new top. If the attachment components are inadequate, install additional ones. This is a simple process.

Remember, a top requires only a few screws to hold it in place, but you must make certain that both the front and the back are properly fastened. Care is important when fastening a top. It is not unusual for a novice to drive a screw that is too long right through the laminate surface. Calculate the size of the screw you need before attaching the top. For example, if the top is ¾" thick and the buildup is ¾", this makes a total of 1½". Add to that ¾" for the attachment component in the cabinet and you have 2¼". Do not use a screw longer than 2¼" to attach the top. In this case you should use 2" screws or 2¼" screws with a washer to make certain you do not get too close to the laminate surface. It is very disheartening to ruin a top in this manner after all that work. After the top has been fastened, caulking should be used to fill all voids.

Special tops - Drawing # 17 illustrates four tops that require special work. Two of them are L shaped, one is U shaped, and the other is more than 8' long. All of these tops must be built using two or more pieces of plywood and gluing them together. First the surface pieces are cut to the appropriate sizes. Take care to make all cuts square and even. Assemble the top on a large flat surface such as a garage floor. Place the pieces of the top in the proper location.

Cut pieces of plywood (the same thickness as the buildups) 8" by 22". These pieces will lap the joints of the top. Apply wood glue liberally on one side of this piece of plywood and apply it over the plywood joints as illustrated in drawing # 17. As shown, allow the buildup to cross over the joint of the surface pieces. This glue up procedure will give the joints great strength. Drawing # 18 illustrates a section of the plywood joints with the plywood lap over.

NOTE: The surface of all four of these special tops can be covered with one piece of laminate. This provides a joint free surface and helps to preclude water damage.

CAUTION: It is best to build tops in one piece as described herein whenever possible. In some cases, especially with U shaped tops, this is not possible because the top is too large to be brought into the kitchen in one piece. In these cases the top will have to be constructed in two or more pieces. Sometimes this problem can be resolved by redesigning the kitchen. Often a range can be relocated to divide the top into 2 sections that can be built and installed in one piece.

CONCLUSION: All laminate-clad tops are done in approximately the same manner. The order of covering the wood is the same regardless of the use the top will get. The splashes are fastened in the same manner. Remember that the buildup can be any size you desire. In this case we used the ¾" plywood to avoid purchasing additional material just for the buildup. But you could make the edge of the top 1" thick by using a ¼" buildup or 1¼" by using a ½" buildup. The 1½" used herein may look good on a kitchen, but it may be too thick for a vanity in a bathroom or for a desk. Use your judgment and build it your way.

By following the steps described herein and working with care, you can build countertops as good as any cabinet shop and better than some.

All of the drawings described in the instructions above begin on the next page and in numerical order. Several drawings appear on each page.

Laminate Drawings
1, 2, 3, 4

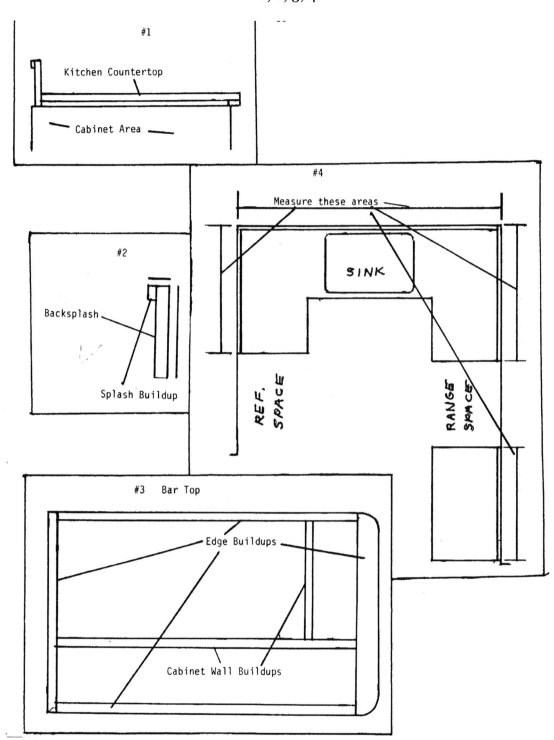

#1

Kitchen Countertop

Cabinet Area

#2

Backsplash

Splash Buildup

#4

Measure these areas

SINK

REF. SPACE

RANGE SPACE

#3   Bar Top

Edge Buildups

Cabinet Wall Buildups

Laminate Drawings
5, 6, 7

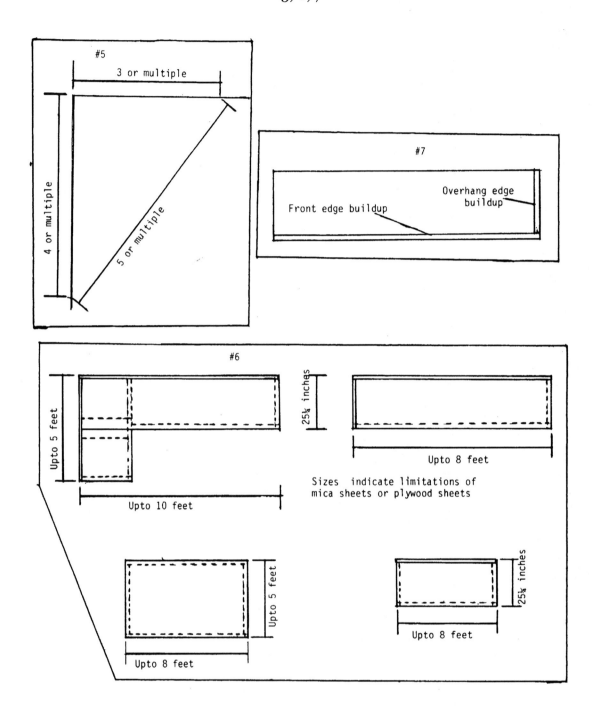

#5

3 or multiple

4 or multiple

5 or multiple

#7

Overhang edge buildup

Front edge buildup

#6

Upto 5 feet

Upto 10 feet

25¼ inches

Upto 8 feet

Sizes indicate limitations of mica sheets or plywood sheets

Upto 5 feet

Upto 8 feet

25¼ inches

Upto 8 feet

Laminate Drawings
8, 9, 10, 11, 12

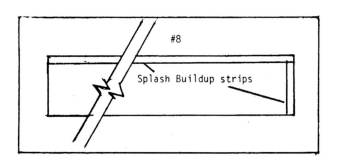

#8

Splash Buildup strips

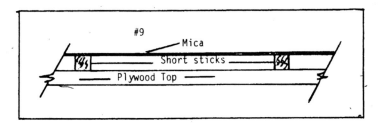

#9

Mica

Short sticks

Plywood Top

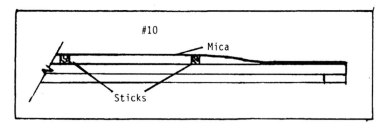

#10

Mica

Sticks

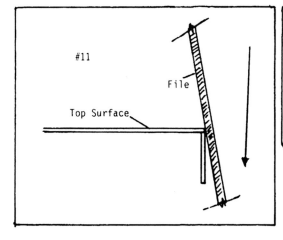

#11

File

Top Surface

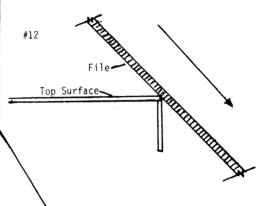

#12

File

Top Surface

Laminate Drawings
13, 14, 15, 16

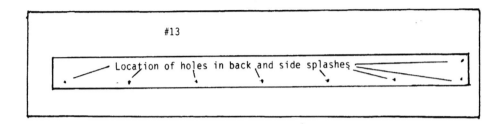

#13

Location of holes in back and side splashes

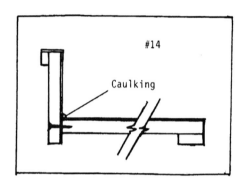

#14

Caulking

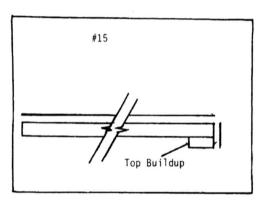

#15

Top Buildup

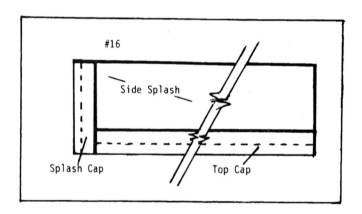

#16

Side Splash

Splash Cap   Top Cap

Laminate Drawings
17, 18

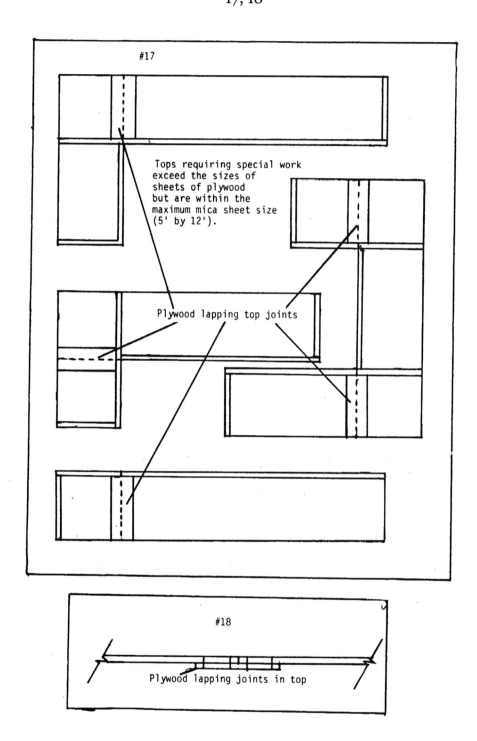

GLOSSARY

Accounting: a precise record of the financial transactions of your business.

Accounting Software: software used to maintain information on the financial transactions of your business.

Accounts Payable: accounts of money you owe to vendors or others.

Accounts Receivable: accounts of money your are owed by customers and others.

Addendum: An addition to a contract to describe additional work or changes to the existing agreement.

Advertising: The activity of attracting public attention to your products or services.

After Market: similar to third party vendors meaning an accessory or attachment made for a tool or product by another manufacturer.

Analyze: to study how best to perform a certain task to maintain safety and avoid injury.

Assembly: The process of putting projects together after all the parts have been cut and sorted.

Assembly Area: The area within your shop that is used to assemble projects.

Backlog: woodwork projects under contract and awaiting completion and delivery to your customers.

Backsplash: The back part of a countertop that goes against the wall.

Band Saw: a power tool that cuts wood or metal using a blade that is a circular tooth band that is driven by two or three wheels.

Bank Account: a fund at a bank where you can deposit and withdraw funds.

Bankruptcy: the process of being declared legally insolvent.

Bartley's: manufacturer of an excellent gel varnish that may be used to stain and varnish products.

Belt Sander: a power tool that uses a circular belt with an abrasive grit for sanding surfaces smooth.

Billing: The process of sending an invoice to your customers for services rendered.

Biscuit Joiner: an excellent woodworking tool used for joinery in cabinets and furniture.

Biscuit Locations: the exact location where slots are cut to accommodate biscuit wafers.

Biscuit Slots: the slots cut with a biscuit joiner to accommodate biscuits.

Biscuits/Wafers: the compressed beech wafers used in biscuit joinery. They come in three sizes, 20, 10 and 0.

Box Nails: Thin nails that are used for assembling crates. They have heads and enter wood easily and hold well.

Budget: an itemized summary of estimated or intended expenditures for a given period of time.

Building Defects: a defect that is inherent in the product as opposed to damage caused by the owner.

Buildup: a strip attached on the bottom of laminated countertops to give the impression of additional thickness.

Butt Joints: a joint where one piece of wood is perpendicularly attached to another with no joinery.

Cabinetmaker: a skilled craftsperson who builds cabinets.

Capital: funds available to pay the costs of operating a business.

Carbide Tipped: blades and bits that have carbide attached so they will cut more efficiently and remain sharp longer.

Carpenter: a skilled worker who makes or repairs wooden objects or structures.

Castors: a small wheel attached under a piece of furniture to make it easier to move from one location to another.

Caulking: a material used for filling cracks or holes.

Caulking Gun: a tool used to apply caulking.

Circular Saw: a power saw for cutting wood consisting of a toothed disk rotating at high speed.

Clamp Marks: the marks made on wood surfaces by metal clamps.

Clamps: metal or wooden instruments used to hold wooden parts together while the glue dries.

Clientele: your list of clients.

Collection: obtaining payment for your work.

Communication Skills: the ability to convey your point regarding your work clearly and concisely to facilitate selling woodwork projects.

Competent: sufficiently qualified to perform the work required.

Complaints: an expression of dissatisfaction with something.

Components: The parts of a woodwork projects.

Compressor: a device that compresses air for use with pneumatic tools.

Consumer Tools: tools that are manufactured to lesser standards because of lighter use by non-professionals.

Contact Cement: glue used especially for plastic laminate. It is characterized by its immediate bonding ability.

Contact Cleaner: a liquid used to remove excess glue from plastic laminate surfaces.

Contract: an agreement between two of more parties to ensure completion of a project and payment for the work.

Corporation: a legal entity often created to protect individuals from the potential liabilities involved in business. Most often used by large companies.

Countertops: the top surface of a cabinet or piece of furniture. This can be plastic laminate or some other material.

Creativity: the ability to be original and to develop new ideas using older ideas as a basis or starting point.

Crosscut Jig: an attachment for the table saw that facilitates crosscutting large plywood pieces.

Crosscutting: cutting lumber across the grain.

Crown Molding: a decorative molding that is applied at the top of a wall against the ceiling.

Custom Cabinets: cabinets that are designed and built for a specific job or location.

Custom Furniture: furniture that is designed and built for a specific customer.

Customer: an individual or company that purchases your products or services.

Cut List: a detailed list of the sizes of all the parts for a specific project.

Cutout: a section of a cabinet or countertop that is cut out to accommodate a sink or other item.

Cutting Area: the area within a shop that is used for cutting cabinet or furniture parts.

Dados: a rectangular groove cut into a board so another board can be fitted into it.

Deed Restrictions: a clause in a warranty deed that prohibits certain actions such as conducting business on residential property.

Deft: a manufacturer of excellent clear finishing products such as Deft Clear Wood Finish and Wood Armor.

Deposit: to put money into a bank or other depository.

Depreciation: a loss in value due to age or wear.

Design: to plan out or create cabinets or furniture.

Design Features: details created to improve the appearance of furniture.

Dimension: the size of a specific portion or part of a cabinet.

Divider Walls: the boards used to divide up the interior of a cabinet.

Dovetails: a fan-shaped tenon that forms an interlocking joint.

Dowels: a round wood pin that fits tightly into a corresponding hole to fasten or align an adjacent board.

Drawings: line sketches that clearly describe the construction details for a cabinet or piece of furniture.

Drill: a power tool for drilling holes in wood or metal.

Drill Press: a tabletop or floor mounted drill

Edge Trimmer: a small mechanical device with dual blades used to trim excess veneer from plywood edges.

Employee: a person who works for you in return for financial or other compensation.

Euro Hinges: hinges made in a European style that facilitates easy adjustments.

Expansion: the growth of your business to the point that additional employees are needed to operate.

Expenses: costs associated with running your business.

Expert: a person with a high degree of skill or knowledge on a particular subject.

Fictitious Name: the name of a business that is not your own name.

Fingerjoints: interlocking straight tenon joints for assembly of wooden projects.

Finish Sander: a vibrating power sander used for the final sanding of a project.

Finishing: the process of applying a clear or painted coating to a project.

Finishing Area: the area within your shop used to finish projects.

Fitness: keeping yourself in good physical, emotional and mental condition.

Flexibility: the ability to respond and deal with change.

Furniture: articles in a home or office used for living and working comfortably.

Gel Varnish: a clear coat finishing product in gel form instead of liquid.

General Contractor: a person who supervises the activities of everyone working on a construction project.

Glue Up: the process as assembling projects with glue.

Gross Income: the total income received from your business activities before expenses are deducted.

Grow or Die: the idea that a business must get larger over time in order to survive and remain viable.

Hand Tools: tools use by individuals for various kinds of work that do not require electrical power.

Hang Rail: wooden supports installed on projects to facilitate secure attachment to walls.

Hardwood Plywood: a multi-layered wood product manufactured with hardwoods only.

Hardwoods: the hard-to-cut woods of broad-leaved trees.

Health Care: the insurance and facilities required to maintain the health of individuals.

Homebuilders: similar to contractors but limited to the construction of homes instead of all kinds of structures.

Hourly Rate: the amount per hour paid to employees.

HVLP Spray Equipment: high-volume low-pressure spray equipment used mostly to spray finish on wooden projects.

Income Tax: the tax required by government from every citizen based on the amount of income they make.

Installation: the procedure of installing a cabinet in a home or building.

Insurance: a contract by a party indemnifying another against a specified loss.

Iron-on Veneer: a strip veneer with a hot melt glue surface used for application to the edges of plywood projects.

IRS: Internal Revenue Service collects income taxes.

J Roller: a tool used to apply pressure to laminate surfaces during the installation of plastic laminates.

Joinery: various methods of strongly fastening wooden parts together.

Lacquer: an excellent clear finish product requiring a respirator to avoid exposure to vapors.

Lacquer Thinner: a liquid used to clean surfaces of lacquer and to thin lacquer.

Laminate: a plastic composite product used to cover tops and other surfaces to protect them from wear.

Laminate Trimmer: a small electrical router used especially to trim excess laminate during the application process.

Laminate-clad: a top or other surface covered with plastic laminate.

Learning: the process of acquiring knowledge about certain skills.

License: an authorization from a government body allowing you to perform some form of business.

Maintenance: keeping tools and buildings in good repair.

Materials: products used to build projects.

MDF: medium density fiberboard sheet goods used to build cabinets and furniture.

Measurements: the dimensions of a specific project used to cut the parts.

Mica: a nickname for plastic laminate coined from the name FORMICA, a legal trademark. This was the company that introduced plastic laminate.

MinWax: a brand of finishing products including stains and polycrylics.

Modules: small components of a wood project assembled on site.

Mortise and Tenon: an excellent and complex joinery method for wood.

Nails: a pointed piece of metal pounded into wood as a fastener.

Net Income: the income left over after all expenses are deducted from the gross income of a business.

Occupational License: an authorization to participate in a certain occupation or business activity.

Online Banking: conducting your banking using the Internet.

Onsite: doing work at the site of the job instead of at a shop.

Ordinances: laws that apply to various aspects of your work activities.

Overhang: the part of a top that overhangs the face of a cabinet.

Overhead: the cost of operating a business.

Paint Thinner: a liquid used to clean or thin paint.

Particle Board: a sheet product created by mixing wood dust and debris with glue and then compressing it to form sheets.

Pattern: a model used to make repetitive parts for a project

Payroll: salary paid to individuals for work performed.

Payroll Taxes: taxes deducted from individuals for payment to the IRS.

Penalties: fees charged for not adhering to regulations.

Permit: an authorization to perform certain tasks.

Petty Cash: funds kept on hand for small purchases.

Piano Hinge: a continuous hinge used on various cabinet and furniture projects.

Pigment: the color in paints.

Planing: using a planer to smooth the surface of wood.

Plastic Laminate: a composite plastic used for counter surfaces.

Pneumatic Nailer: a pneumatic tool that drives nails into wood.

Pneumatic Stapler: a pneumatic tool that drives staples into wood.

Podium/Lecterns: a stand for holding a microphone and the notes of a public speaker.

Polycrylic: a clear finish for wood.

Polyurethane: a clear finish for wood.

Post-form: a type of plastic laminate that can be shaped with heat.

Pre-stain: a liquid that partially seals wood surfaces to reduce splotching.

Product Consistency: maintaining the same dimensions and colors when building several of the same item.

Professional: a person engaged in a certain activity for their livelihood.

Profit: what is left after all operating expenses are deducted from gross income.

Project: a specific job involving one or more products.

Radial Arm Saw: a power saw with a sliding track.

Radius: one fourth of a circle.

Random Orbit Sander: a power sander that rotates and orbits to sand rapidly without creating circular marks on a wood surface.

Reserve Fund: money set aside for one or more specific purposes.

Reveals: a decorative feature on a cabinet or piece of furniture.

Rip Fence: a straight edge or bar used to guide wood during the ripping process.

Ripping: the process of cutting wood into strips of various width.

Router: a power tool with a sharp bit used to cut grooves and decorative edges.

Saber Saw: a power saw used to cut various radius and cutouts on wood.

Safety: steps taken to remain free from danger, risk or injury.

Salary: compensation paid to an individual for services rendered.
Sales Technique: a method used to sell items to someone.
Sanding: the process of smoothing wood in preparation for finishing.
Sanding Belts: circular sanding strips used on belt sanders to sand wood.
Sanding Block: a wooden block with a piece of sandpaper attached.
Sandpaper: abrasive sheets used to smooth wood surfaces.
Sawhorses: four legged supports to raise work from floor level.
Screws: a metal pin with incised threads used as fasteners.
Security: the idea or concern of being secure.
Self-Employed: working for yourself in a business.
Self-Analyses: a critical look at yourself and your life.
Self-disciplined: being able to perform required tasks without having someone to make certain things are done.
Self-motivated: being a self starter who does not require an external motivating force.
Shop: a work area for building wood products.
Shop Layout: a plan for an efficient work area.
Shop Space: the space used for the building of wood products.
Side Splash: the laminated board on the right or left side of a countertop.
Simple Methods: more efficient ways of performing tasks.
Simplified Methods: simpler ways to perform various tasks.
Simplified Woodworking: alternative woodworking methods intended to allow faster completion of wood projects.
Sliding Compound Miter Saw: a miter saws that facilitate compound cuts and slides to allow for cutting through wide boards.
Sliding Table: a table added to a table saw to facilitate crosscutting wide boards.
Slip-Sheet: a sheet used to facilitate application of plastic laminate sheets.
Slitter: a mechanical tool used to slit strips from sheets of plastic laminate.
Small Business: varying definitions exist but basically it is a business that is not considered large.
Social Security: a fund that individuals pay into in order to have funds available for retirement.
Specifications: details that describe the specifics of a job or project.
Splitter: a flat metal piece behind the table saw blade to keep cuts from binding.
Splotching: discoloration of stains that are applied without a pre-stain.
Spray Gun: a tool used to apply finishes by spraying them on the surface.
Spring-Loaded: something that maintains pressure to remain in a certain position.
Square: an instrument to test right angles.
Square Formula: the 3,4,5 formula used to test squareness.
Squareness: a cabinet with corners at exact 90 degree right angles.
Stain: a penetrating liquid used to color wood.
Standard Grade Laminate: the thickest grade of laminate, normally used for countertops.
Stationary Tools: floor standing power tools intended to remain in one location.
Straight Edge: a straight board used to guide a saw through a long cut.
Straight Lining: the process of creating a straight edge on rough lumber.

Subcontractor: a self-employed individual who works on a project or projects for the individual who is running the project.

Supply and Demand: the process of setting prices on products based on the demand for it.

Table Saw: a stationary power saw used to rip and crosscut lumber and plywood.

Template: a pattern used to replicate an item.

Thickness Planer: a power tool used to smooth off wood.

Toe Space: The space at the base of cabinets that allows you to stand closer to the top.

Trade Tools: tools manufactured for professionals in various fields.

Traditional Methods: acceptable woodworking methods that can be replaced with simplified methods for faster production.

Utility Knife: a short bladed knife with a metal or plastic handle used for trimming edging.

Varnish: a clear coat liquid for finishing.

Veneer: a very thin wood product that is applied to sheet products to give the appearance of wood.

Vertical Grade Laminate: a thin laminate used on the vertical surfaces of cabinets.

Visualize: to study the steps involved in safely cutting a board or sheet of plywood.

Wages: hourly fee paid to employees.

Waste Factor: the amount of material that must be calculated in a job because it will be wasted during the cutting.

Wax Stick: a stick used to lubricate the laminate surfaces to avoid damage during trimming.

Wood Edging: especially cut strips applied to the edges of plywood and particleboard sheets to protect the edges and improve the appearance.

Worker's Compensation: fees paid by employers to protect employees while they are unemployed or injured.

Other Books Published By Positive Imaging, LLC

Simplified Woodworking: A Business Guide For Woodworkers
by A. William Benitez

The Self Employment Survival Manual:
How To Start and Operate a One-Person Business Successfully
by A. William Benitez

Good Relationships 101:
Keeping Relationships Happy and Healthy
by A. William Benitez

Lottie's Adventure:
A Kidnapping Unraveled
by Barbara Frances

LaVergne, TN USA
30 September 2009

159454LV00002B/53/P